THE GOD BEAT

THE
GOD
BEAT

WHAT JOURNALISM SAYS ABOUT
FAITH AND WHY IT MATTERS

COSTICA BRADATAN
and ED SIMON

Editors

 Broadleaf Books

Minneapolis

THE GOD BEAT
What Journalism Says about Faith and Why It Matters

Cover image: shutterstock/photka
Cover design: FaceOut

Print ISBN: 978-1-5064-6577-7
eBook ISBN: 978-1-5064-6578-4

Contents

Part III—Natural Agon: Science & Technology

Part IV—Divine Agon: Theology & Philosophy

Introduction

Even the most sober and analytical of seemingly objective reporting has a *story* to tell. Plot, narration, and character come together in journalism as surely as they do in fiction, and it doesn't court relativism to acknowledge that journalists always have to make literary choices that structure, shape, and alter what they have to say. Journalism may be defined by that famous interrogative sestet—who, what, where, when, how, and why—yet by deciding what to focus on, what to let in and what to leave out, how to shape the material and how to plot it, objective reporting still constructs its own world—whether or not the facts themselves are unassailable. That insight was at the core of the New Journalism movement, which emerged in the 1960s and 1970s. Writers such as Truman Capote, Joan Didion, Gay Talese, Hunter S. Thompson, and Tom Wolfe revolutionized journalism by writing brash, innovative, and stylistically sophisticated essays and books that covered everything from Florida's orange juice industry to the space program. Most of all, the New Journalists had no compunction about inserting themselves into the story, embracing Thompson's claim that "there is no such thing as Objective Journalism. The phrase itself is a pompous contradiction in terms."

For all its merits, the New Journalism had a secularism problem: it often ignored the questions of meaning and transcendence that lay at the center of the human experience. While the New Journalists revolutionized how politics, culture, and sports were covered in the media, the so-called "God beat" journalists remained much more staid in their approach, dutifully reporting the election of new popes or the goings-on at Christian colleges more than a reporter's own interaction with their faith—or lack thereof. More subjective articles on religion hewed to the evangelical, the New Age, or the atheistic, with all positions uncomfortable exploring the ambiguity that defines the actual religious experience. Secular newspapers, even the largest and the best of them, always tended to have fewer reporters working on the God beat than on politics, culture, sports, or even the weather page. A perhaps unconscious promotion of the "secularization hypothesis": the dubious notion that religion would become less important over time.

That was until the turn of the millennium, when the 9/11 terrorist attacks reminded secular writers and readers that religion, for good and bad, was still very much pertinent in the modern world. One of the results of this new awareness was a corollary to that experimental reporting of half a century ago: a New Religion Journalism emerging to cover issues of faith with the same literary panache as a Didion or a Talese. At the *Los Angeles Review of Books* (itself an occasional home for New Religion Journalists), Ed Simon defined the New Religion Journalism as being a "mode of nonfiction in which often personal questions of faith are interrogated against the backdrop of wider issues, where authors frequently insert themselves into the story in a manner in which more traditional 'God beat' reporters wouldn't, and most importantly, where the theism/atheism binary is questioned and the full ambiguity and ambivalence of belief can be displayed."

If this new movement has a place of birth, it's probably Jeff Sharlet and Peter Manseau's provocatively named site, *Killing the Buddha*. Drawing its name from a Zen koan on the need to disavow ourselves of idols in the search for truth, *Killing the Buddha* promoted itself as a religion site for people made uncomfortable by church, publishing neither religious apologetics nor secular diatribe but a new type of writing that was thriving in the borderlands between faith and doubt.

Such writing has covered a wide range of issues, from politics (the puzzling support of some evangelical Christians for an overtly immoral president or the emergence of important dissenting evangelical voices) to liberal social activism (the popularity of a pope who is regularly seen as "progressive" or to the increasing acceptance of homosexuality in mainstream denominations) to science and bioethics. When Kelly Baker writes on the role of racism in the institutional church, Ann Neumann on palliative medical care and faith, Patrick Blanchfield on religion and firearms, Nick Ripatrazone on Catholicism and literature, Jeff Kripal on New Age and paranormal faith, and Meghan O'Gieblyn on evangelical identity, to give just a handful of examples, all use tropes and techniques associated with the New Journalism but applied to issues of faith. Even as mainstream journalism is besieged, both politically and economically, editors have realized the crucial role that religion reporting plays, as evidenced, for instance, by the Lilly Endowment's new grant program in support of hiring new religion reporters at the Religion News Service, the Conversation, and the Associated Press. Even though the phenomenon has attracted the attention of perceptive analysts and scholars, it has remained relatively neglected and understudied. Hopefully this anthology will help address this lacuna.

This collection of essays is neither exhaustive nor very systematic. Indeed, it is limited to the English-speaking world, with a focus on the US journalistic scene. The selection is meant to serve as a sampler—to make people want to know more. Without a doubt, the twenty-six pieces gathered here cannot do justice to an increasingly rich, textured, and diverse journalistic literature that has religion at its center. Yet *The God Beat* does bring together some of the finest and most representative examples of this emerging genre—from sites that focus on religion, such as *Killing the Buddha*, *Religion Dispatches*, and the *Revealer,* to generalist venues that are conversant with issues of religion, such as *Aeon* and the *Los Angeles Review of Books*.

If journalism involves the use of the storyteller's tools (narrative, dramatization, characterization, and suchlike), then it should be interpreted as such. Indeed, at the heart of *The God Beat* lies the conceit that since any good journalism seeks to tell a story, we should expect a narrative of conflict. Directly or indirectly, explicitly or implicitly, then, an agon is to be found at the core of any good piece of journalism—and the New Journalism in particular. Giving what is due to literary conventions, we've structured our anthology around essays that concern a dialectic of personal, political, scientific, and theological conflict. In other words, you will find here stories involving some sort of disjunction within the self, within society, within the natural world, and within our definitions of the divine. In each of these conflicts there are intimations of the sacred and the profane, the holy and the heretical, the blessed and the blasphemous.

PART I

Personal Agon:
Experience & Identity

Introduction

Spiritual autobiography is one of the most venerable of genres associated with religious writing. Saint Augustine's *Confessions*, Saint Teresa of Avila's *Autobiography*, John Bunyan's *Grace Abounding to the Chief of Sinners*, Thomas Merton's *The Seven Storey Mountain*, and Alex Haley's *The Autobiography of Malcolm X*— all, in differing ways, express something about what it means to be an individual caught up in the forge of religious transformation. While it can be tempting to reduce religion to an issue of individual self-definition and to erroneously define faith as a mere private matter, it is undeniable that the recounted experience of the solitary initiate has a long history within religion, from the Buddha under the bodhi tree to Saul on the road to Damascus to the latest conversion story that you read in the news.

The New Religion Journalism is not without its share of conversion narratives, though the nature of those conversions can be ambiguous. If individuality is the primary medium of our culture, then personal narrative can become a means of complicating and challenging our received notions of what it means to be an individual—especially as concerns definitions of belief. Nat Case, for instance, provides a variation on the traditional statement of faith in his *Aeon* piece, asking what it means to be both an atheist and a Quaker. "I do not believe in God," he offers his antidoxology, and yet "*these* stories, *this magic* . . . they don't bore me. . . . Even though I know they are fiction, I believe in them." For Case, faith is an issue of constructed narrative—not an indictment, but an observation. Burke Gerstenschlager notes something similar in his piece from *Image*, recounting how, as a jaded ex-seminarian, he still wishes to impart the worthiness of faith to his son, realizing that narrative is at the core of any such endeavor: "I want him to create his own world filled with meaning, gleaned from and created by the images and stories around him."

The creation and employment of narratives doesn't necessitate that they be positive ones. Both Tara Isabella Burton and Sands Hall grapple with those noxious creations of the human mind and heart we sometimes call "cults." William Blake famously admitted that he had to create his own system lest he be enslaved by another man's, and while the anarchic generation of new faiths and doctrines can embody a certain hope, both Burton and Hall consider the ways in which the arbitrariness of this freedom can go in darker directions. Burton observes, while remaining honest and respectful about her subjects, that "the uncomfortable truth here is that even *true church* . . . and *cult* aren't so far apart."

As a reaction (or overreaction) to such trends, some people make a conscious decision not to join any church or cult. When asked to respond to Pew Research polls on religious affiliation, they check "none of the above." They form their own church—the religion of the "nones"—which makes the object of Brook Wilensky-Lanford's piece (originally published in *Religion Dispatches*), "How to Talk to 'Nones.'" There is also, unfortunately, the church of those abused and humiliated, to which Patrick

Blanchfield dedicates his piece "Soul Murder" from the *Revealer*, about the clerical sexual abuse scandal within the Roman Catholic Church. Here he presents a spiritual autobiography about how he "left the church for good."

Essays of personal agon are concerned with how an individual struggles with faith or its absence, with God or the opposite. The writing of religion is often a recounting of such struggles. True to the ambiguities at the core of the New Religion Journalism, spiritual autobiography is a genre that can go in uncertain or unusual directions. Yet all of these authors see writing as a means of exploration, definition, and discovery. They are willing to examine the soul as a location to report from; as Briallen Hopper says in her piece from the *Revealer*, "I'd try to write myself towards or away from something. I'd write to uncover and discover."

CHAPTER 1

Learning to Write about Religion

Briallen Hopper

"Writing about religion is both freeing and scary." —*Laura Ferris*

On a gray fall morning in a Queens College classroom, I ask the students in my Writing about Religion class to take out a piece of paper and write about what it's like to write about religion. I tell them I'm working on a piece about it, and I'd love their help thinking it through. As they settle into their thoughts, the room grows quiet, and I see their heads bowed over their work as if in prayer.

> *"I was nervous because I didn't know what to expect. [But] once the class started and we began our assignments I fell in love with the class. I like being able to write about my own religion because it is so personal. It has given me lots of opportunities to self-reflect."* —*Katarzyna Szmuc*

We started the semester by reflecting on what we think religion is. I've taught this class many times, and on the first day I always bring in a bag of objects for my students to ponder: a book of yoga poses, a dollar bill, a colander, a tiny bottle of High John the Conqueror oil, a sprig of mistletoe, a box of incense with a lotus on the label, a box of Manischewitz matzo ball mix, a plain Goya-brand novena candle from the bodega or one with a picture of the Golden Girls on it from Etsy . . . I ask the students to choose an object and work together in pairs to come up with answers: What are some reasons why it might be religious, and some reasons why it might not be? Afterwards we all discuss: Is "religiousness" inherent in an object itself, or does it reside in the object's use? Is religion reliant on community, or personal intention, or tradition, or labeling? Can satire be religion? Or commerce? Or pop culture? Their answers vary, and I write them all on the board.

One year, a student improvised a spell on the spot, anointing the dollar bill with High John oil after she googled to find out who High John was and how conjuring worked. I felt a twinge of secular anxiety in that moment, alongside a sense of wonder. Should a creative writing class be a place where we interrogate our assumptions about religion, or a place where we learn to cast spells? Or both?

"When it came to the initial thought of writing about religion in class it was a bit nerve wracking. Religion has always been a touchy subject and gets touched with a 10[-]foot pole often. . . . I never want to come off ignorant or pushy so I only bring up my religion when asked about it. . . . I was interested to hear about other people's walks with religion. Was it long? Was it short? Is

the walk still happening? Did you two sit on a bench and take a break? You learn a lot from other people's experiences and stories and that's what really help[s] motivate me to keep telling my stories." —Kayla Saxton

At the midpoint in a semester of writing about religion, the students have listened to Harry Potter and the Sacred Text, a podcast that models its textual interpretation on the Jewish practice of havruta (study partners) and the Catholic practice of Lectio Divina (monastic textual reading), and they have applied these ways of reading to texts that are sacred to them: an autographed novel by Maaza Mengiste, a Top 40 song, and a red envelope covered with good-luck messages in Chinese characters. They have read Mary Antin's migration memoir and Flannery O'Connor's prayer journal; they have read religious coming-of-age stories by Langston Hughes, Laila Lalami, and Jia Tolentino; and they have watched a documentary film by Zareena Grewal about Mahmoud Abdul-Rauf, the NBA player who converted to Islam and then refused to stand for the national anthem. They have interviewed classmates and family members and friends. And they have written personal essays about doubt and grief and memory and joy; essays illuminated by church candles on sale for *ena dólario* and household shrines bedecked with gold velvet and Bic lighters. Soon they will write presentations on visits they make to sacred sites. And they will embark on research essays in which they will seek answers to questions that might not have answers.

"It's like soul searching without physically going anywhere. It's like your self, your spiritual self, is being discovered, being understood." —Isabella Costa

"Stories travel." This is the reassurance my graduate school advisor gave me when I was worried about writing about literary traditions other than my own. I see religious stories and forms traveling across time, space, and religious traditions in the texts my students and I read together, and in the ways we use these texts to write stories ourselves.

In the prayer journal she kept as a student in her early twenties, Flannery O'Connor expressed her Catholic faith and doubt in the traditionally Protestant form of extemporaneous prayer, writing informal epistolary entries addressed to "My Dear God." Later, my friend Ashley and I wrote an essay in response to hers, in the form of letters to God, Flannery, and each other. (I've been reliably informed that I'm relentlessly Protestant, and Ashley, the child of a Coptic Christian father from Egypt and a Pentecostal mother from Alabama, identifies as "Copticostal." Like O'Connor, we both believe in borrowing the religious and literary forms we need.)

> *"I do not mean to deny the traditional prayers I have said all my life; but I have been saying them and not feeling them."*
> *—Flannery O'Connor*

A hundred years ago, Mary Antin repurposed stories about the Exodus and the Promised Land to tell a story about fleeing pogroms in Eastern Europe and going to public school in Boston as a secular Jew. Antin's stories traveled from the Pale to the United States, and now I see them traveling through the work of a student who cites Antin as an influence, and whose own story brought her from China to the United States, from Buddhist altars to an altar of language:

"Seemingly, the Chinese have constantly recorded their ideologies into books of prayers and chants, to have language ground their belief—to somehow give it tangibility. During this semester, our class did something similar. We collected our ideologies, specifically our religions, and tied them down to our writing. Though we took it one step further through reflective reinvention. Language is perhaps the most tangible, yet abstract, medium—almost ideological itself. Perhaps, what we did was substitute one ideology for another. In other words, substituting religion [with] a belief that exists outside the sphere of any systematic ideology we had previously been tied down to. When I was younger, religion was mandatory, severe, and repressive. By taking control and writing about it, religion has been replaced by something else—by a reinvention of a religion into a liberated belief outside of any type of familial or national conditioning."—Amanda Long

Writing about religion encompasses stories of deracination and alienation as well as their opposite: the literal racination of anointing with oil distilled from a root. Especially at a college where a third of the students were born outside the United States and two-thirds have parents who were born outside the United States, writing about religion often involves a reckoning with origins both national and existential.

"On a simple piece of paper, the pen glides through, embedding all my feelings into words. Ink splatter[s] throughout the paper as it spills my thoughts and emotions. It allows me to find my deeper feelings and understand who I am as a person. Writing about religion has humbled me and allowed me to touch base

*with my faith. It leads me back to my origins, and remind[s]
me of who God is and what my faith teaches. Throughout this
course, I have learned a great deal about who I am and how I
want to embody Islam." —Maria Sultana*

I ponder the histories that brought us all here. Recently or
long ago, our families found their way to New York City from
China, Colombia, the Czech Republic, the Dominican Republic,
Germany, Greece, Guyana, Honduras, Korea, the Netherlands,
the Philippines, Poland, Puerto Rico, Trinidad, and elsewhere.
In Queens I am often conscious of my status as a white Protestant in a country that has been settled and dominated by white
Protestants, in a borough and on a campus where most people are
neither Protestant nor white. There are many chasms between my
experience and my students'—chasms that I sometimes marvel
at, and sometimes try to bridge. In many ways, we are so different from each other. But for all of us, religion has been a thread
that connected us across continents, or tangled, or snapped. It has
been braided with new threads or left to fray.

*"Why do I pray? Why do I fast? Religion writing demands ask-
ing questions and investigation." —Zainab Gani*

Like I did at their age, and like many college students, my
students are reckoning with a religious inheritance that may
seem tenuous or overwhelming or sometimes both. As a college
student, I often felt estranged from my two worlds: the evangelical subculture I was leaving behind and the secular world around
me that seemed stripped of meaning. My religious struggle was
not a crisis of piety or belief but a crisis of community. I had
no trouble praying or affirming creeds, but I couldn't imagine

a permanent place for myself in a religious world where women were expected to marry young and submit to men, and where women could not become scholars or writers. I survived that time by writing myself through it. When I felt brave enough, I'd try to write myself towards or away from something. I'd write to uncover and discover.

"It really challenges you to think deeper. Not only on your own but also [with or about] your family." —Ivana Cruz

Unlike many people in this country, but like most of my students, I lived with my family during college. Writing was my privacy and my escape. By going to a secular college and pursuing an academic career, I was slowly writing myself out of a community that practiced excommunication and shunning of wayward women—a community my family had made their life in for decades. I felt that writing had the power to free me, but I didn't yet know what I was writing myself into.

"The experience was cathartic. The ability to get your own feelings out and ask all these important questions everyone asks but are too afraid to admit it is something very enchanting." —Elisabeth Mercado

I wrote to God, I wrote to my professors, I wrote to no one. Like some of my students, I didn't have a computer. When I was writing to meet deadlines, I stayed up late at a communal computer on campus, sipping surreptitiously from some smuggled-in caffeine, fueling my papers on Louisa May Alcott and Frederick Douglass with the restlessness of my faith and doubt. At home in bed as I lay with my notebooks, I wrote words over and over in a self-soothing trance that felt like transcribing glossolalia, channeling syllables in flowing ink that turned language into shapes and lines. Lifelines.

> *"Writing about religion this semester has been difficult. However it has been so therapeutic for me because of my experiences, which were not all good. Writing about it has helped me reevaluate my relationship with it and put some of my hateful experiences in perspective."* —Qadeera Murphy

For me and for some of my students, religion has sometimes been an encounter with hate. How do we find the courage to resist the rules that would condemn us? I was told that sex outside of heterosexual marriage made women as worthless as crumpled paper. I was able to embrace my life as a fallen woman when I decided my body was as God breathed it in Scripture. I decided to live as if my experience was a source of authority. Writing about religion requires a sense of one's own authority.

> *"My self and experiences that I had are the sources and proofs of my writing."* —Eunice Chang

Treating one's experience as a sacred text to ponder and to wrestle with, or as a ritual to reinvent: this is the work of an essayist and a memoirist. It might also be the work of any religion writer. What you have witnessed, you must testify. In a world full of libraries and search engines, your own varieties of experience are still evidence. Your experience of libraries and search engines is evidence too.

> *"To write about religion means to write from the heart, to be truthful and transparent. I think it has little to do with*

persuasion[;] rather it serves as a testimony/recollection of one part of a person's life. . . . It brings perspective." —*Jaylin Yee*

My testimony is that after a turbulent time in my teens and twenties, when my religious life was in chronic crisis and my writing life was punctuated by panic attacks, I arrived at a tenable truce in both. I'm now an amateur believer, a professional writer, and midwife to the writing of others. My writing no longer feels like spirit writing. Instead it feels like a daily service that must be rendered, as comforting and tiring as any other ritual practice that feels both optional and not.

"Having faith in something . . . It brings people a lot of comfort but also a lot of frustration." —*Maggie Chen*

The best writing advice I ever received was from a graduate school professor who told me to write out of a sense of unease. I'd already been doing this all my life, but she gave it the stamp of approval I needed. I tell my students that uneasily mixed feelings are a writer's gift, and nothing creates more mixed feelings than religion. One of the taglines of Killing the Buddha, the publication I coedit, is "a religion magazine for people made anxious by churches." Are you exasperated by the smell of incense? Are the prayer beads in your palm getting slick with sweat? Does the sound of a Hammond organ start to dissolve your own organs? Maybe you, too, might be a religion writer.

Or maybe your unease is the unease of homesickness, and an uncertainty about where home might be.

"I've felt the urge to want to connect with religion. I distanced myself and had doubted God because of all the faults I have

made. Writing made me realize that I do believe in God and have faith. It is challenging because although I want to reconnect myself with religion, I don't know if it'll be as a Catholic. . . . I am open to anything." —Chelseajoy Cabrega

Not all my students are on a personal religious quest. Many end up taking the class because it fulfills a writing requirement and fits with their work schedules. Some use it as a way of learning about their friends or neighborhoods. Others take the opportunity to write about their preexisting interests in *The Handmaid's Tale* or astrology or digital art. Regardless of why they are here, I want them to have the time and opportunity to find their visceral curiosity and write from it. In the midst of long commutes and long days, I want their writing to make them feel alive. I want them to be thinking about their research questions as they stand and sway on the subway. I want them to experience their own uncertainty as a place to begin.

"I always figured that in order to write about religion, you need to know your views the way you know the back of your hand. I've found that this is actually not true." —Nick Armont

For the past two weeks the back of my hand has been recovering from a burn that turned it brown, then fuchsia. For a while the skin swelled like a water balloon and then it collapsed and wrinkled like an elephant's hide. I can't give a clear account of my religious views, and I don't know the back of my hand at all. Some people write to find out what they know. It's also worth turning to writing as an alternative to knowing.

"I've truly come to believe none of it and all of it. So now my question isn't why *people believe or* what *they believe, but* how *they believe in* just one thing." —Allison McFarlane

How *do* other people believe what they do? How do they pray as they do, and eat as they do, and desire as they do, and mourn as they do? How do they live? These are questions that express a desire for connection, and they motivate so much of what my students and I have read together: Zora Neale Hurston apprenticing herself to a practitioner of hoodoo in New Orleans; Ellen Willis arguing with her Orthodox family in Israel; James Baldwin sitting down to a meal with Elijah Muhammad. These questions express a desire to understand others beyond the self, even and especially when they mystify us most. They are outward looking in a way that I aspire to be when I think about writing and religion. My own religion writing started with my internal struggle, and it has turned into a social practice. I wrote a syllabus that starts with writing about ourselves and ends with research about the world around us. But of course this is a false dichotomy: because writing is a conversation between multiple voices, a dynamic between different worlds and selves.

> *"Most of the time it feels LOVELY to hear [about] the lives of other people. I learn a lot from others when they speak of their lives. But sometimes it can feel very difficult to speak about myself and the things I've dealt with. What really resonates with me is to hear my classmates' stories and how they have dealt with hardship much worse than mine. This class teaches me how to figure out my religion while observing and respecting other religions. And with the multiple stories we read, I can say I'm getting closer to becoming a much more peaceful and accepting person." —Antonio Martinez*

Eleven years ago, I thought God might be calling me to be an academic chaplain—a minister to college students. I applied to academic jobs and divinity schools and decided to let God decide.

God chose Yale Divinity School, where for two years I trained to minister and to preach. But in the end God was no match for my student loans. After sinking deeper and deeper into debt, I realized I needed a job with benefits as soon as possible, and I left divinity school a year early to become a writing teacher. In the years since then, I've mostly stopped preaching. Instead, I've been listening to the sermons and khutbahs and letters and blessings and sacred texts and incantations my students are writing—to me, to each other, and maybe to you—as they learn to write about religion from classes, from novels, from radio waves, from tarot cards, from grieving, or from Friday Prayer:

> *"When I write I am able to come to terms with doubt and fear. When I write about religion, I am able to look God in the face and the world in the face through pen and paper and say that I am in control of my life. When I write about religion I find the divine in those I love. I find religion in things not usually considered religious. I find holy the body, the mind, the inter-connectedness of society." —Sayyid Mohammed*

CHAPTER 2

In Praise of Gods
That Don't Exist

Nat Case

I read voraciously as a child, even obsessively. Our family drove across the United States when I was thirteen, and I hardly noticed the scenery, eyes glued to a mammoth book of classic science-fiction stories. As I recall, this ticked off my parents.

Magical stories moved me to tears. I vividly remember, at the age of eight, being surprised at how deeply the second chapter of Astrid Lindgren's *The Brothers Lionheart* (1973) affected me. The narrator dies and goes to the land where sagas come from, and when he arrives he finds that all that he had wanted—to be strong, healthy, and beautiful like his older brother—has come to be, and that his beloved brother is there, too. And this is just the beginning of the story. I remember arriving at the end of Penelope Farmer's *The Summer Birds* (1962) and weeping bitterly as the children, who have spent the summer flying about the English countryside, return gravity-bound to school while their lonely classmate and the strange bird-boy fly off together over the ocean.

This essay wasn't supposed to be about the stories I read as a child. It was supposed to be about how I manage to be an atheist within a religious community, and why I dislike the term "atheism." But however I wrote that essay, the words died on the page. *That* story comes down to this: I do not believe in God, and I am bored with atheism. But *these* stories, *this* magic, and their presence in my heart, they don't bore me—they are alive. Even though I know they are fiction, I believe in them.

> "Truth," in the sense that it was used by seventeenth-century Friends, had less to do with verifiable evidence and more to do with sense of being a "true friend," an arrow flying true.

My main religious practice today is meeting for worship with the Religious Society of Friends: I am a Quaker. Meeting for worship, to a newcomer, can feel like a blank page. Within the tradition of Friends, it is anything but blank: it is a *religious* service, expectant waiting upon the presence of God. So it's not meditation, or "free time." But that's how I came to it at first, at the Quaker high school I attended.

After almost fifteen years away, I returned to Quakerism in 1997. During a difficult patch of my life, a friend said I needed to do something for myself. So I started going to the meetinghouse on Sunday mornings. What I rediscovered was the simple fact of space. It was a hiatus, a parenthesis inserted into a complicated, twisty life. Even if it held nothing but breath, it was a relief, and in that relief, quiet notions emerged that had been trampled into the ground of everyday life.

I am an atheist, but I've been bothered for a long time by the mushiness I've found in the liberal spiritual communities that admit nonbelievers such as me. I've spent the better part of two decades trying to put my finger on the source of this unease, but it is not a question to be solved by the intellect: it must be lived through.

Several years ago, Marshall Massey, a fellow Friend, pointed out to me that "truth," in the sense that it was used by seventeenth-century Friends, had less to do with verifiable evidence and more to do with sense of being a "true friend," an arrow flying true. It was about remaining on a path, not about conforming to the facts of the world. This points to a deep truth: we humans are built for a different kind of rigor than that of evidentiary fact. It is at least as much about consistency, discipline, and loyalty as it is about the kinds of repeatable truth that we hold up in a scientific world as fundamental.

This is a large part of what drew me to the Friends rather than the Unitarians or other study groups. Binding oneself to specific patterns, habits, and language seems to have the effect of providing a spine, and Quakers seemed to have more of this spine than other groups I was attracted to. It was a partial solution to my sense of mushiness, but it certainly didn't solve everything.

If you are really going to be part of a community, just showing up for the main meal is not enough: you need to help cook and clean up. So it has been with me and the Quakers: I'm concerned with how my community works, and so I've served on committees (Quakerism is all about committees). There's pastoral care to accomplish, a building to maintain, First-Day School (Quakerese for Sunday School) to organize. And there's the matter of how we as a religious community will bring our witness into the world. Perhaps this language sounds odd coming from a nontheist, but as I hope I've shown, I'm not a nontheist first. I've been involved in prison visiting and have been struck at the variety of religious attitudes among volunteers: some for whom the visiting is in itself ministry, and others for whom it's simply social action towards justice (the program grew out of visiting conscientious objectors in the Vietnam era). The point is: theological differences are not necessarily an issue when there's work to be done.

But the committees I've been in have also had a curious sense of unease too, a sense of something missing, and I've now been on three committees that were specifically charged with addressing aspects of a sense of malaise and communal disconnect. The openness of liberal religion resonates strongly with me. It means I *do* have a place, and not just in the closet or as a hypocrite. But I wonder if my presence, and the presence of atheists and skeptics such as me, is part of the problem.

People need focus. There's a reason why the American mythologist Joseph Campbell chose the hero's journey as his fundamental myth: we don't give out faith and loyalty to an idea nearly as readily as we give it to a hero, a person. And so a God whom we understand not as a vague notion or spirit, but as a living presence, with voice and face and will and command—this is what I think most people want in a visceral way. In some ways, it's what we need.

And I do not believe such a God exists in our universe.

Here's a peculiar sense I've been getting in Friends committee meetings: we often don't know *how* to seek the will of God; we are uncertain whether God actually *possesses* will. And yet, I suspect that the way out of our tortuous debates is to stop arguing and submit. That submission—because that's what it is, in the same sense that *islam* means "submission"—is what pulls us out of ourselves and gets us lined up to do what needs doing instead of arguing about whose idea is better.

In the seventeenth century, the Quaker theologian Robert Barclay argued for the bodiless Holy Spirit as the only way to reach Christ and then God. Nowadays, we might find comfort in the spirit alone, or the Light, as Quakers describe an inwardly detected sense of the divine. But submission to something so vague is difficult. We might love and treasure and "hold our beloved friends in the Light," but that's not a humbling of self, a laying low of ego, and that is what I believe we are missing.

How can we do that? How can *I* do that? Submitting to something I am pretty sure doesn't exist? How can I bow down to a fiction? I did it all the time as a child. Open the cover of the book, and I'm in that world. If I'm lucky, and the book is good enough, some of that world comes with me out into the world of atoms and weather, taxes and death. It's a story, and sometimes stories are stronger than stuff.

Maybe part of the trick is realizing that it doesn't have to be just *my* little bubble of fiction. I can read a novel, or I can go gaming into the evening with friends. I can watch a ballet on a darkened stage, or I can roar along to my favorite band in the mosh pit. I hated school dances with a passion, yet I have been a morris dancer for twenty-three years now: I just had to find the form that was a right fit. I don't pray aloud, or with prescribed formulas. But I can ask Whatever-There-Is a question, or ask for help from the universe, or say thank you. And now that I'm in a place with a better fit, sometimes I get answers back. And so there I am, a confirmed skeptic, praying in a congregation.

A year and a half ago, our family began worshipping with a smaller Conservative Friends group. Conservative Friends are socially and theologically liberal but stricter in adhering to older Quaker practices. The group uses the Montessori-based Godly Play curriculum for the children: it's all about stories. Every session begins with a quieting and a focusing. The leader tells a story from the Bible or from the Quaker story book. Then "wondering" questions are asked that spur the children to reflect on what's going on, and what they would do in the same situation.

> Maybe that god would tell us not to tramp over the earth in armies, pretending we are bigger than we are, and that dying is okay.

I wish I'd had this great program as a child. The teacher is a good storyteller who clearly loves the kids, and they love the stories and the time with their friends. To me, it's such an improvement on school-style lessons. It says: this is a different kind of knowing and learning—this is not about facts and theories you need to learn, but about the stories we want to become part of your life.

I love facts and theories, the stuff of the world. I spend most of my life wrestling and dancing with all this amazing matter. As the Australian comic Tim Minchin says in his rant-poem "Storm" (2008): "Isn't this enough? Just this world? Just this beautiful, complex, wonderfully unfathomable world?" And yes, it's enough. We don't need to tell lies about the real world in order to make it magical. But we do still need impossible magic for our own irrational selves. At any rate, I do.

Because I don't *feel* stuff-and-logic-based explanations deep down in my toes. There are no miracle stories of flying children there, or brothers reborn into the land where the sagas come from. The language of "stuff is all there is" tells me that I *can*—even *ought* to—be rational and sensible, but it doesn't make me *want* to be. "Atheism" tells me what I am not, and I yearn to know what I *am*. What I am has a spine, it's a thing I must be true to, because otherwise it evaporates into the air, dirt, and water of the hard world.

Maybe I—we—need to start small, rebuilding gods that we talk to, and who talk back. Or just one whom we can plausibly imagine, our invisible friend. Maybe part of our problem is that we don't actually *want* to talk to the voice of Everything, because Everything has gotten so unfathomably huge. George Fox, the founder of Quakerism, didn't have to think about light-years, let alone billions of light-years. The stars now are too far away to be our friends or speak to us in our need. Maybe we could talk to a god whom we imagined in our house. Maybe we could ask what is wanted, and hear what is needed. Maybe that god would tell us not to tramp over the earth in armies, pretending we are bigger than we are, and that dying is okay, because it's just something that happens when your life is over. Maybe we would ask for help and comfort from unexpected places, and often enough receive it and be thankful for it.

Maybe we need to name that little god something other than God, because maybe our God has a boss who has a boss whose boss runs the universe. Maybe we name this god Ethel, or Larry, or Murgatroyd. Maybe there is no god but God . . . or maybe there just is no God. And maybe it doesn't matter. Maybe we just tell stories that ring true to us and say up front that we know they are fiction. We can let people love these stories or hate them. Maybe imagining impossible things—such as flying, the land where sagas come from, God—is what is needed. Maybe we don't need the gods to be real. Maybe all we need is to trust more leaps of the imagination.

CHAPTER 3

What Is a Cult?

Tara Isabella Burton

Cults, generally speaking, are a lot like pornography: *you know them when you see them.* It would be hard to avoid the label on encountering (as I did, carrying out field work last year) twenty people toiling unpaid on a Christian farming compound in rural Wisconsin—people who venerated their leader as the closest thing to God's representative on Earth. Of course, *they* argued vehemently that they were not a cult. Ditto for the two-thousand-member church I visited outside Nashville, whose parishioners had been convinced by an ostensibly Christian diet program to sell their houses and move to the "one square mile" of the New Jerusalem promised by their charismatic church leader. Here they could eat—and live—in accordance with God and their leader's commands. It's easy enough, as an outsider, to say, instinctively: *yes, this is a cult.*

Less easy, though, is identifying *why*. Knee-jerk reactions make for poor sociology, and delineating what, exactly, makes a cult (as opposed to a "proper" religious movement) often comes down to judgment calls based on perceived legitimacy. Prod that perception of legitimacy, however, and you find value judgments based on age, tradition, or "respectability" (that nice middle-class couple down the street, say, as opposed to Tom Cruise jumping up and down on a couch). At the same time, the markers of cultism as applied more theoretically—a single charismatic leader, an insular structure, seeming religious ecstasy, a financial burden on members—can also be applied to any number of new or burgeoning religious movements that we *don't* call cults.

Often (just as with pornography), what we choose to see as a cult tells us as much about ourselves as about what we're looking at.

Historically, our obsession with cults seems to thrive in periods of wider religious uncertainty, with "anticult" activism in the United States peaking in the 1960s and '70s, when the United States religious landscape was growing more diverse, and the sway of traditional institutions of religious power was eroding. This period, dubbed by the economic historian Robert Fogel as the "Fourth Great Awakening," saw interest in personal spiritual and religious practice spike alongside a decline in mainline Protestantism, giving rise to numerous new movements. Some of these were Christian in nature, for example the "Jesus Movement"; others were heavily influenced by the pop-cultural ubiquity of pseudo-Eastern and New Age thought: the International Society for Krishna Consciousness (aka the Hare Krishna), modern Wicca, Scientology. Plenty of these movements were associated with young people—especially young countercultural people with suspicious politics—adding a particular political tenor to the discourse surrounding them.

Against these there sprang a network of "anticult" movements uniting former members of sects, their families, and other objectors. Institutions such as the Cult Awareness Network (CAN) formed in 1978 after the poison fruit-drink (urban legend says Kool-Aid) suicides of Jim Jones and his Peoples Temple. The anticult networks believed that cults brainwashed their members (the idea of *mind control*, as scholars such as Margaret Singer point out, originated in media coverage of torture techniques supposedly used by North Korea during the Korean War). To counter brainwashing, activists controversially abducted and forcibly "deprogrammed" members who'd fallen under a cult's sway. CAN itself was cofounded by a professional deprogrammer, Ted Patrick, who later faced scrutiny for accepting $27,000 from the concerned parents of a woman involved in Leftist politics to, essentially, handcuff her to a bed for two weeks.

But that wasn't all. An equal and no less fervent network of what became known as *countercult* activists emerged among Christians who opposed cults on *theological* grounds and who were as worried about the state of adherents' souls as of their psyches. The Baptist pastor Walter Ralston Martin was sufficiently disturbed by the proliferation of religious pluralism in the United States to write *The Kingdom of the Cults* (1965), which delineated in detail the theologies of those religious movements Martin identified as toxic and provided biblical avenues for the enterprising mainstream Christian minister to oppose them. With more than half a million copies sold, it was one of the top-selling spiritual books of the era.

Writing the history of cults in the United States, therefore, is also writing the history of a discourse of fear: of the unknown, of the decline in mainstream institutions, of change.

Every cultish upsurge—the Mansons, the Peoples Temple, the Sun Myung Moon's Unification Church (or Moonies)—met with an equal and opposite wave of hysteria. In 1979, US sociologists Anson D. Shupe, J. C. Ventimiglia, and David G. Bromley coined the term "atrocity tale" to describe lurid media narratives about the Moonies. Particularly gruesome anecdotes (often told by emotionally compromised former members) worked to place the entire religious movement beyond the bounds of cultural legitimacy and to justify extreme measures—from deprogramming to robust conservatorship laws—to prevent vulnerable people falling victim to the cultic peril. True or not, the "'atrocity tale" allowed anticult activists and families worried about their children's well-being (or their suspicious politics) to replace sociological or legal arguments with emotional ones.

This terror peaked when atrocity tales began outnumbering genuine horrors. The "Satanic panic" of the 1980s brought with it a wave of mass hysteria over cult Satanists ritually abusing children in day care centers, something that seems entirely to have been the product of false memories. In the now-discredited bestselling book *Michelle Remembers* (1980) by the psychiatrist Lawrence Pazder and his patient Michelle Smith (later, Mrs. Lawrence Pazder), the lead author relates how he unlocked Smith's memories of Satanic childhood. This influential atrocity tale influenced the three-year case in the 1980s against an administrator of the McMartin Preschool in Los Angeles and her son, a teacher, that racked up sixty-five crimes. The prosecution spun a fear-stoking narrative around outlandish claims, including bloody animal mutilations. The number of convictions? Zero. But mass-media hysteria made Satanic panic a national crisis, and a pastime.

And yet it is impossible to dismiss anticult work as pure hysteria. There might not be Satanists lurking round every corner, lying in wait to kidnap children or sacrifice bunny rabbits to Satan, but

the dangers of spiritual, emotional, and sexual abuse in small-scale, unsupervised religious communities, particularly those isolated from the mainstream or dominant culture, is real enough.

It is also keenly contemporary. The decentered quality of the US religious landscape, the proliferation of storefront churches and "home churches," not to mention the potential of the internet, makes it easier than ever for groups to splinter and fragment without the oversight of a particular religious or spiritual tradition. And some groups are, without a doubt, toxic. I've been to compounds, home churches, and private churches where children are taught to obey community leaders so unquestioningly that they have no contact with the outside world; where the death of some children as a result of corporal punishment has gone unacknowledged by church hierarchy; or where members have died because group leaders discouraged them from seeking medical treatment. I've spoken to people who have left some of these movements utterly broken—having lost jobs, savings, their sense of self, and even their children (powerful religious groups frequently use child custody battles to maintain a hold over members).

In one Reddit post, James Chatham, formerly a member of the Remnant Fellowship, a controversial church founded by the Christian diet guru Gwen Shamblin, listed every reason he'd been punished as a child:

Allow me to give you a short list of the super-crazy things I recieved [*sic*] "Gods loving discipline" for.
Opening my eyes during a prayer
Joking with adults (That joked back with me) . . .
Saying that i don't trust "Leaders" (Their name for those that run the church)

Asking almost any question about the bible.

Trying to stop another kid from beating my skull in . . .

Sneezing . . .

Not being able to stand for 30 minutes straight with no break.

Asking if my mother loved me more than god.

Does such extreme disciplinarianism make the Remnant Fellowship a cult? Or does the question of labeling distract us from wider issues at hand?

The historian J. Gordon Melton of Baylor University in Texas says that the word *cult* is meaningless: it merely assumes a normative framework that legitimizes some exertions of religious power—those associated with mainstream organizations—while condemning others. Groups that have approved, "orthodox" beliefs are considered legitimate, while groups whose interpretation of a sacred text differs from established norms are delegitimized *on that basis alone.* Such definitions also depend on who is doing the defining. Plenty of "cults" identified by anticult and countercult groups, particularly Christian countercult groups such as the EMNR (Evangelical Ministries to New Religions), are recognized elsewhere as "legitimate" religions: Jehovah's Witnesses, the Church of Jesus Christ of Latter-Day Saints, even the Catholic Church have all come under fire, alongside the Moonies or the Peoples Temple.

> **We label cults "cults" because they're easy pickings . . . even if their beliefs are no more outlandish, in theory, than reincarnation.**

To deny a so-called "cult" legitimacy based on its size, or beliefs, or on atrocity tales alone is, for Melton, to play straight into normative definitions of power. We label cults "cults" because they're easy pickings, in a sense; even if their beliefs are no more outlandish, in theory, than reincarnation or the transubstantiation of the wafer in the Catholic Eucharist.

In a paper delivered before the Center for Studies on New Religions in 1999, Melton said: "we have reached a general consensus that New Religions are genuine and valid religions. A few may be bad religion and some may be led by evil people, but they are religions." To call a group—be it Scientology or the Moonies or the Peoples Church—a cult is to obscure the fact that to study it and understand it *properly*, both sociologically and theologically, we must treat it like any other religion (Melton prefers the term "New Religious Movements"). His point underscores the fact that questions of legitimacy, of authority and hierarchy, and of delineation between inner and outer circles are as much the provenance of "classical" religious studies as of any analysis of cults.

Whatever our knee-jerk reaction to Scientology, say, and however much we *know* that compounds where members voluntarily hand over their savings to charismatic leaders are creepy and/or wrong, we cannot forget that the history of Christianity (and other faiths) is no less pockmarked by accusations of cultism. Each wave of so-called "heresy" in the chaotic and contradictory history of the Christian churches was accompanied by a host of atrocity tales that served to legitimize one or another form of practice. This was hardly one-sided. Charges were levied against groups we might now see as "orthodox" as well as at groups that history consigns to the dustbin of heresy: issues of ecclesiastical management (as in the Donatist controversy) or semantics (the heresies of Arianism, for example) could—and did—result in mutual anathema: *we are the true church; you are a cult.*

Of course, the uncomfortable truth here is that even *true church* (large, established, tradition-claiming church) and *cult* aren't so far apart—at least when it comes to counting up red flags. The presence of a charismatic leader? What was John Calvin? (Heck, what was Jesus Christ?) A tradition of secrecy around specialized texts or practices divulged only to select initiates? Just look at the practitioners of the Eleusinian mysteries in ancient Greece, or contemporary mystics in a variety of spiritual traditions, from the Jewish Kabbalah to the Vajrayāna Buddhist tradition. Isolated living on a compound? Consider contemporary convents or monasteries. A financial obligation? Christianity, Judaism, and Islam all promote regular tithing back into the religious community. A toxic relationship of abuse between spiritual leaders and their flock? The instances are too numerous and obvious to list.

If we refuse any neat separation between *cult* and *religion*, aren't we therefore obligated to condemn both? Only ontological metaphysical truth can possibly justify the demands that any religion makes upon its adherents. And if we take as writ the proposition that God isn't real (or that we can never know what God wants), it's easy to collapse the distinction with a wave of a hand: all religions are cults, and all are probably pretty bad for you. The problem with this argument is that it, too, falls down when it comes to creating labels. If we take Melton's argument further, the debate over what makes a cult, writ large, might just as easily be relabeled: what makes a religion?

Besides, accusations of cultism have been leveled at secular or semi-secular organizations as well as metaphysically inclined ones. Any organization offering identity-building rituals and a coherent narrative of the world and how to live in it is a target, from Alcoholics Anonymous to the vegan restaurant chain the Loving Hut, founded by the Vietnamese entrepreneur-cum-spiritual leader Ching Hai, to the practice of yoga (itself rife with structural issues of spiritual and sexual abuse), to the modern phenomenon of the popular, paleo-associated sport-exercise program CrossFit, which a Harvard Divinity School study used as an example of contemporary "religious" identity. If the boundaries between *cult* and *religion* are already slippery, those between *religion* and *culture* are more porous still.

In his seminal book on religion, *The Interpretation of Cultures* (1973), the anthropologist Clifford Geertz denies that human beings can live outside culture (what he calls the capital-M "Man"). Everything about how we see the world and ascribe meanings to symbols, at a linguistic as well as a spiritual level, is mediated by the semiotic network in which we operate. Religion, too, functions within culture as a series of ascriptions of meaning that define how we see ourselves, others, and the world. Geertz writes:

> Without further ado, then, a *religion* is:
> *(1) a system of symbols which acts to (2) establish powerful, pervasive, and long-lasting moods in men by (3) formulating conceptions of a general order of existence and (4) clothing those conceptions with such an aura of factuality that (5) the moods and motivations seem uniquely realistic.*

Such a definition of religion isn't limited to groups with formal doctrines about "'God," but encompasses any wider cultural narrative of the self in the world.

Geertz's definition—somewhat dated now—has been updated: most notably by postcolonial thinkers such as Talal Asad, who argue that Geertz overlooks one of the most significant mechanisms for meaning-making: *power.* How we conceive of God, our world, our spiritual values (a hunger for "cleansing" in yoga, or for proof of strength, as in CrossFit, or for salvific grace) is inextricable from both our own identities and our position within a group in which questions of power are never, can never be, absent.

Even the narratives that many religions, cults, and religious-type groups promulgate—that they are in some sense separate from "the others" (the Hebrew word for "holiness," *qadosh*, derives from the word for separation)—are themselves tragically flawed: they are both apart from and firmly within the problems of a wider culture.

> Cults don't come out of nowhere; they fill a vacuum, for individuals and, as we've seen, for society at large.

Take, for example, the cultural pervasiveness of ideals of female thinness. It is precisely the aspirational desire to be Kate Moss skinny that allows a Christian diet program such as Remnant to attract members in the first place (*don't eat too much; it's a sin!*). So too does it allow cults of "wellness" to take hold: a woman who is already obsessed with cleansing toxins, making her body "perfect" and "clean," and "purifying" herself is more likely to get involved with a cultlike yoga practice and/or be susceptible to sexual abuse by her guru (a not uncommon occurrence).

Likewise, the no less culturally pervasive failure of mainstream institutions—from the health care system to mainline Protestant churches—to address the needs of their members gives rise, with equal potency, to individuals susceptible to conspiracy theories, or cultish behaviors: to anything that might provide them with meaningfulness.

The very collapse of wider religious narratives—an established cultural collectivism—seems inevitably to leave space for smaller, more intense, and often more toxic groups to reconfigure those Geertzian symbols as they see fit. Cults don't come out of nowhere; they fill a vacuum, for individuals and, as we've seen, for society at large. Even Christianity itself proliferated most widely as a result of a similar vacuum: the relative decline of state religious observance, and political hegemony, in the Roman Empire.

After all, the converse of the argument *"If God isn't real then all religions are probably cults"* is this: if a given religion or cult is *right*, metaphysically speaking, then that rightness is the most important thing in the universe. If a deity really, truly wants you to, say, flagellate yourself with a whip (as Catholic penitents once did), or burn yourself on your husband's funeral pyre, then no amount of commonsense reasoning can amount to a legitimate deterrent: the ultimate cosmic meaningfulness of one's actions transcends any other potential need. And to be in a *community* of people who can help reinforce that truth, whose rituals and discourse and symbols help not only to strengthen a sense of meaningfulness but also to ground it in a sense of collective purpose, then that meaningfulness becomes more vital still: it sits at the core of what it is to be human.

To talk about religion as a *de facto* abuse vector of hierarchical power (in other words, a cult writ large) is a meaningless oversimplification. It's less an arrow than a circle: a cycle of power, meaning, identity, and ritual. We define ourselves by participating in something, just as we define ourselves against those who *don't* participate in something. Our understanding of ourselves— whether we're cradle Catholics, newly joined-up members of the Hare Krishna, or members of a particularly rabid internet fandom—as people whose actions have cosmic if not metaphysical significance gives us a symbolic framework in which to live our lives, even as it proscribes our options. Every time we repeat a ritual, from the Catholic Mass to a prayer circle on a farm compound to a CrossFit workout, it defines us—and we define the people around us.

Today's cults might be secular, or they might be theistic. But they arise from the same place of need, and from the failure of other, more "mainstream" cultural institutions to fill it. If God did not exist, as Voltaire said, we would have to invent him. The same is true for cults.

CHAPTER 4

Light a Candle

Sands Hall

Julie Christofferson was a devoted Scientologist. But one weekend, while she was visiting her parents, her distraught mother took the doorknobs off the doors, hired a deprogrammer, and didn't let her daughter out of the house until Julie had been convinced that the Church of Scientology was a con. Christofferson sued the church, claiming it had misrepresented L. Ron Hubbard's credentials (that he was a graduate of Princeton, that he'd served in the navy) and promised things it didn't deliver (improve her eyesight, raise her intelligence). Above all, she sought restitution for the years she'd devoted to Scientology, which had, she said, *derailed her life's plans*. In 1977, she won $2 million. The Church demanded a retrial. In May of 1985, a Portland jury gave Christofferson Titchbourne (in the intervening years she'd married) $39 million.

The Scientology lawyers swore she'd never see a penny of it. The organization itself exhorted all Scientologists to immediately travel to Oregon, to protest this attack on religious freedom.

At the time, I was living in Los Angeles, immersed in Scientology. I studied at a place called Celebrity Center. Three years before, when I'd been introduced to Scientology, I might have been considered a bit of a celebrity, at least by Scientologists: seasons with the Oregon and Colorado Shakespeare Festivals and the Old Globe Theatre, a stint on a soap opera, an occasional "guest star" on popular sitcoms. But that career had flagged: I spent a lot of time in Scientology course rooms studying concepts that would, I was convinced, improve my life.

In any case. A bus had been hired to take a load of L.A. Scientologists to Portland.

"Sweetheart," my boyfriend Skye said. "We have to get on that bus."

"I don't want to," I said, but I knew protest was futile. By then I was familiar with what Hubbard called "Tone 40"—a command that expects and receives total compliance—and I went to pack a bag.

The next morning, a bus belched diesel outside Celebrity Center, a lovely building that looked as if it been lifted from a gothic fairy tale and plonked down on Franklin Avenue. Once upon a time, I thought, as I walked down the filthy aisle to settle into a dilapidated seat next to a dirty window, I'd believed in fairy tales, and I'd believed in my own bright future. But these days, even as I persuaded myself that I was a happy Scientologist, I often felt like a princess that had been captured, locked away from the world.

As the bus headed north, I was surly, unresponsive to the cheer emanating from my fellow Scientologists, wondering if I, like Ms. Christofferson, had "derailed my life's plans." My comrades were bursting with pride and excitement at the idea of marching for their religion. Chick Corea had canceled a concert to be there! John Travolta was flying in! They began to sing songs from the civil rights movement: "Kumbaya," "We Shall Overcome." My heroes, Joan Baez and Pete Seeger, had sung these songs, and I could not help but join in. "Someone's prayin', Lord," I sang, thinking, though, that in Scientology there wasn't much praying. "We shall live in peace," I sang, wondering how I'd ever find peace with my deeply distressed parents, who were frantic over what I was doing with my life. "We shall not be moved," we sang, my friends Kanga and Margie providing beautiful, soaring harmonies.

And then, halfway to Portland, the bus broke down. I was thrilled.

One of the things I noticed about Scientology, and then tried not to notice—a self-imposed mind control that both fascinates and horrifies me now—was that this happened a lot with Scientology's equipment. This was in the 1980s, before Hubbard died and David Miscavige became head of the church and began to lavish money on what he terms "Ideal Organizations"; ever since, anything physically related to Scientology has tended to be impressively new and shiny, thick and glossy, trumpeting its expense and thereby (at least implied) the church's success. But even in those days, we all understood that the equipment did not fail because it was ancient or uncared for or put away improperly; no, that was never the reason. The reason was that a Suppressive Person was in the vicinity. The SP caused the malfunction, the missed connection, the breakdown.

It was quite possible that I was the Suppressive Person. Because unlike my friends, who were frustrated not to be in Portland, marching, I was delighted to spend hours sitting on a dirty linoleum floor waiting for a second chartered bus. People dozed on knapsacks or smoked outside. Leaning my back against a wall, I closed my eyes, marveling, as I did all those days, how I could be so confused. Hadn't I always wanted to be involved in a "movement"? Here was this opportunity to march for something important. Wasn't religious freedom as important as civil rights? Or peace? Isn't the right to worship as we choose supposedly bedrock in this country? Shouldn't I be proud to be involved in such an important cause?

But another voice spoke with snide authority: Really, Sands? *Scientology* is where you want to pour those energies?

I scrubbed my head with the fingers of both hands and gave a little groan. But a phrase I'd only recently heard started to run through my head: *it is better to light a candle than to curse the darkness*. I liked the message. With an effort akin to heaving a loose bra strap back into place, I focused on that idea. Throughout history, candles had been kept flickering in spite of astounding darknesses: the Inquisition, the Holocaust, the Communist crackdown in China. Then I wondered why I was pondering religious tyrannies, and pulled my mind away from that (I was always doing this) to gaze about the bleak bus station, and from there back inward to the bleakness I felt about my continued involvement in what, in spite of constant reassurances from those around me, I worried was, indeed, a cult. Some part of me wished my own mother would take the doorknobs off the doors and hire a deprogrammer, but although she hated—*hated*—that I was "snared" by Scientology, she would never do that. Ironically, she had too much respect for me.

Light a candle for freedom

The words arrived with music in my mind, forming like a fast-motion crystal.

Hold it up for all to see

In the last few years, songwriting, that beloved dance with lyric and music, had become increasingly rare. But this song tugged at me. I pulled my journal from my bag and scribbled the words as fast as they came.

Spark a flame around the world
To burn towards being free

Three years previously, my older brother had suffered a terrible fall that left him brain-damaged, unrecognizable as the charismatic mentor who'd been for me a vital force: he'd led the way into drama as a major; I'd followed him to New York City, where he and friends were creating a theater company. But he'd almost died, and for me in many ways he had. Not understanding that I was grieving, I'd fled New York, convincing myself I was headed to Hollywood to expand my acting career. A chaotic year and a half later, after flinging myself into uncharacteristic activities like sleeping with married men and snorting cocaine, I plunged into marriage with a Scientologist. Only now is it clear to me that I married Jamie, at least in part, for the order Scientology appeared to offer, order that was balm to my churning, unhappy soul.

Light a candle, the tune developed in my head, *light a candle*. This would be the chorus.

To burn towards being free
Light a candle for freedom
To burn eternally

I'd first seen Jamie playing upright bass, brilliantly, in a jazz trio. New to jazz, I fell in love with the music as I fell in love with him. But he scoffed at my folky, Joni Mitchell–inspired song-writing. "Pretty," he said. "But not interesting. Now jazz—jazz is music." I began to find reason to crumple up my songwriting efforts and put them in the trash, where the pages would fill with the brown seepage of coffee grounds. A year after marrying Jamie, I'd divorced him, but not the church; I met Skye, also a Scientologist, soon after. Even divorced from Jamie, his patronizing contempt hovered over my songwriting. Yet these lines appeared:

The truth is in each one of us
To show us how to go

A thought zipped by: show us how to go—*where?*

I would not actually process this for years: that the lyrics were not in support of a religious rally, or even of religious freedom. They were a protest *against* the church, the control it seems to wield over so many lives, a control that makes one feel powerless, that makes one doubt one's own intelligence, that forces one to convince oneself, again and again, that Scientology has the answers. This was true for me, then. It remains true for many, still.

Scientology is masterful at handling doubt: doubt means you have committed a transgression. (Doubt itself is a transgression, which leads one around an endless Möbius strip of reasoning.) Once you face whatever you've done or said, or not done or not said—all of this "processed" with Scientology's assistance—you have an epiphanic realization: You've been "bad"! That made you doubt Scientology. But now that you've cleared all that up, you're "good," and Scientology, just as Hubbard promises, is once again the way, the truth, the light.

Until the next bout of doubt arrives.

It's exhausting. It's impossible to comprehend, now, how I opted to live like that, perpetually off-kilter, so deeply unhappy, for so long.

There's a reason it's called a cult.

I got up and walked over to settle in next to Kanga. Holding the scribbled lyrics before us, I began to sing. She added a harmony. Margie, sitting on the other side, found a fifth. Their harmonies made it sound like a hymn. It *was* a hymn. To candles, to holding a light up in the darkness—even when we're not sure which is the darkness and which the light.

Another bus eventually arrived, and off we went to join the Scientologists who'd flown and driven and hitchhiked and bused to Portland to protest the jury's decision to hand Julie Christofferson Titchbourne those $39 million. Even after we all headed home, we were not allowed to forget this attack on our religion: hammered on us through phone calls, home visits, and endless rallies, we were reminded that every resource of every Scientologist must be devoted to fighting for this cause.

Money, of course. Money, always.

Back in Los Angeles, I booked time in a studio, and Kanga and Margie and I recorded "Light a Candle." I played the song for a Scientologist friend and singer, Gayle. Gayle was very much a celebrity, and she thought it would be perfect for one of these religious freedom rallies. Which is how, one night, I came to be in a backstage honeywagon listening to an impressive array of Scientology musicians performing to thousands who sat entranced by the spectacular nature of the event.

I was once again being treated like a celebrity. That was nice. My song—a song I had written!—would be, because of Gayle's involvement, a focus of the event (Margie had been replaced by

Gayle, "for the good of the cause"). And like my heroes, Joan Baez and Pete Seeger, I was about to sing in support of . . . something important!

But I felt as if I had the flu. My face, reflected in one of the trailer's mirrors, gleamed a pale green, like the interior of celery. A slime of sweat was everywhere: forehead, underarms, the backs of my knees. As I left the honeywagon and headed backstage to join Kanga and Gayle, the music stopped. Now, religious leaders from other Los Angeles churches—Catholic, Baptist, and was that a rabbi?—thanked Scientologists for the work they were doing for this vital cause. The talking went on and on, including, of course, a pitch for donations, but finally the stage manager led us up the back stairs. Our names were announced. Three mic stands seemed to materialize even as we crossed the stage. As we took our places around them, a roar from out front engulfed us. The lights were blinding. Gayle hummed a note. It would be the right one; she had perfect pitch. We took a breath.

Light a candle for freedom

What came out of my throat was not a series of notes. It was a bleat. For the rest of that verse and the chorus, my voice humped along, barely audible. Then came verse two. I was to sing the first line alone. It came out as a croak. Kanga and Gayle's concern radiated off of them in almost visible waves, but what was there to do but forge on? Kanga floated in on the second line and riding the upper harmony, Gayle joined us: *the truth is in each one of us* . . . Their beautiful, full voices almost made up for the lack of mine.

We headed into the final verse, which was to be sung quietly, before we were to explode into the final lyric, with all the energy and power we could muster. But by this time I was pretty much mouthing the words. And while Kanga and Gayle's voices could more than compensate for the absence of mine, without me, we lacked the melody. Worst was the final note of the song: during the *ly* of *to burn eternally*, I was to sustain a note around which Kanga and Gayle marched a series of Bach-like harmonies, until we hit the final triad and swelled into a long and triumphant finish. But that pedal tone, needed to anchor all that delicious, cathedral-evoking polyphony, was inaudible.

Nevertheless, the crowd went wild. We headed offstage, Gayle waving a loving hand.

They tried to tell me it really wasn't that bad. But it was that bad. The song was performed at a few more rallies, but they got someone else to sing my part until that particular *cause célèbre* was replaced by some other infamy the church could use to galvanize its supporters.

"I lost my voice!" I said, laughing, as I told the story a couple of times. Then what I was saying hit me: I had literally *lost my voice*.

And it stayed lost. It wavered whenever I tried to sing. I picked up my guitar less often. I wrote even fewer songs.

I wish I could say that all this led to a massive epiphany and I left Scientology behind. That would make such a tidy story. But I did not. I stayed and stayed.

In fact, until a few years ago, I didn't remember any of this.

I did finally manage to leave Scientology. I was accepted into the Iowa Writers' Workshop, and the distance from Los Angeles, as well as the workshop's fierce intellectual energy, forced me to confront the seven years I'd devoted to the church. I suffered terrible insomnia; I'd steep three bags of Sleepytime tea, drinking the bitter brew right before bed, and plunge briefly into sleep before waking to ponder what would happen to the soul I'd come to believe was everlasting. It took three more years before I was certain the church would not find a way to pull me back. Pre-internet, and the information it provides, there was no way to find out that with the ascendency of David Miscavige—which, I realized only later, coincided with my own departure—thousands were abandoning Scientology. I did not know this. I felt massively alone. Deeply ashamed, I confided in almost no one. I carried my wonderful old Martin guitar with me wherever I went, and I moved many times in those years, but for sometimes a year at a time it stayed in its case.

Eventually I found my way to a small town in the Sierra. I joined a theater company. I taught writing. I sold a novel. My guitar began to stay out of its case. Now and again I scribbled lyrics. Friends encouraged my music. The songs began to come again. Only then did it occur to me that while I had managed to write the words to this particular song, I couldn't sing them—not until I understood what I was saying, not until I could believe it. I could not sing about freedom when I was, myself, in thrall.

Julie Christofferson Titchbourne never got that $39 million. But not due to Scientology's efforts. A few weeks after the jury award, Judge Londer declared a mistrial, saying that Christofferson Titchbourne's lawyer had erred: in his closing remarks, he'd called Scientology a "terrorist organization," and thus, said the judge, had put the religion itself on trial rather than the actual issues at hand, which included misrepresentation and fraud.

To my mind—distressed though I was by that judge's decision—I see it as a kind of candle: he looked beyond his own opinion and, even though it meant admitting a flaw in his original reasoning, he issued a judgment based on precedent and the Constitution. I can only imagine Mrs. Christofferson Titchbourne's disappointment. And while I'm sorry she didn't get at least some of that money, I do hope she managed to get her life back on the rails.

It took a while, after I left Scientology, to feel my own life was on the rails again. But eventually I recorded an album, which includes "Light a Candle," digitized from the original tapes. That a capella hymn to freedom of thought leaps across the years to connect the person I was when I wrote it to the person I am now. Oddly, sadly, so much of what I chafed against while in Scientology is part of today's world, as if Donald Trump had studied Hubbard's doctrines. What's branded as "fake news" now is called, in Scientology, "Black PR"—anything that criticizes is not only labeled wrong, but assigned nefarious intent—no matter if there are sources cited, or facts to back the claims. *Never defend! Always attack!*—something we see every day, especially on a particular Twitter feed—is an idea straight out of a Hubbard Policy Letter (December 26, 1966), as is the idea of diverting attention from what is actually going on by making a large noise about something else (August 15, 1960). Above all, as Scientology's top management acquires property, and thereby influence, in every major city in the world, there's the cynical certainty that money can buy anything—that Epstein's money could purchase the silence of both the police and the courts, that American money can buy compliance, that Russian money can purchase elections.

But then there are people like investigative journalist Julie K. Brown, who used a lot of wattage to expose Epstein's activity in a series in the *Miami Herald*. There are people like that judge in Portland. There are those who donated to a GoFundMe to provide toothbrushes, soap, and blankets to the incarcerated children of migrants; or there's a friend's daughter, who is in Greece volunteering at a refugee camp. Innumerable artists, over millennia, have held up lamps, from Euripides in *The Trojan Women*, to Picasso with *Guernica*, to Morrison in *Beloved*. "Democracy Dies in Darkness," reads the epigraph on every issue of the *Washington Post,* and these days (indeed, as they always have) journalists are lighting the way through some pretty dense and gloomy forests, including the aforementioned Brown regarding Epstein, Ronan Farrow's bombshell reporting regarding Matt Lauer and Harvey Weinstein, the steadfast reporters keeping us abreast of fast-breaking news regarding Ukraine and its connections to our politics, and—back to the matter at hand—Leah Remini, with her HBO series *Scientology and the Aftermath*, and Tony Ortega, with his blog *The Underground Bunker,* calling out the egregious abuse the church has inflicted on so many—just a few of those who light candles and keep them burning all over the world.

CHAPTER 5

How to Talk to "Nones" and Influence People: Rob Bell's Transrational Experience

Brook Wilensky-Lanford

Did I really need to learn *How to Be Here*, urgently, right now? The book's publisher had sent me not one advance reading copy, but three. A sign from the universe?

I decided to read the book to find out.

Or rather, to *experience* the book.

Because that's the one word that is associated with the work of Rob Bell, a "contemporary Christian" thinker who is at once renegade and establishment.

Whether lectures or workshops or books, it's all part of the Rob Bell Experience. So when I learned that Bell would be stopping in nearby Durham, North Carolina, for an all-day, in-person event, I was excited to attend. The book has a lot of white space.

Short sentences that force you to stop. And think. And start again. What would Rob Bell do to fill up eight hours in person?

The message of the book is simple: look around at your life, decide if it's what you want, then devote all your energy to living the best life you can. Don't stop yourself from doing something you want to do. Just do it. Even if that thing is being an assistant regional manager of an insurance company—he actually says this—be the best assistant regional manager of an insurance company you can be.

Work on something called your "craft." (Even the insurance agent has a craft.) Also, pay attention to the details of life. Use the fine china. Unplug and play with your kids. Take a "Sabbath" from email. And you, too, will learn how to be here.

Rob Bell, for most of us, will be best known as the guy who declared hell doesn't exist—and caught hell for it from his fellow evangelicals. The author of *Love Wins: A Book about Heaven, Hell, and the Fate of Every Person Who Ever Lived* (and many, many other books), he is the former founder and pastor of the Mars Hill Bible megachurch in Grandville, Michigan, from which platform he resigned after the controversy.

Since leaving Mars Hill, Rob Bell has found an even sturdier platform. He writes a book a year, produces short films and a podcast, and goes on speaking tours with high-profile self-help personalities. But he would emphatically resist the notion that he is an "institution," or an "industry." He thinks of himself as a pastor without a church—without, that is, a *building*.

Buildings come in for a lot of flak from Bell. At most megachurches, he says, preachers preach sermons to fill seats, to win donations, to "buy a new building." Although Bell's original authority comes from his status as a megachurch pastor, these days he seems to get equal status from his choice—whether voluntary or under pressure—to leave that setting.

Whatever it is he's doing now, it seems to be a mirror of the zeitgeist. We hear a lot about that portion of the population the media likes to call "nones," those who respond to Pew Research polls on religious affiliation by checking "D: none of the above." Mostly composed of eighteen- to thirty-four-year-olds, this cohort sees affiliation with a religious institution to be neither necessary nor desirable, even if they are looking to do good work in the world, or to remain "spiritual but not religious."

Rob Bell may not have a building anymore, but he does have a space—or rather, many spaces. For this latest book, he's going on what he calls a "living room" tour.

On April 9th, the day of the How to Be Here Experience in Durham, I was running late, and only found the place—a distillery-turned-events-space with an unmarked address—almost by accident. I saw that the wide metal-plated door of a low-slung brick building was propped open, and on the stoop outside stood a tall skinny guy in hipster glasses, manning a card table with a laptop. "Is this the Rob Bell Experience?" I asked. He nodded. I gave him my name and entered the building.

Along the edge of the wood-and-brick interior was a ring of black café tables with fresh flowers. On one side of the room was a glass wall that afforded a view of gigantic ancient copper kettles and brewing machines. Folding chairs had been arranged in concentric circles radiating outward from an empty space in the middle; a hundred or so people milled about, friendly, excited to be there. There were long beards and shaved heads, T-shirts reading "Spiritual Angst" and "Sons of Dominion," and strewn on the café tables were leather-bound journals, handmade scrapbooks, and sets of markers.

Over the course of the next eight hours Rob Bell held forth from the center of that circle of folding chairs. He began with a walk-through of the new book, chapter by chapter. At the end of each section, Bell would ask for "requests," and audience members would call out topics: *empire building, the Eucharist rhythm, raising kids!*

Soon the event started to feel less like a book talk and more like a sprawling conversation. The audience seemed not only comfortable with the stories and the message, but actually hungry for both.

When I spoke to Bell on the phone a couple weeks after the event in Durham, he told me,

> In some ways what I do is basic pastoring. It's, you give people an idea, you let them respond to it, you give them another idea . . . it's basic spiritual direction. Like the itinerant rabbi, the guru—not to say that I'm a guru—but there's a long tradition [of that kind of work]. But so many people right now are rethinking everything . . . saying *wait, is this it*? They've been handed a way of experiencing the world that's not right for them. . . . Or they've experienced some kind of loss, and they don't have the rituals, rites, forms to express it.

Instead, what they have is this. And what *is* this exactly? Occasionally after a particularly pithy inspiration point, there would be applause or an "Amen!" from the crowd. It wasn't church, but there was a church-shaped hole in the room. Were these the fabled "nones" that I had heard so much about?

"Yeah," Bell told me,

> It's funny, when I hear the latest Pew research I'm like, "I could introduce you to nine thousand of those people next

week." But if I were to then say "I'm the leader of the nones," everyone would be like "That guy sucks!" Because as soon as someone has named it and made a pamphlet, you've killed it. . . . Headlines kill it. Don't keep naming it. Just let it be a pop-up . . . therapy/performance art/meditation/ritual in Durham. Just enjoy it!

So I asked Bell if it had to expand: did the pop-up have to become a franchise?

You know, denominations start with people saying "We need to do this differently," and then organizing it. That's not me. I'm not the organizer guy. I like to say my basic ministry is "You're not alone." It's people learning there's a bigger conversation going on out there, like in the audience in Durham.

Some kind of conversation did seem to be happening in that unlabeled brick building, though I wasn't quite sure what to make of its nonorganizer. In the morning, the light shining through the large industrial windows in the front of the Rickhouse made Bell appear to me as a dark, featureless silhouette. The silhouette had a tall, gangly build (as a kid, Bell says, he always looked up to Larry Bird) and the squared shoulders of a stylish, Chairman Mao–style jacket.

Bell was giving our side of the room a lot of attention, possibly because to turn in the opposite direction would have been blinding. At one point I turned to the young woman next to me and asked if she, too, was having trouble seeing Bell's face. "Yeah," she said, "I keep squinting at him, but I don't want him to think I was crying." It was a fair concern; emotions were high in the room.

"The greatest lie of the modern world," Bell said to the crowd, "is that *anyone* has it figured out." He proceeded to tell a story about going on tour with Oprah, and watching her work a stadium crowd, then leaving the stage, changing clothes, and going up to another room where she would meet "three or four hundred people" individually for photographs. "And every single person, she would be completely present for," he said, amazed. But the real ending to that story was months later, when he talked to Oprah about watching her do that, and she said something like "Yeah, that was too much." Even Oprah, Bell revealed, sometimes has trouble saying no. If *she* does, we are not alone.

The Oprah parable is meant as a teaching tool. But it also, of course, reminds us that he has intimate access to Oprah. In the book and in person, many of the examples he uses to illustrate his principles come from his own life. He's an L.A. surfer and musician who hobnobs with vegan restaurateurs and Silicon Valley moguls. He does a two-man show with comedian Pete Holmes at an L.A. club called Largo. (After the show, Bell told me, some people have told him "It's the best church I've ever been to.")

If there's a clash between his insistence that anybody can do this being-here thing and the distinctly celebrity-culture incidents he uses to prove that, Rob Bell isn't interested in pointing it out. That's just his life, his material.

And of course people do treat Bell like a celebrity. A man who said he drove to Durham from Columbus, Ohio, was starting an online ministry known as "Radical Nation," and he wanted Bell's advice on making the decision to go "radically inclusive" (or "gay-friendly," to the rest of us), and on how to sustain his and his wife's energies for pastoring. A serene woman in an orange scarf announced that she had opened what she called "a gym for body and soul," and she wanted advice on how to reach people who didn't want to be reached. Someone else described at length a Sunday School class he taught that was based entirely on improv-comedy techniques. He described responding to a woman's fear of death by enacting an improvised funeral for her, in which she had to lie still and listen to people say nice things to her.

All of this was met with enthusiastic if sometimes bemused support from Bell.

Still thinking about Bell's audience a couple weeks later when I spoke to him, I asked him about all those group-builders; did he get that a lot? The "spiritual entrepreneurs," he said, are indeed "pretty typical," for this tour.

So many people at the Experience, in fact, had announced that they came from out of town with their own spiritual entre-preneurship project that someone asked us all to raise our hands if we were actually *from* Durham, so that she could see if there were enough people to start to build a group with.

All of this was right in line with what Bell had been saying all along: everybody has spiritual questions, and they need a place to bring them. A place that doesn't judge them, or expect allegiance like an institution would.

After lunch, Bell signed copies of the book. The long line moved slowly, because Bell spent time with everyone, autograph-ing, chatting, posing for photographs. Like Oprah. And as with Oprah, there was something cozy about this process. Bell would chalk this feeling up to the "living room" atmosphere he's created.

Part of it is what I've been doing for twenty-five years, but now I can control the setup of the space even more. There's a power of a space that's spiritual, but hasn't already been co-opted by some institution, some religion.

All day, when people would call out topics for him to discuss, Bell kept adding one of his own, "Oh, and we're going to talk about the transrational; don't let me forget." So finally someone shouted out: "Tell us about the transrational!"

Bell formulated it like this, in historical stages. First, there was the prerational, which attributed false causes to supernatural entities—*my rain dance made it rain*; *God found me a parking space*. Then came the rational, the enlightened, the scientific, the mindset that knows that rain comes not from dances but from water molecules. This mindset, Bell was repeatedly careful to point out, has given us a lot: schools and iPads and cars and cures for diseases. But as he explained, it has its drawbacks, which is why we need the transrational—or the rational understanding that that rationality itself has limits.

When I asked him where the concept came from, Bell credited philosopher Ken Wilber. "You know that gift of people who put language to something you've always experienced but never had words for?" Bell knew this concept would be very difficult for many people: "The mind is very good at parts versus wholes, but there are things in the world that the mind doesn't know what to do with, and then it kind of loops in on itself."

This kind of "doubling down" on rationality is happening all over our society, according to Bell. He sees it in the fact that TED Talks require you to talk about topics that you can prove with evidence—no spirituality allowed. You can hear it in New Atheist rhetoric, which, according to Bell, often mistakes the transrational for the *pre*rational. "Right, the prerational and the transrational may be using the same language, but coming from a different perspective," Bell told me.

> Like when someone says "I'm praying for you," and you think, well [that sounds crazy]. Well I actually *am* doing that, I actually am sending you all the best energies and thoughts on your behalf . . . yes, I know exactly how that sounds in the modern world and I'm still doing that.

Bell wants society to open up to the transrational, starting with those in his living room and moving out to unexpected venues.

> Whatever awesome things science brings us, we are still desperate for the inner life. And you saw at the event in Durham, we were talking about things that can't be accessed with the five senses—meaning the sacred, hope, joy, love. And these are not aberrations but normal ways of living. Part of what I'm doing is normalizing—normalizing sanity in a fragmented world.

At first, I wasn't feeling the Rob Bell Experience; the three copies of *How to Be Here* I'd received had not worked their magic. I was, however, intrigued by the charming Larry Bird–meets–Chairman Mao figure in the middle of a circle of folding chairs, telling me things I mostly already knew, but in a way that made me feel like maybe I didn't.

As a non-Christian, I kept waiting to notice the fact that I was listening to an evangelical pastor, but what Jesus talk there was seemed designed to float by. It did seem to mean something to many of those seated around me, though. Audience members asked Bell how to teach their children about Jesus without repeating anything they didn't believe themselves, or how to respond to parents of the youth-group they lead who want to know how much they taught the kids about Jesus. "Isn't that *their* job?" Bell asked, to murmured assent. He clearly had no patience for conservative theology, for institutions that insist, for example, that women should be submissive.

More than once, in answering an audience question, Bell would say, "People won't go to a church that sends them backwards. They just won't do it!"

I sympathized with the predicament of the isolated Christian trying make her way in the world without the comfort of church. But, never having been a churchgoer, it was hard for me to grasp this feeling of being unmoored. Until I realized, sitting in my folding chair, that there *was* something that was making me feel unwelcome in my community, something that was "sending me backwards." I had moved to North Carolina almost a year before, from New York, in order to get my PhD in religion at UNC Chapel Hill. A good northeastern liberal, I'd read the warning articles in the *New Republic* before I went, and I knew the Tea Party had taken over the state, but I could not have imagined something like the "bathroom bill," or HB2.

When I sat in Bell's audience in Durham in March, the fall-out from the state's recent anti-LGBT legislation was just beginning. Still, I kept waiting for someone in the audience to ask: What do we do if it's not our church but our *government* sending us backwards? But no one did. Politics writ large seemed to fall outside the living room walls.

At some point some provocateur did ask Bell "the race question," that is: "Why is everyone in this room white?" People shifted in their folding chairs. If these ideas about how to create your life and inhabit transrational spaces are so powerful, so world-changing, why are they only being shared with people who by definition already have the (white) privilege to hear them?

Bell took the question seriously. He acknowledged that the disproportionately nonwhite poor and disenfranchised may not have the luxury to "create their lives," and that that is not okay. "Politically, people are starting to realize this doesn't work." But then he made a sort of trickle-down argument: when traveling to a new city, he doesn't make efforts to recruit people from populations that wouldn't ordinarily know or care about Rob Bell. He was fully aware that his audience consisted of people "high up on the pyramid," and it was exactly by "changing the hearts of the people who run the system" that he hoped his work would begin to effect unspecified larger change.

"But I'm not going to apologize for the people in this room," he concluded. And the people in the room applauded.

After that, I knew I wasn't going to ask the HB2 question in front of that crowd. I also wasn't quite sure how to formulate the query: I am a cisgender white woman, not especially connected to the transgender community.

Why did the law feel like a personal affront? By the time I had the opportunity to speak to Bell again, I understood why.

I live in a state that is now a national embarrassment for transgender rights, which are *civil rights*. My elected government treats my (and lots of other North Carolinians') values like so much heresy. Every time I buy something with sales tax, I tacitly support that government. So I *do* feel personally out of place, without recourse, isolated, backward.

I offered this concern to Bell when we spoke on the phone. He responded thoughtfully, but cautiously. "Oh yeah. See the thing is: we actually do have real, life-or-death problems going on. And many of us are totally convinced that this"—he meant the stated reason for the law, the phantom possibility of trans, or fake-trans, people preying on young women in bathrooms—"is not one of them."

True enough, but to say that HB2 is essentially a solution in search of a problem is kind of understated for someone who prides himself on being "radically inclusive." Wasn't it a real, life-or-death problem that a discriminatory bill *could* get passed? Bell did go on: "This is not us. We are better than this."

Bell was telling me that I was not alone in feeling betrayed by HB2—but I wasn't entirely reassured. We may be better than this, but it is not "we" who passed the law. It was state assembly-men who voted largely on party lines, in a state that has recently been mandated to redraw its heavily gerrymandered congressional districts. They drafted the bill to appeal to a particular socially conservative group of Republican donors. They showed their Tea Party "small government" rhetoric to be hypocritical by overruling the city of Charlotte's democratic process. And even *they* had to call a special session in order to sweep the law through.

The bill also bans further antidiscrimination protection for any group (including, for example, disabled veterans), and makes it impossible for localities to raise their minimum wage. And that was before the risk of the state's public education system (one which I work for and am invested in) losing billions of dollars of federal Title IX funding became real. How do we mobilize the part of us as individuals that is "better than this" to address these systemic issues?

Bell is authentically rankled by preachers in their big buildings who want to send people backward. And he does want to lead people into spiritual-but-not-institutional spaces where they can work out something better. But he actively resists telling them what that something better should be. In a way his aversion to politics echoes a much older style of American evangelicalism, where spirituality was not meant to be contaminated by the world.

And perhaps Bell knows his audience. Last month the Raleigh *News & Observer* published a basic explainer on transgender issues. What is "gender identity"? What is "gender expression"? What does it mean to say "transgender man" or "transgender woman"? If this had appeared in the *New York Times*, people would have been baffled, or complained of condescension. But maybe the local paper just really knows their readership. They know that even those with whom HB2 doesn't sit well don't necessarily understand why; readers need information, but don't know where to begin asking.

Rob Bell might be serving a similar function. As he told me, people make a lot of very basic assumptions when it comes to religion. And they are not assumptions based on knowledge. "I'll just ask people, 'What do you mean?' Even the word 'God'—what do you mean by that? And you'll talk to them and it'll end up like 'basically an old man in the sky who either gets involved or not.' Well, no wonder it doesn't work! And you just say 'There are other ways to conceptualize the possible existence of a divine being.' And sometimes that's all you have to say."

I hope he's right.

CHAPTER 6

The Lonely Boy: A Catechism of Backyard Saints

Burke Gerstenschlager

Living in brownstone south Brooklyn, we walk everywhere. There is always something to look at. This is an Italian Catholic neighborhood; a casual atmosphere of bathtub Marys and various saints lounge in the front yards. Some are well attended, brightly white, watching over manicured lawns. Others crumble in silence, their owners old mainstays in a swiftly gentrifying neighborhood.

In his skinny jeans and black hoodie, my son looms large among his classmates, looking painfully northern European with his blond shock of hair. Five-year-old Søren has his mother's sharp blue eyes in the almond shape of his father's. He is ours, but, living up to his namesake, Søren Kierkegaard, he is most definitely his own person. Søren is my maelstrom, a whirlwind of energy and inquiry.

On the way to the park, we stroll past an empty lot where Mary stands beneath a flowering garden trestle. She looks over the various exceedingly well-fed stray cats. We've named her "Mary of the Cats." "Meow meow, Mary!" we call to her and wave. During Advent, in the adjacent wooden crèche, the cats huddle together for warmth under the lamp before the appearance of Baby Jesus. I think they shove him out.

His questions have a catechetical cadence to them.

"Who is Mary?"

"That is the Lonely Boy's mama," I reply.

"What does she say?"

"Listen to the Lonely Boy."

"Tell me a story about Mary."

"Once upon a time there was a wedding at a place called Cana . . ."

So who is the Lonely Boy? It began when he first saw Jesus dead in the churchyard of a local Catholic parish. Walking, he points to the man hanging from a cross.

"Who is that?" he asks.

"Who do you think it is?" I say, encouraging him to explore.

After a moment staring, he decides, "That's the Lonely Boy!"

Shocked, I say, "Why is he the Lonely Boy?"

Soberly, Søren says, "Because all of his friends have left him."

"Why is he on a stick?" he continues.

This is our son's entry point into Christianity: an abandoned boy, alone on a stick.

"Because," I offer, "some people didn't like that he said to love one another."

"Oh."

And we continue walking home. For us, Jesus has been the Lonely Boy ever since.

"What does the Lonely Boy say?" he asks later, working to wrap his head around this strange image.

"He says to love one another." I don't offer easy answers. Words like "atonement" and "sedition" aren't helpful.

How does a world-weary divinity school alum go about teaching his young son about Christianity? For me, these years are an easy moment, when the meanings of time and event are more pliable and less causal. I read him myths and we ground them in the Greco-Roman statues and vases at the Metropolitan Museum of Art. They're as real as the statuary and frescoes of Jesus and the saints in the Medieval Wing. They're as real as the four statues of Saint Anthony of Padua in the front yards of a single block of our neighborhood. Stories are what is most significant in a child's world. They define, articulate, and describe the world. Love and acceptance ground and glue that world together.

Søren does not know what a Bible is, but he knows storytellers with names like Mark and John. He knows that Jesus was transfigured and that his clothes turned white. He knows that a Samaritan was a good neighbor and helped someone who was beaten and different. I do not want him to understand the Bible as a monolithic text, some object of idolatry.

We do not talk about God, either in identity or in action. There is no God, only the Lonely Boy and his mother and the saints who talk about him. Trained in theology and learning to parent, I've learned how to pick my battles. "Transcendence" and "immanence" are fool's errands at his age and probably at mine, too. Why muddle things with "theodicy" and "kenosis"? Why wrestle with the existence of God at all right now? A bird just flew into that bush and he wants to find it.

I want to give him a foundation. I want him to create his own world filled with meaning, gleaned from and created by the images and stories around him. The Met. MoMA. The city's skyline in the morning. I want his world to be rich with imagination and description and the ineffable, the indescribable and unknowable.

The yard saints ground a complex and maddening religion. It is something that Catholicism has always done better than Protestantism. In its iconoclasm, Protestantism objectifies a book at risk of kitschy pictures and clumsy proof texts.

I am trying to explain aspects of Christianity through these common objects along our streets. And yet, these saints are not for children. Much of the Bible is not for children. It's not about an elect zoo floating over humanity's graveyard.

He already knows some Greek letters. One day he will learn well about the iconoclast for whom he is named. The angst will come. For now I tell him stories about a man and his friends who will leave him and his mother who will be sad.

"Her heart was on fire when he was handed over to the bad Romans," he says.

I hold his hand on our way to our subway station. We hold hands all the time, as much for comfort as for stability.

"I love you, Dad," he says. He says it often. We tell each other this truth all the time. Søren does not like to be lonely.

CHAPTER 7

Soul Murder

Patrick Blanchfield

On Tuesday, a grand jury in Pennsylvania released a report about seven decades of sexual abuse by Catholic clergy and systematic cover-ups by church authorities. The report is the product of two years of investigation, encompassing dozens of witness interviews and the review of half a million pages of documents. Carried out in the face of opposition from two dioceses (Harrisburg and Greensburg, which sought to quash the investigation prematurely), it is the single largest such investigation in American history, naming three hundred priests as perpetrators, and establishing a tally of at least one thousand identifiable victims, many of whom were continually abused over the course of years.

The Pennsylvania report is being covered intensively by practically every major news outlet, with each publication's reportage including multiple brief vignettes of abuse. The reason the cases summarized in each outlet are different is because there are hundreds upon hundreds of different episodes to choose from. Their horror beggars imagination. A priest rapes a young boy so violently he damages the child's spine, consigning him to years of painkiller dependency, and ultimately to overdose and death. A priest rapes a girl while she is in a hospital bed recovering from having her tonsils out. A group of priests whip boys with belts and force them to pose for photographs, naked, as though crucified. A priest rapes a girl and then arranges for her to receive an abortion—with the subsequent blessing and sympathy of his superiors. The sadism and perversion the report documents is so heinous that readers with a Christian upbringing may find themselves reaching for the vocabulary of demons and the demonic. So, too, did one priest, who, in warning his superiors about a sexual predator colleague, described him as an "incubus."

Despite that warning, that predator's superiors effectively did nothing about it. And this is the other half of the report's story: the revelation of sophisticated and elaborate mechanisms for shielding predators, avoiding public scrutiny, escaping legal accountability, and even punishing victims and families. Time and again, whistle-blowing clerics and parishioners (including some who worked in law enforcement) approached their pastors and bishops to report abuse, confident the church would act decisively. And time and again, the reports were ignored or rejected, and abusive priests were transferred to other parishes, not infrequently being promoted and given even greater access to vulnerable children. These stories, too, beggar belief. When a father shows up to a rectory in Pittsburgh with a shotgun to confront his daughter's abuser in the 1960s, the church responds by sending the priest to a church-run mental health facility for "evaluation"—and then assigns him to teach middle school in San Diego for the next two decades. When another priest dogged by child sex abuse allegations eventually resigns, his superiors write him a letter of reference—for a job at Walt Disney World.

For seven decades, priests who were known, and self-admitted, abusers were laundered within the system. "The bishops weren't just aware of what was going on; they were immersed in it," observes the report. "And they went to great lengths to keep it secret." Those lengths included "continuing to fund abusive priests, providing them with housing, transportation, benefits, and stipends—and leaving abusers with the resources to locate, groom and assault more children." Indeed, in numerous cases, as the report makes clear, the church lavished money on dubious "treatments" for abusers, and paid large sums to abusers in order ease their departure from the clergy, all while running out the statute-of-limitations clock on legal actions by victims and fighting over pennies necessary for their medical and mental health treatment. The report refers to this edifice of cover-ups and wrongdoing as "The Circle of Secrecy"—noting this phrase is not its own devising, but rather the coinage of former bishop of Pittsburgh Donald Wuerl.

For his part, Wuerl is no longer in Pittsburgh—he's now archbishop of Washington, DC. But the response of the church in Pennsylvania to the report is stunning in its own right. "Sadly, abuse still is part of the society in which we live," writes Alfred A. Schlert, bishop of Allentown. "We acknowledge our past failures, and we are determined to do what is necessary to protect the innocent, now and in the future."

Perhaps Bishop Schlert is sincere in his concerns about "society," though one might suspect that he and other apologists want to have things both ways—to keep the City of God hygienically *apart* from earthly "society," while also strategically shifting any blame for clerical misconduct onto contagion *from* it. But, in any event, let's consider the abstraction of blaming "society" alongside the concrete details of the following episode, included in the grand jury materials, which occurred near Pittsburgh in the 1960s.

In his message, the victim revealed that while living in West Newton when he was around seven years old, he was told by a Sunday school teacher that missing mass could make you die. Concerned for his mother who was missing mass, the victim went down to the church to plead the case of his mother. The victim related that "Father Gooth" [Guth] took the victim into the rectory office where Guth sat in a chair as the victim stood before him, sobbing and pleading for his mother's soul. Guth asked the victim whether he believed that Jesus suffered and died for our sins, in response to which the victim said "of course" as that is what he was taught. Guth talked about penance and having crosses to bear and asked the victim if he would do anything to save his mother. Guth then spoke of secret confessions and penance before reaching over and unbuckling the victim's pants, pulling them down, fondling him, and sticking his finger up the victim's anus. The victim believed Guth then spoke in Latin. The victim stated he was frozen stiff when the abuse was occurring and that when Guth was done, he was instructed to pull up his pants and that if he told anyone about the secret penance, not only would his mother go to hell, but he [the victim] would burn with her. Guth then gave the victim a nickel and warned him again not to say anything to anyone or his whole family would burn in hell.

Or consider this episode, which occurred in the very diocese of Allentown itself—Schlert's current bishopric—back in the early 1980s.

> The victim said that his first memory of abuse happened while he attended CCD [Confraternity of Christian Doctrine, aka "Sunday School"] class at St. Bernard's, where [Monsignor J.] Benestad was assigned. The victim was taken out of class by a nun and delivered to Benestad in his office. The victim had worn shorts to CCD, which was against the rules. The victim was told that shorts were not proper attire and that not wearing proper attire was sinful. The victim was told to get on his knees and start praying. Benestad unzipped his pants and told the victim to perform oral sex on him. The victim did as he was told. Benestad also performed oral sex on the victim. The victim recalls that, after the abuse, Benestad would produce a clear bottle of holy water and squirt it into the victim's mouth to purify him.

Whatever the problems of "society" more broadly, it is impossible not to see in these horrors very particularly Catholic features: tropes, however twisted, of sin, penance, mortification, and punishment, concepts and ritual items wielded as tools of abuse. These priests, in other words, did not just rape children using their hands, mouths, and genitals. They also raped them using their faith.

———

I grew up around priests, and in the church. I served as an altar boy, first in my local parish church and then in a cathedral, for almost ten years. I received an impeccable education from Jesuits, for free, a gift for which I am still grateful. To this day, I count priests among my friends. Liturgical music can still transport me, and the slightest whiff of incense—Jerusalem brand—opens up Proustian vistas of memory.

But I left the church for good in the summer of 2002. I was in Massachusetts, right as the first, explosive investigations of clerical sexual abuse were being made public by the *Boston Globe*. During the Sunday homily at my then parish in Cambridge, the pastor read us a letter, sent by the archbishop of Boston, Bernard Law. The topic was a legislative effort to add a so-called "Protection of Marriage Amendment" to the state constitution, which would have preemptively denied efforts to legalize same-sex marriage. Unsurprisingly, Law urged support for the amendment, in the most strenuous terms; it was our duty as Catholics, a decent people with family values, to pressure our legislators accordingly.

Our pastor read the letter, and then, to his credit, spoke briefly for himself. In so many words, he admitted that he only read it because he had to, and that he felt uncomfortable with it. He expressed particular hesitation with the linchpin of Law's argument: that same-sex marriage would be "damaging to children." In light of breaking news about the diocese's history of covering up sexual abuse, and particularly given our parish's thriving youth choir program, he felt it was not his place, let alone Law's, to make any such pronouncements.

I forget the exact words the priest used, but I suddenly felt moved to tears by his candor and even bravery. I also found myself realizing, with almost crystalline clarity, that I was crying about something else, too: that this was it for me, that there was nothing there for me, that I wanted no part in an institution that could produce such a scene. The contortions of loyalty and pain, the suffering it generated and the empathy it at once made possible and denied—I couldn't bear it. I don't remember if I left while everyone else shuffled around for Communion. But I do remember walking out and telling myself not to look back.

To be sure, I was never, in retrospect, or even as I saw it at the time, a "Good Catholic." In fact, to be perfectly frank about it, the phrase and idea of being a "Good Catholic" always struck me, if not as an oxymoron, then at least a kind of provocative irony. The very core of Catholicism as I was raised in it hinged on a self-critical, precarious relationship to the idea of goodness. Your Goodness as a Catholic was always ever only provisional, contingent upon a logic of confession and atonement in this life, and of final judgment in the next. At one point, in a theology class, a priest asked us what our favorite words in the liturgy were. I knew the whole thing by heart, and my response was immediate: "Lord, I am not worthy to receive you, but only say the word and I shall be healed." These words are said right before Communion—or at least they were (a recent update to the English liturgy brings the expression closer to its origin in Matthew 8:8). They paint a poignant picture: the finite human, mortal and frail, begging only a single, transformative gesture of healing from the infinite divine.

Reading the grand jury report today, those words keep coming back to me. Their power still speaks to me, but now I detect something else in them. On the one hand, they express a posture of beseeching receptivity towards the divine; on the other, they signal profound vulnerability to all-too-human abuse. The episode in West Newton, with the child begging for intercession on behalf of his mother, looms. How vulnerable is a seven-year-old, burdened with the ontological guilt of Original Sin, and navigating an austere calculus of punishment according to which his mother can go to hell for missing Mass? If you carry within you some basic fault, some constant taint of dirtiness and shame, does it not follow that further debasement is somehow inevitable? That you can never be entirely sure if you're getting what you deserve—or what you want? Or that, in the muck and sinfulness of your humanity, if goodness and healing *were* to come you, you might mistake them for exploitation and filth—or vice versa? And if the whole enterprise of sin and forgiveness is so overcoded by themes of concealment and privileged divulgement—the very logic of confession—does that flow seamlessly into relationships of being groomed and then keeping silent—of understanding that You Keep the Secret, or You Go to Hell?

I should say: I was never abused. The closest I came was a strange encounter with a layperson CCD instructor, a stockbroker in his thirties, in what was supposed to be some sort of sex-ed/theology class, yelling at me and some other pubescent boys, veins popping in his neck, about how *"Jesus didn't get nailed to a telephone pole so you could drop your shorts!"* My friends and I just looked at each other, completely uncertain what the guy was talking about. The priests my friends and I knew, as altar servers and teachers in our all-boys school, were nowhere near as florid or erratic. And besides, you made allowances for priests—didn't you have to be a little weird, a little "queer" (in the old sense), to become one in the first place? Their frequent oddity was part and parcel, a necessary evil, so to speak.

Of course, some were weirder than others. The priest who was a little too enthusiastic about hugs. The priest who was always hanging around groups of athletes, who was always ready with pats on the back after a game, who had clear favorites on the team, who would sometimes massage a boy's shoulders. The priests we made snickering jokes about in locker rooms; jokes that served, not coincidentally, to defuse and redirect pervasive homosocial tension.

To be clear, I do not think these men ever crossed certain lines—or at least, I do not know if they did. For what it's worth, they never *seemed* predatory. The affect they broadcast instead was more a kind of sadness. You could see it when they didn't think we were watching. Glimpses in their eyes and faces of deep loneliness and frustration, the tells of bodies and souls too long macerated in yearning and lack. The sadness they'd struggle to disguise when talking of former colleagues and seminarian friends who had left the cloth behind to marry women, and, in at least one case I knew, to marry a man. The same tonalities of sadness you might sometimes perceive learning of the priests who, having given up possession of significant worldly assets, spent their meager funds overindulging on liquor and tobacco and fatty food.

I leave it to others to address the delicate questions of how celibacy or the oppression of the closet are implicated in clerical abuse. Likewise, I cannot stress enough there is to be no question of excusing such behavior in the guise of "explaining" it—if anything, as the grand jury report documents, this bait and switch has been an integral part of the church hierarchy's own cynical publicity MO for years. By the same token, we must always reject as obscene any attempt to equate sexual abuse to nonheterosexual orientation (another classic misdirection). After all, as the report makes painfully clear, the targets of abuse in

Pennsylvania included not just boys but girls too, both women and men. And the psychology research on sexual predators is unequivocal: abuse is first and foremost about availability and vulnerability—it is about power, and about being able to get away with it.

But, again, there is *something* in the episodes the report contains, something that resonates with the core of my experience of Catholicism—and I suspect I am not alone. A particular configuration of innocence and guilt, of expiation and profanation, that suggests some deeply flawed, corrosive worldview, a sadistic-erotic matrix of pleasure, suffering, secrecy, and guilt. This suspicion is underscored every time some bishop or professional apologist circles the wagons and takes every discussion of abuse or abusers as an assault on Catholicism itself. What if, you start to wonder, in some way—they're right? What if, in a basic way, these outrages are not incidentally Catholic, but essentially so? And what are we supposed to do, then?

Reading the report, I feel many things at once. Part of me wants to smash altars with a sledgehammer. Part of me wants RICO investigations into every archdiocese and diocese in the country. And part of me wants a priest to put a hand on my shoulder while I cry, to tell me that everything will be all right, that these were not *real* priests, that all this, somehow, can be made understandable and redeemed in light of God's love.

No matter what I do, there's some part of me that wants nothing more than to feel the forgiveness of grace, some feeling of total forgiveness, acceptance, and love that undoes the most basic of faults. I feel this even as I understand that, in large measure, that conviction of a fault in the first place is something that was put in me by the institution that I want to heal it. What the church shaped in me was a conviction of fallenness, of brokenness, of sinfulness, of a fundamental pain and tragedy and unworthiness written through all of human existence that cried out for the healing transformation of grace. And what the church took from me was the belief that any such transfiguration was possible through it. Reading the grand jury report, I suspect that, in this too, I am not alone.

PART II

Political Agon:
Politics & Society

Introduction

With the collapse of the Soviet Union, political theorist–cum-pundit Francis Fukuyama famously claimed that a postideological "end of history" had begun. Central to some versions of this argument was a variation of the "secularization hypothesis": the notion that politics and society would become largely neutered of religion, and faith merely a private practice. History, however, had different ideas. The new century began with 9/11, a spectacularly violent display of religion's continuing influence in the world. The two decades since have seen copious evidence that history is a never-ending story.

In the United States, religion has been evident in a variety of political movements, from Black Lives Matter and Occupy on the left to the revanchist doctrines of racialized white nationalism on the right. "It's hard to think of any place where religion's revolutionary potential has been more fully realized than the United States," writes Nathan Schneider, "both for good and for evil." New Religion Journalists such as Schneider have illuminated the ways in which faith has played a role in politics, society, and culture in the new millennium. In an essay that initially ran in *Occupy!,* he looks at the role that progressive Christianity played in the Occupy Wall Street movement. Schneider analyzes Occupy (of which he was a participant) as a type of utopian revival.

Kaya Oakes writes about another seminal social-political movement in her *Killing the Buddha* piece "Forgiveness in the Epoch of Me Too." Arguably exacerbated by the frustration and rage at the election of Donald Trump, Me Too emerged years earlier from the work of activists such as Tarana Burke. The movement focuses on women's dignity and autonomy, demanding that sexual assault, abuse, and harassment be properly identified and addressed. Calls for justice have naturally also included discussions about forgiveness and redemption, which has inaugurated its own genre of the inadequate apologies written by accused figures who don't express as much contrition as respective situations might dictate. Oakes writes that "we have had little in the way of a national conversation about what it would mean to forgive men for harassment, abuse, or rape."

Questions of contrition, redemption, and grace were at the heart of Lutheran theologian Dietrich Bonhoeffer's writings. The German thinker was martyred by the Nazis in the waning days of World War II, and he has become a particularly relevant figure as authoritarian governments have proliferated in recent years. Joel Looper examines how his memory is deployed across the political spectrum in his *Los Angeles Review of Books* piece, "How Would Bonhoeffer Vote?" Looper's cultural analysis is a reminder of the ways in which historical extrapolation and conjecture don't always render helpful conclusions, as he argues that it "would seem that Americans, particularly American Christians, are at an impasse with Bonhoeffer." Pastor Sam Washington also examines the ways in which politics and religion intersect, sometimes to the detriment of the latter, in his confession "A Welcoming

Church No More," also published in *Los Angeles Review of Books*. As an African American man raised in the Pentecostal tradition, Washington interrogates how white evangelicalism has become enthralled to seemingly very un-Christian values in the pursuit of temporal power. He writes: "I'm no longer comfortable with the label of 'evangelical' because I have become slack-jawed with disgust at friends who will defend Trump harder than they defend the gospel."

Trump's ascendancy, and the election of like-minded authoritarian leaders around the world, has meant an increasingly precarious position for religious minorities. The massacre at the Tree of Life synagogue in Pittsburgh was the most violent pogrom in recent American history, perpetrated by a killer who'd been propagandized by internet communities into far-right beliefs. Emma Green eulogizes the victims in her powerful piece from the *Atlantic*, "Will Anyone Remember Eleven Dead Jews?," writing about the purpose of memory, whereby archives "neither predict nor prevent atrocities. They document what has happened"—which can be radical enough.

Despite the United States' self-understanding as a land of religious liberty, persecution has marked religious minorities throughout our history. Our own homegrown faith of Mormonism has had its share of stigmatization. Simon Critchley redresses that legacy in his *New York Times* piece "Why I Love Mormonism." While not a member of the church himself, Critchley bemoans casual anti-Mormon bigotry. "Among my horribly overeducated and hugely liberal friends," he writes, "expressions of racism are completely out of the question . . . [b]ut anti-Mormonism is another matter."

Tolerance is, in part, an issue of pedagogy, something addressed by Jennifer Ratner-Rosenhagen's *Los Angeles Review of*

Books piece "Zen and the Art of a Higher Education." A reflection on Robert Pirsig's classic account of western Buddhism, *Zen and the Art of Motorcycle Maintenance*, it examines the ways in which intentionality, thought, and education all intersect. Ratner-Rosenhagen writes that "intellectual engagement happens all over the place—in the sun and in the seminar, alone on dirt roads and together with students in the classroom," a moving invocation of how education as an antidote to political despair can have its own charged omnipresence.

CHAPTER 8

Why I Love Mormonism

Simon Critchley

I've spent what is rapidly becoming nine years in New York
City. It's been a total blast. But as a transplanted English-
man, one thing to which I've become rather sensitive in that
time is which prejudices New Yorkers are permitted to express
in public. Among my horribly overeducated and hugely liberal
friends, expressions of racism are completely out of the question,
Islamophobia is greeted with a slow shaking of the head and anti-
Semitism is a memory associated with distant places that one
sometimes visits—like France.

Why is it okay to say totally uninformed things about
Mormonism?

But anti-Mormonism is another matter. It's really fine to say
totally uninformed things about Mormonism in public, at dinner
parties or wherever. "It's a cult," says one. "With thirteen million
followers and counting?" I reply. "Polygamy is disgusting," says
another. "It was made illegal in Utah and banned by the church
in 1890, wasn't it?" I counter. And so on. This is a *casual* prejudice

that is not like the visceral hatred that plagued the early decades of Mormonism—lest it be forgotten, Joseph Smith was shot to death on June 27, 1844, by an angry mob who broke into a jail where he was detained—but a symptom of a thoughtless incuriousness.

There is just something *weird* about Mormonism, and the very mention of the Book of Mormon invites smirks and giggles, which is why choosing it as the name for one of Broadway's most hard-to-get-into shows was a smart move. As a scholar of Mormonism once remarked, one does not need to read the Book of Mormon in order to have an opinion about it.

But every now and then during one of those New York soirées, when anti-Mormon prejudice is persistently pressed and expressed, and I perhaps feel momentarily and un-Mormonly emboldened by wine, I begin to try and share my slim understanding of Joseph Smith and my fascination with the Latter-day Saints. After about forty-five seconds, sometimes less, it becomes apparent that the prejudice is based on sheer ignorance of the peculiar splendors of Mormon theology. "They are all Republicans anyway," they add in conclusion. "I mean, just look at that Mitbot Romney. He's an alien." As an alien myself, I find this thoughtless anti-Mormon sentiment a little bewildering.

This is mainly because my experience with Mormonism was somewhat different. Very early on in my philosophical travels, near the Italian city of Perugia to be precise, I met Mormon philosophers—Heideggerians, actually, but this was the 1980s when many such dinosaurs roamed the earth—and got to know them quite well. They were from Brigham Young University, and they were some of the kindest, most self-effacing and honest people I have ever met. They were also funny, warm, genuine, completely open-minded, smart, and terribly well read. We became friends.

There was still suspicion, of course, perhaps even more so back then. I remember being pulled aside late at night by an American friend and told, "You know that guy from BYU. They say he's a bishop and conducts secret services." "Does he eat babies too?" I wondered out loud.

Thereby hangs a story. Because of my convivial contact with these philosophers from BYU, I was invited in 1994 to give a series of lectures. I stayed for more than a week in Provo, Utah. The absence of caffeine or any other stimulants was tough, but the hospitality was fulsome, and I was welcomed into people's homes and treated with great civility and care. My topic was romanticism, and the argument kicked off from the idea that the extraordinary burst of creative energy that we associate with romantic poetry comes out of a disappointment with a religious, specifically Christian, worldview. Poetry becomes secular scripture. In other words, romantic art announces the death of God, an idea that catches fire in the later nineteenth century. It's a familiar story.

Things went pretty well. But right at the end of the final lecture, something peculiar happened. A member of the audience asked me a question. He said, "What you have been telling us this week about romanticism and the death of God where religion becomes art is premised on a certain understanding of God, namely that God is unitary and infinite. Would you agree?" "Sure," I said. "At least two of the predicates of the divinity are that he/she/it is unitary and infinite." Gosh, I was smart back then. "But what if," he went on, "God were plural and finite?"

Concealing my slight shock, I simply said, "Pray, tell." Everyone in the room laughed, somewhat knowingly. And with that the chairman closed the session. I went straight up to my questioner and pleaded, "Tell me more." Thirty minutes later, over a caffeine-free Diet Coke in the university cafeteria, he explained what lay behind his question.

"You see," my questioner said, "in his late sermons, Joseph Smith developed some really radical ideas. For a start, God did not create space and time, but is subject to them and therefore a finite being. The Mormon God is somewhat hedged in by the universe, and not master of it. The text to look at here is an amazing sermon called 'King Follett,' which was named after an elder who had just died and was delivered in Nauvoo, Illinois, a few months before the prophet was murdered. He asks repeatedly, 'What kind of being is God?' And his reply is that God himself was once as we are now."

He leaned in closer to me and continued in a lower voice, "If you were to see God right now, Smith says, *right now*, you would see a being just like you, the very form of a man. The great secret is that, through heroic effort and striving, God was a man who became exalted and now sits enthroned in the heavens. You see, God was not God from all eternity, but *became* God. Now, the flip side of this claim is that if God is an exalted man, then we, too, can become exalted. The prophet says to the company of the saints something like, 'You have to learn how to be Gods. You have to inherit the same power and glory as God and become exalted like him.' Namely, you can arrive at the station of God. One of our early leaders summarized the King Follett sermon with the words 'As man now is, God once was. As God now is, man may be.'"

"So, dear Simon," my new friend concluded, "we, too, can become Gods, American Gods, no less." He chuckled. I was astonished.

My host, Jim, arrived to pick me up for an early dinner at his home and then drove me back to Salt Lake City to make a late flight to Chicago. I kept looking at the vast night sky in the Utah desert and thinking about what my interlocutor had said. I read the King Follett sermon and anything else I could find, particularly a very late sermon by Smith on the plurality of Gods, given around ten days before the prophet's murder. They totally blew me away. I also stole a copy of the Book of Mormon from the Marriott hotel in Chicago and waded through as much of it as I could. To be honest, it's somewhat tedious.

Of course, I knew that what the audience member told me was heresy. Christianity is premised on the fact of the incarnation. There was a God-man rabbi in occupied Palestine a couple of millenniums ago. But that doesn't mean that *anyone* can go around claiming divinity, like Joachim of Fiore in the twelfth century or the recently deceased and much missed Reverend Sun Myung Moon. There was only one incarnation. God became man, was crucified and resurrected, and we're still waiting for him to come back. The New Testament, especially the Book of Revelation, is very clear that he is coming soon. Admittedly, it's been a while.

In order to explain the consubstantiality of God and man in the person of Christ, third- and fourth-century Christian Fathers, including Saint Augustine, built up the wonderful theological edifice of the Trinity. The three persons of the Trinity, the Father, Son, and Holy Ghost, are distinct but participate in the same substance. Three in one is one in three. It is a heretical act of arrogance to arrogate divinity for oneself or to claim multiple incarnations. God is indeed unitary and infinite.

Joseph Smith believed none of that. He taught that God the Father and the Son were separate substances, both of them material. Speaking directly of the Trinity, Smith remarked, "I say that is a strange God," and goes on, in a line that must have got big laughs back in 1844, "It would make the biggest God in the world. He would be a wonderfully big God—he would be a giant or a monster." Not only is the Mormon God not as big as the Christian God, there are any number of Gods within Mormonism. In the late sermons, Smith repeatedly talks about a council of the Gods that was meant to take place sometime before the Book of Genesis begins. This is based on a rather windy interpretation of various Hebrew words, which concludes with the claim, "The head God called together the Gods and sat in grand council to bring forth the world."

But wait, things get even weirder. Smith accepts that Jesus Christ had a father, namely God, but goes on, "You may suppose that He had a Father," adding, "Was there ever a son without a father?" Common sense would answer no, but Christians must answer "Yes, there was." Namely that God created all creatures but was himself uncreated. God is causa sui, a self-caused cause. Smith explicitly rejects this idea, saying, "We say that God Himself is a self-existing being. Who told you so?" He goes on, "I might with boldness proclaim from the house-tops that God never had the power to create the spirit of man at all. God himself could not create himself." God is not an uncaused cause, but himself part of the chain of causation.

> Divinity is the object of that much-admired Mormon striving.

This is a little like that amazing exchange said to have taken place following Bertrand Russell's lecture "Why I Am Not a Christian," given at Battersea Town Hall in South London in 1927. After Russell had made his case for atheism, a female questioner asked him, "What Mr. Russell has said is well enough, but he has forgotten that the entire universe stands on the back of a turtle." Quite unfazed, Russell answered, "Madam, upon what does the turtle stand?" "Oh," she said, "it's turtles all the way down."

For Joseph Smith, it is turtles all the way down. There is an endless regress of Gods which beget one another, but which do not beget the universe. That is, creation is not ex nihilo, as it is in Christianity, where God created heaven and earth, as it says at the beginning of the Bible. Rather, matter precedes creation. This makes the Mormon God like the Demiurge in Plato's pagan creation myth in the *Timaeus*. The Mormon God does not create matter. He simply organizes it. Admittedly, he organized it pretty impressively. Just look at the design of trees.

The great thing about Mormonism is that Mormons take very seriously the doctrine of incarnation. So seriously, indeed, that they have succeeded in partially democratizing it. For Christians, incarnation is a onetime, long-distance ski jump from the divine to the human. But for Joseph Smith, incarnation is more of a two-way street, and potentially a rather congested thoroughfare. If God becomes man, then man can become God. And the word "man" has to be understood literally here. Women cannot be priests or prophets or aspire to an exclusively masculine divinity, which seems petty, a pity, and rather silly to me. But there we are. And I don't even want to get into questions of race and the historical exclusion of Blacks from the Mormon priesthood until 1978.

The point is that any number of Mormon men can become God—potentially even you-know-who. It's an intriguing thought.

There is a potential equality of the human and the divine within Mormonism, at least in the extraordinary theology that Joseph Smith speedily sketched in the King Follett sermon. Divinity is the object of that much-admired Mormon striving. Perhaps this is why Mormons are so hardworking.

Smith says, and one gets a clear sense of the persecution that he felt and that indeed engulfed and killed him, "They found fault with Jesus Christ because He said He was the Son of God, and made Himself equal with God. They say of me, like they did of the apostles of old, that I must be put down. What did Jesus say? 'Is it not written in your law, I said: Ye are Gods' . . . Why should it be blasphemy that I should say I am the son of God?"

Of course, for Christians, this is the highest blasphemy. But the Mormon vision is very distinctive. The idea is that within each of us is a spirit, or what Smith calls an "intelligence," that is co-equal with God. Smith says in the King Follett sermon, "The first principles of man are self-existent with God." This intelligence is immortal. Smith goes on, "There never was a time when there were not spirits, for they are co-equal (co-eternal) with our father in heaven." If God could not create himself, then one might say that each of us has within us something uncreated, something that precedes God and that is itself divine.

Having accepted to be sent into the world, as Mormons sometimes put it, the task is to exalt ourselves such that we, too, can become Gods. God the Father was just a stronger, more intelligent God capable of guiding the weaker intelligences, like us.

As Smith says in a marvelously sensuous, indeed gustatory, turn of phrase, "This is good doctrine. It tastes good. I can taste the principles of eternal life, and so can you." Who wouldn't want a taste of God or to taste what it might be like to be a God oneself?

The heretical vistas of Mormonism, particularly the idea of something uncreated within the human being, excited the self-described Gnostic Jew Harold Bloom. I read his wonderful 1992 book, *The American Religion*, shortly after my trip to Utah and just reread it recently with great pleasure. Bloom sees Mormonism as the quintessential expression of an American religion and controversially links the idea of the plurality of Gods to plural marriage. The argument is very simple: if you are or have the potential to become divine, and divinity is corporeal, then plural marriage is the way to create as many potential saints, prophets, and Gods as possible. Indeed, plural marriage has to be seen as a Mormon obligation: if divinity tastes so good, then why keep all the goodness to oneself? Spread the big love. It makes perfect sense (at least for heterosexual men).

In his quasiprophetic manner, Bloom thought the future belonged to Mormonism, concluding, "I cheerfully prophesy that some day, not too far in the twenty-first century, the Mormons will have enough political and financial power to sanction polygamy again. Without it, in some form or other, the complete vision of Joseph Smith never can be fulfilled."

It makes little sense to say that Mormonism is *not* Christian. It's right there in the Mormon articles of faith that were adapted from Smith's famous Wentworth Letter from 1842. Article 1 reads, "We believe in God, the Eternal Father, and in his Son, Jesus Christ, and in the Holy Ghost." But, as Bloom makes compellingly clear, Mormonism is not *just* Christian. The new revelation given to Joseph Smith in his visions and the annual visits of the angel Moroni from 1820 onward is a new gospel for the New World. Mormonism is an American religion, which beautifully, if fallaciously, understands the native inhabitants of the New World as ancient descendants of inhabitants of the Old World, the scattered tribes of Israel. Article 10 reads, "We believe in the literal gathering of Israel and the restoration of the ten tribes; that Zion (the New Jerusalem) will be built upon the American continent." I don't know whether Prime Minister Benjamin Netanyahu has read this article of faith, but it might have some specific consequences for American foreign policy should his close friend and former colleague at the Boston Consulting Group, Mitt Romney, be elected.

Mormonism is properly and powerfully *post*-Christian, as Islam is post-Christian. Where Islam, which also has a prophet, claims the transcendence of God, Mormonism makes God radically immanent. Where Islam unifies all creatures under one mighty God to whom we must submit, Mormonism pluralizes divinity, making it an immanent, corporeal matter and making God a more fragile, hemmed-in, and finite being. And obviously, both Islam and Mormonism have a complex relation to the practice of plural marriage.

Yet unlike Islam, for which Muhammad is the last prophet, Mormonism allows for *continuing* revelation. In a way, it is very democratic, very American. Article 9 reads, "We believe all that God has revealed, all that He does now reveal, and we believe that He will yet reveal many great and important things pertaining to the Kingdom of God." In principle, any male saint can add to the stock and never-ending story of revelation and thereby become exalted. From the standpoint of Christianity, both Islam and Mormonism are heresies and—if one is genuine about one's theology, and religion is not reduced to a set of banal moral platitudes—should be treated as such.

Like Bloom, I see Joseph Smith's apostasy as strong poetry, a gloriously presumptive and delusional creation from the same climate as Whitman, if not enjoying quite the same air quality. Perhaps Mormonism is not so far from romanticism after all. To claim that it is simply Christian is to fail to grasp its theological, poetic, and political audacity. It is much more than mere Christianity. Why are Mormons so keen to conceal their pearl of the greatest price? Why is no one really talking about this? In the context of you-know-who's presidential bid, people *appear* to be endlessly talking about Mormonism, but its true theological challenge is entirely absent from the discussion.

CHAPTER 9

Will Anyone Remember Eleven Dead Jews?

Emma Green

Eric Lidji is a man who cares deeply about modest ambitions. He has lived in Pittsburgh on and off for twenty years. It is a city perfectly sized to his sensibility, neither very small nor very large—a place known to but mostly ignored by those who do not live there. Lidji, thirty-six, has held many jobs; most recently, in late 2017, he became the director and only permanent staff member of the Rauh Jewish History Program & Archives, a repository of early twentieth-century local Yiddish theater posters as well as records from dozens of small-town synagogues in western Pennsylvania. But even before he became an archivist, Lidji's work has always been the same: he is a diarist of small delights, a chronicler of curios, an ardent psalmist of Pittsburgh's quirky charms.

Like many of the forty-nine thousand other Jews in the Pittsburgh area, Lidji was socializing at a local synagogue on the final Saturday in October last year when he heard the first rumors of a shooting at the nearby Tree of Life synagogue. The news was soon confirmed: eleven Jewish worshippers had been murdered. Lidji felt paralyzed: Shabbat, the Jewish day of rest, was still ongoing, and he wasn't sure what to do. It wasn't until a few hours later that something clicked, and Lidji felt a certain desperation stirring alongside his sorrow. Already, people were laying artwork and stones, which Jews customarily place on graves, on the sidewalk around the synagogue where the shooting had taken place. Many of the accumulating objects were fragile and homemade, with no clear owner or steward, left outside without protection against Pittsburgh's notoriously wet weather. This was not just an outpouring of grief, but a proliferation of artifacts—artifacts that, in Lidji's view, should be preserved.

On the Monday morning after the shooting, Lidji met with half a dozen colleagues who work in other divisions of Pittsburgh's Heinz History Center, where the Jewish archives are housed. Together they formed a task force, fanning out to as many vigils, funerals, and religious services as they could. They filled their bags with copies of programs and approached speakers after public events, asking them for their notes. Whenever Lidji spotted someone carrying a sign, he would hurry over and hand them a business card, hoping they would call him when the card reappeared at the bottom of a purse or in a pocket emptied for laundry and offer to donate what they had made. Sometimes he felt overwhelmed. On the Tuesday after the shooting, he showed up at a protest against President Donald Trump in Squirrel Hill, Pittsburgh's historic Jewish neighborhood, to find thousands of people gathered in the streets carrying signs and banners. "It felt like . . . archiving the ocean," he told me.

The grim reality of Jewish history is that Lidji is not the first archivist of his kind. Medieval Jews buried family heirlooms in the walls of their houses in times of plague, fearing that they might be blamed for the disease. Scholars founded the Yiddish institute YIVO in the early twentieth century, recruiting ordinary Eastern European villagers to collect photographs and folktales of a culture threatened by pogroms and mass migration. Emanuel Ringelblum led a covert effort to collect and bury artifacts documenting life in the Warsaw Ghetto in the early years of the Holocaust, before its inhabitants were murdered and its remaining structures burned to the ground.

Archives neither predict nor prevent atrocities. They document what has happened, but remain neutral about what is to come. Their purpose is to endure as a monument to smallness, a reminder that history is in part a composite of stories about little lives. The purpose of Lidji's archive is to keep what happened at Tree of Life from being reduced to "Pittsburgh, synagogue shooting, eleven dead," and nothing more.

Every morning, Lidji rises in the four o'clock hour, when it is still dark. He was in the midst of renovations on his house in the Garfield neighborhood when he got the job at the archives and now lives spartanly in three semihabitable rooms upstairs. His morning ritual begins with grinding coffee beans from Zeke's, the shop beloved by locals in East Liberty, the next neighborhood over. Then he puts on a pot of beans and rice or something similar for breakfast. He glances at the *New York Times* and local Pittsburgh papers to read the headlines and, only a little jokingly, to make sure Jews are still allowed in this country. He finally takes his place at his desk and begins to write.

Lidji started keeping a new kind of diary on October 27: notes about what he's collected, whom he's talked to, what the community seems to be feeling. He types quickly, with no poetry or flourish—the goal is to export as much as he can from memory to paper. After a couple of hours, he packs up his things and leaves for the next stop in his day: morning minyan, a gathering of ten or more Jews for prayer.

Since the attack, Lidji has experienced a personal religious transformation: After nearly fifteen years of haphazard Jewish observance, he started attending services every day. But there were other reasons to show up for prayer: it has proved a useful venue for winning people over to the cause of archival collection.

Documenting history is often the last task on any community's mind, all the more so during a time of grief. Prior to the shooting, the archives mainly served as a repository for records from at least three dozen local synagogues, each with its own distinct religious identity or immigrant population; for miscellanea, such as World War II–era correspondence and photographs of big groups at synagogue anniversary dinners and holiday events; and for files from seventy-five small-town Jewish communities scattered across western Pennsylvania. It holds at least one item from nearly every Jewish organization that has ever existed in Pittsburgh, Lidji told me.

And yet, that work was largely hidden to all but the city's biggest history buffs. After the attack, Lidji's first big challenge was becoming more visible to the community: being unobtrusively, insistently present at memorial events, and building relationships with community leaders. His second big challenge was convincing the Pittsburgh Jewish community that its history is worth preserving.

The first time Lidji felt "any sense of accomplishment," he told me, was when a man who had been "polite but reticent" about the archival project came over during morning minyan one day and announced that he had found "the perfect object." On the day of the shooting, a boy had been celebrating his bar mitzvah at an Orthodox synagogue about a mile away from Tree of Life and continued the service even as news of the shooting reached the community. The *bentscher*, or book containing the prayers said after meals, captured the moment perfectly, the man told Lidji: it featured the boy's name and the starry Pittsburgh Steelers logo wrapped around the date, 10.27.18. Lidji eventually got hold of one of the bentschers.

The most significant items Lidji has collected have what he calls "the shine," a certain raw, emotional quality that indicates an object's clear connection to the past. In the week after the attack, students at the Hillel Jewish University Center of Pittsburgh gathered and expressed their feelings on Post-its. "My childhood illusion of security as a Jew was shattered," one student wrote. Lidji and his colleagues collected programs from memorial events, some more pointed than others: a community with a large Bhutanese population hosted a vigil, where attendees seemed to feel acutely the dangers of being an ethnic minority. A large Reform Jewish congregation, Rodef Shalom, hosted a small event where the preschool director reported that ever since the attack, the children had been obsessed with building elaborate protective structures out of blocks.

For whatever reason, people donated stacks upon stacks of "I voted" stickers from the November 6, 2018, election printed with the "Stronger than hate" logo designed to commemorate the attack. Lidji also collected bags of black paper strips, which protesters had torn, mimicking a Jewish funeral custom, during the Trump protest to symbolize their grief over the shooting and their dismay at the president's arrival. Eighteen days after the shooting, the impromptu memorial that had covered the sidewalks, fences, and bushes around the Tree of Life synagogue finally came down; it took roughly a dozen people nine hours to take it apart. They laid everything out on paper, and a local business owner agreed to take the flowers for composting. Some of the volunteers, however, felt too pained to throw the stems away, so they made bundles to dry and preserve. Once summer arrived, the dried bouquets threatened to start decomposing in the business owner's un-air-conditioned house, so he asked Lidji to come get them. Lidji now has crates of these flowers in his house.

A few weeks after the attack, Lidji got a call from a local family who wanted to donate a sign they made for the first memorial vigil, on the night of the shooting. When the mother brought her two children, three and five, to the archives, the older child asked why they had to give the sign away. Sometimes, Lidji told her, things are so important that we have to make sure they will be around for a really long time. Right, the girl's mom added. One day, *you* will be able to bring *your* grandchildren to see this sign.

In late summer, Lidji picked up several vanloads' worth of material from Jewish organizations around town, ranging from condolence notes to quilts to paper cranes they had received in the preceding months. Lidji said it will probably take him at least a year to go through it all. And there's more: Tree of Life and the other two congregations that were in the building during the shooting received an estimated ten thousand letters in the days after the attack. It is unclear where they will end up.

"People will tell this story someday, and they're going to tell it using this information that we've all left behind for them," Lidji told me. "We've only done as good a job as we could do. We couldn't save everything."

The Heinz History Center is in a brick warehouse, the site of an old ice company in Pittsburgh's Strip District, within sight of the Allegheny River. Named for Senator H. John Heinz III, the heir to the Heinz ketchup fortune, the center holds a variety of collections pertaining to western Pennsylvania, about such topics as the history of sports and the French and Indian War. The Rauh Jewish Archives—really just Lidji's cubicle—sit on the sixth floor.

When I met Lidji there late last spring, he seemed exhausted. By now he really had two full-time jobs: Pittsburgh's Jewish archivist, and archivist of the Tree of Life attack. The trove he is building will one day contain a large portion of the shooting's physical imprint. Alone, these objects may seem insignificant, but together, they show the arc of this community's grief: Poster-board signs made in solidarity, and in protest. Letters from around the world. Handicrafts and other offerings. A digital collection of community members' posts and messages about the attack. Clips from local news outlets and Jewish media. Programs from events, the texts of speeches and sermons. Anything and everything that can be touched and seen, Lidji hopes to collect.

Dispositionally speaking, Lidji is geared much more toward pleasantly mundane local drama than toward grand narratives of history. He had been devising small-scale local-history projects long before he took up his formal post at the archives. Before last October, one of his projects at the archives was tracing the rivalry between two competing Yiddish theater producers who had set up shop in Pittsburgh in the 1920s. He loved that the letters outlining their feuds were written in a spirit of high dudgeon, befitting their craft.

Lidji has had to figure out how to start telling the story of the Pittsburgh shooting, a story with much larger and darker implications than any he's had to tell before. At first, it was Jewish organizations in and around Pittsburgh that approached him to help them make sense of the shooting—the Orthodox yeshiva where he went to high school, an area synagogue where one of the victims' children attends services. Eventually, he started getting requests from people who live farther afield. In June, Lidji spoke at a convention in Colorado of mostly non-Orthodox *chevrot kadisha*, or sacred societies, made up of the members of Jewish communities who oversee the washing and burial of the dead. The convention was held not long after a gunman allegedly killed fifty-one people and wounded dozens more in a mosque in Christchurch, New Zealand, and also not long after a nineteen-year-old man allegedly opened fire in a synagogue in Poway, California, murdering one woman and injuring three others, including a rabbi and an eight-year-old girl.

Lidji began his talk with a story he sometimes tells when he's trying to explain the deeper meaning of the archives project. Psalm 90 begins, "A prayer of Moses, the man of God." According to Jewish tradition, most of the psalms were composed by King David, who was born centuries after Moses died. How, Lidji asked, could David have known what Moses had said in his prayers?

In answer, Lidji offered his interpretation of a line from the Radak, a medieval Jewish commentator, painting a scene of dramatic discovery: King David, unable to sleep and wandering around his palace at night, finds a pottery jar containing a mysterious scroll bearing Moses's prayers. How meaningful it must have been, Lidji said, for David to hold in his hands the words of the Jewish tradition's greatest prophet. Psalm 90 itself describes how insignificant human events must seem to God: *For in Your sight, a thousand years are like . . . a watch of the night.* And yet the Jewish people, Lidji explained, have been able to maintain continuity in part because their archives have let them "come back later and be reminded."

The bar mitzvah boy who persevered through his prayers even as his synagogue went on lockdown will one day die. The little girl who gave her sign to the archives will one day die. From dust to dust: a century hence, no one who witnessed the Pittsburgh synagogue shooting and its aftermath will be around to explain why they loved Squirrel Hill. If it survives, Lidji's archive will be all that's left to tell a more textured story. Depending on what comes next, those stones and signs and notes of grief could tell radically different stories: of a rare aberration in American Jewish history, or the restarting of an ancient clock.

CHAPTER 10

No Revolution without Religion

Nathan Schneider

There was a flash of wisdom in Occupy Wall Street's controversial and otherwise unsuccessful attempt to occupy a plot of land owned by Trinity Church on December 17 of 2011: if the movement is going to last much longer, it is going to have to occupy, and be supported by, faith. By "faith" I mean religion—the more organized the better. "Hey, church," one could almost hear the Occupiers saying, as they mounted the giant yellow ladder over the fence and dropped down on the other side, "act like a church." And, this being just a month after the eviction from Zuccotti Park, "We need you."

The Occupy movement has been largely a white, urban phenomenon, and one with a bit of a tendency toward vanguardism, which makes it not entirely surprising that it's often blind to the fact that there is no force more potentially revolutionary in US history or in the country today than religion. But the movement remains oblivious to this fact at its own peril. You who are blind, see.

On the other side of the Atlantic, left intellectuals have been starting to discover what they have to learn from religion about revolution. Slavoj Žižek, Alain Badiou, and Giorgio Agamben have all written about the apostle Paul in recent years: he stood at the intersection of Judaism and Christianity and was the architect of an underground movement that eventually subsumed the Roman Empire. During the early days on Liberty Plaza, actually, I felt like I was witnessing a glimpse of how Paul described his early church: the holding of all things in common, a single-minded asceticism, and local cells miraculously spreading throughout the known world. Living in societies far less religious than ours, thinkers on the European left are realizing that the loss of religious imagination can mean losing the capacity to imagine and take steps toward a radically different kind of society.

It's hard to think of any place where religion's revolutionary potential has been more fully realized than the United States—both for good and for evil. Many activists nowadays assume the completely nonempirical notion that religion in this country today is a wholly owned subsidiary of the Republican Party. But this impression is the result of a very temporary and partial—if singularly effective—alliance forged at the onset of the Reagan era. This alliance need not last. American religion is nothing if not finicky with regard to politics, and highly troublesome to those in power.

———————

The colonial impulse itself, of course, originated among Puritan congregationalists—utopians who sought to create autonomous communities apart from monarchs. This impulse, further radicalized, gave us the concept of religious liberty and the legal right to free thought. In the decades before independence, anti-imperialist ideas spread through the revivals of the First Great Awakening. Quakers, working in leaderless and consensus-based communities, resisted conscription and oath-taking at the behest of the state; in the mid-nineteenth century, they also led the crusade to abolish slavery. Facing discrimination and lack of access to services, Catholic immigrants created a whole system of parallel schools, hospitals, and charities. The Northeast of the nineteenth century was dotted with off-the-grid communes and experimental lifestyles, run according to the dictates of various religious and spiritualist sects; it was from these that we get Americanisms from Shaker furniture to graham crackers. The insurrectionary and separatist Mormons emerged from this milieu as well, until being driven westward to found their socialist Zion in the desert, which they defended from the feds by force of arms.

These are not the exceptions of American religion; inventiveness, suspicion of authority, and autonomy are really right in the mainstream, however cleverly disguised for the sake of bourgeois decency. Want to see mutual aid? Look no further than the nearest suburban, nondenominational megachurch, where members find free day care, credit unions, employment services, good works for the poor, support in times of crisis, and access to a political machine.

While these political machines have tended of late to be co-opted by the 1 percent, in the past they were engines that helped drive (as well as suppress) the early labor movement, and women's suffrage, together with just about every other political movement with any major impact on American history. And how could it not? About 14 million people belong to labor unions in the United States; closer to 120 million attend religious services regularly. Most of them, at least some of the time, are told in those services to do good, seek justice, and rescue the oppressed. Whether it's on behalf of affordable housing or the unborn or for an end to AIDS and human trafficking, religion represents an enormous proportion of how people in this country organize.

———————

The Occupy movement has already caught some of the bounty that faith-based organizing has to offer. Before and especially after last fall's wave of evictions, Occupiers have met, slept, and eaten in houses of worship. Religious communities possess tremendous quantities of real estate, no small amount of it unused. Such spaces could become available to the movement, and by means more diplomatic than the failed, forced occupations of church property tried in New York and, most recently, San Francisco. Far preferable, I would think, are Occupiers' successes in defending from closure an historic Black church in Atlanta and a Catholic homeless center in Providence.

Meanwhile, for a movement that has still failed to bring eviction-defense and antiforeclosure action to a mass scale, religious groups provide the ideal platform for doing so; equip them with the right tools and strategies, and when some of their own are threatened by the banks, their fellow faithful will rally to save their homes—not merely on the basis of political ideology, but with the far more powerful motivation of looking out for the community. This kind of action also has special resonance in religious traditions, from the debt-forgiving Jubilee of the Hebrew scriptures to the radical aid for those in need taught and practiced by Jesus Christ to the ban on usury in Islamic law. An act may be civil disobedience by temporal standards, but to a higher law, resisting oppression is a basic requirement.

One need only think of the civil rights movement, arguably the last mass resistance movement in the United States to win decisive political gains. In it, churches were often the basic units of organizing. Clergy locked arms with activists at the front lines, and together they won.

The tryst between activists and churches, however, is not always a happy one. Saul Alinsky claimed that he never got anywhere appealing to clergy by the precepts of their faith. "Instead," he wrote, "I approach them on the basis of their own self-interest, the welfare of their Church, even its physical property." An eminent religion reporter I know says he deals with them like he used to deal with the mob. The clergy-driven Occupy Faith network has been created to be an interface between the leaderless movement and the needs of professional religious leaders. It's not an easy task, Occupy Faith's organizers realize, but it needs to be done. The alliance between churches and civil rights ultimately worked because courageous people made clear that it had to.

While most religious communities don't come anywhere near the Occupy standard for horizontality and transparency—nor does Occupy, for that matter—they're not as bad as an outsider might think. The flock often finds plenty of ways of scaring the shepherd—from the power of the pocketbook to steering committees and boards to the threat of simply picking up and going elsewhere. That's why, as with unions, Occupy isn't going to get anywhere with religious communities until it wins over the rank and file. Then, leaders will have to show support for the movement, or else.

As I stood waiting for the action against Trinity Church to begin on December 17, I struck up a conversation with a man in a Roman collar and a black beret, Father Paul Mayer—a formerly married Catholic priest and veteran of every major American social justice movement since he marched with Martin Luther King Jr. in the 1960s. Trinity is an Episcopal church; I asked him what he thought Catholics would do if OWS were making a demand like this of us.

"We'd be worse," he replied.

I didn't know it at the time, but, together with Episcopal Bishop George Packard and Sister Susan Wilcox, a Catholic nun, Mayer was about to lead the charge over the fence, down onto Trinity property, and promptly into police custody. The following night, out of jail, he and Wilcox joined me and a lapsed cradle Catholic, a theologian, and a sociology student for the first meeting of Occupy Catholics at a bar near Zuccotti Park. We came together with a common but still not quite clarified desire to create an affinity group of Catholics involved with the movement, as well as to take what the movement was teaching us and bring it to our church. Maybe, someday, we could help Catholic churches respond better to Occupiers than Trinity did, and vice versa.

So far our emphasis has been on reaching out to laypeople, online and through the social justice ministries of nearby churches. We've held a general assembly at Maryhouse Catholic Worker, part of the organization Dorothy Day cofounded with Christian anarchist principles to serve the poor and struggle for justice and peace. For months we've been slowly growing, planning, and praying about how to lead our church, the biggest landowner in

New York City, to join Occupy's call for a more righteous society. We've been teaching Catholics about the movement and Occupiers about the long and deep Catholic social justice tradition. We got this group going because the connection between Occupy and our faith was so obvious we couldn't ignore it. We needed this movement, and we know that the movement no less needs us.

This past Good Friday, the most solemn day of the Christian year, we stood in front of Saint Patrick's Cathedral and sang, "Were you there when they crucified the poor?" against the bishops' silence on a budget in Congress poised to slash services upon which the 99 percent depends. "We love our church," we cried with the people's mic, "and right now the church needs to speak." So we did. Maybe next time we go to Saint Patrick's, we'll be sleeping on the sidewalk.

CHAPTER 11

Forgiveness in the Epoch of Me Too

Kaya Oakes

The predator was revealed in a post on social media, written by a woman, circulated by women. Years ago, he and I were members of a loosely connected group of writers; not really friends, just acquaintances working on opposite sides of the country. The Internet shrinks our worlds, however, and we emailed and chatted enough for me to get uncomfortable with things he suggested a number of times. Nothing like violence, nothing like sustained harassment or stalking, but an ongoing irritation, like a night mosquito.

The post, written by a woman he'd been involved with, revealed worse: physically and emotionally abusive patterns of behavior with different women that went on for years. They were always younger, always emerging in their careers. Some of the names of women who reported interactions with him were familiar: the web of relationships was tightly woven. It made it easier for him to find someone to move on to. Apparently he'd sobered up, yet the pattern still seemed to be happening. So I did what we do these days when we find out a man in our lives is problematic: I activated the whisper network and shared the information with a few women, and severed digital connections with him.

A few days later, a Facebook message. I'd hurt his feelings and disappointed him by terminating our relationship. He was working on his "spiritual life," which I knew involved Catholicism because we'd talked about Thomas Merton. He was sober now, and what had happened, had happened while he was drinking, and "everyone knew" he was a wreck at that point. Could I forgive him?

I considered this for a few weeks. It seemed the Christian thing to do, the ethical move of a good person. Plenty of men had done much worse to me, from my childhood and into my adulthood. Many of them had also asked for forgiveness. And then I discovered that the agonized note he had sent was a form message. He'd sent the exact same note to friends, male and female, one by one, as they dropped him.

We are in a peak moment right now when it comes to men asking women for forgiveness. And in each case, before any of the violations make it to court—which they rarely do—the forgiveness is meted out not by the judicial system, with its mythologies of checks and balances, but by the person who was violated. The onus for forgiving, over and over again, is laid at the feet of the victim. What are these men really asking women to do? To absolve them and clear their consciences, so they can move on. Meanwhile, the women are left behind to grapple with the repercussions of the abuse.

Sexual harassment and sexual violence tend to occur in a serial manner, one violation after another, on and on, until someone has enough of the silencing and speaks out. Then come the apologies, so many apologies, riddled with "but" and "however" and "although I recall things differently." Since the Me Too floodgates opened, we have had little in the way of a national conversation about what it would mean to forgive men for harassment, abuse, or rape. But we have also had to read a series of apologies. Many do not explicitly ask for forgiveness, but they do acknowledge the damage they have done. And in that, even in our secular era, there is an implied request for repentance and absolution. The man asks to be cleansed of his sins because he is so very sorry for committing them.

In February of 2018, the novelist Sherman Alexie began his apology by acknowledging that he had "harmed other people." Victims had described a series of verbal and physical incidents, mostly between younger female writers and the powerful, older writer, sometimes involving Alexie threatening to damage their literary careers. But Alexie then spent three paragraphs disparaging one of his accusers, whose tweets had opened the floodgates for others, finally saying that he had made "poor decisions," but that he had never threatened anyone's career, which would be "completely out of character." Multiple women contradicted this statement. Did he earn their forgiveness by dismissing their claims?

After being accused by multiple women of masturbating in front of them, the comic Louis CK admitted that what they said was true. "There is nothing about this that I forgive myself for," he wrote. "And I have to reconcile it with who I am." CK at least shouldered his responsibility, and acknowledged the damage he'd done. And while what CK did was truly odious, there are also horrifying monsters on the continuum of harassment and abuse, serial violators of bodies and minds. The monsters would also like to be forgiven.

Larry Nassar, the Michigan State doctor to the USA women's gymnastics teams, was sentenced in January of 2018 for sexually assaulting a series of girls and women over the course of more than a decade. At least 150 women and girls have come forward; Nassar pleaded guilty to assaulting seven of them. In his written statement, Nassar said that their words had shaken him "to the core" and that he would carry those words for the rest of his days. He also said that an acceptable apology was "impossible to write and convey." Nassar, too, was asking for absolution. He was admitting to his sins, which makes sense, because by all accounts, he is a faithful Catholic.

Nassar was a catechist and Eucharistic minister at Saint Thomas Aquinas Catholic church in East Lansing, Michigan. The diocese confirmed that Nassar had completed the mandated "safe environment" training for parishioners who work with children, and it appears he was involved in catechesis with children up until 2016, a year after he was fired by USA Gymnastics, after the first wave of victims had come forward. The AP reported in February that a bill inspired by the Nassar scandal that "would retroactively extend the amount of time child victims of sexual abuse have to sue their abusers" was "drawing concerns from the Catholic church," which worried about the financial implications of giving victims extended time to come forward. The church Nassar belongs to was shattered by abuse, but in this situation, it appears its greatest concern is not the well-being of its victims.

Christians would like to pretend that we understand what forgiveness means. We march into confessionals to be forgiven. We ask our brothers and sisters to forgive us every Sunday. We have Lent and Advent, entire liturgical seasons focused on penitence. Jesus's own words about forgiveness from Luke are drilled into us in our catechesis: "even if they sin against you seven times in a day and seven times come back saying 'I repent,' you must forgive them." It is Holy Week as I write this, just a few days from Good Friday, when Jesus pleads with God to forgive his killers "who know not what they do."

Abusers will emphasize this: they knew not what they did. "I was drunk. I understood the situation differently. I assumed it was consensual. My recollection is different than hers." And in the context of situations like Larry Nassar's, Christ's emphasis on forgiving no matter how many times someone sins against us is nearly impossible to comprehend. Many of those girls were too young to understand they were being sexually violated. They took years to come forward because it took years for them to understand that what happened to them was deeply sick and wrong.

So, too, does this idea that forgiveness on the part of the victims should be automatic fail in the Catholic church's own history. At the height of the Boston scandal, Cardinal Law stated that he apologized and begged forgiveness from those "who have suffered from my shortcomings and my mistakes." Law's funeral in December of 2017, held in the Vatican and in the thick of rising numbers of Me Too accusations, contained no mention of his years of cover-ups of abuse. The presiding cardinal, Angelo Sodano, mentioned only that Law had dedicated his life to the church, but added that "each of us can sometimes be lacking in our mission." Pope Francis, to the chagrin of many, delivered the benediction over Law's coffin. A month later, the pope flew to Chile, where he begged forgiveness for the church's history of abuse under Bishop Barrios, and then, almost immediately, turned around and accused the victims of "calumny."

The Catholic Church wears a Janus face when it comes to forgiveness. It looks to a future where, ideally, abuse has ended and there is nothing to forgive. But it also looks to a past where protecting the institution, its finances, and its leadership led to years of silencing, which damaged victims even further. This same Janus face has revealed itself in entertainment, politics, sports, universities, and workplaces, as the sins of harassment and abuse continue to be aired. On the one side, we see a future where abuse and harassment might happen less often thanks to those who have come forward. On the other: millennia of silencing, skepticism, and doubt.

In researching this essay, I found surprisingly little written in Catholic theology about sexual harassment, abuse, or forgiveness. Even after Boston, even after the Magdalene Laundries, after commission after commission, not much has been written about what forgiving abusers might mean. Much more has been written about this by female Protestant theologians, and particularly by female Protestant ethicists from denominations where women have been ordained for some time.

Perhaps having women in leadership positions means that this reckoning with abuse and forgiveness is able to be more of an open conversation. Perhaps, too, those women, many from the first generations to be ordained, had to deal with harassment and systemic misogyny themselves. Perhaps women in their congregations who'd been uncomfortable talking to male pastors about domestic and sexual violence were finally able to open up to these female religious leaders. And perhaps it's just how pervasive this problem is across every religious denomination, in every part of the country, and in nearly every workplace. An ABC News/*Washington Post* poll revealed that over half of American women have been sexually harassed, particularly in work environments. The dominant numbers of these women described their emotional state as angry or humiliated. These are not emotional states that easily lead to forgiveness.

In an essay entitled "Love Your Enemy: Sex, Power and Christian Ethics," Karen Lebacqz writes that the problem of expecting forgiveness is that it fails to understand that abused women "need to operate out of a 'hermeneutic of suspicion.'" In this mindset, forgiveness can appear to "ignore the role-conditioning or status of men and women in this culture." Lebacqz writes that forgiveness means "loving your enemy," not losing "the self or the self's perspective, for this contradicts the value of survival." Another part of the problem is that we conceive forgiveness as a kind of sentimentality, when in fact it is an issue of justice, both in recognizing injustice and in redressing it. In Lebacqz's understanding, forgiveness means that "the enemy remains the enemy," but victims can "seek a relationship with that group that is a relationship free of injustice."

For Serene Jones, the president of Union Theological Seminary, the problem of forgiveness is tied up in the notion of universal sin, which she wrote about in *Sojourners* in February of 2018. In the Christian tradition, Jones writes, sin and sinfulness "pervades all of life." In terms of male sexual violence, this universal sin "names how some are guilty of perpetrating grave harms, while others bear the direct effects of this sin on their victimized, traumatized bodies and minds." For Jones, the challenge for Christians is both admitting that the "war against women is real, ongoing, and church-sanctioned" and understanding that God "rejects this violence as sin and evil and stands beside all those who suffer from it and who fight against it."

In 1976, Marie Fortune founded the FaithTrust Institute, which works to help religious leaders address issues of sexual and domestic violence. The institute is still in operation today, working with interfaith clergy and laypeople. In an essay entitled "Preaching Forgiveness?" Fortune frames the issue by first defining what forgiveness is *not*. According to her, forgiveness is not "condoning or pardoning harmful behavior, which is a sin," or "healing the wound lightly." Forgiveness is not "always possible," and not "an expectation of any degree of future relationship with the person who caused the harm."

One Catholic theologian who has written on forgiveness and the sexual abuse of women is M. Shawn Copeland of Boston College. In her book *Enfleshing Freedom*, she discusses forgiveness through the lens of slavery, which "rendered black women's bodies objects of property, of production, of reproduction, of sexual violence." These women could not forgive their slave masters because "a human subject cannot consent to any treatment or condition that is intended to usurp the transcendental end or purpose for which human beings are divinely created." For Black Christian women in particular, Copeland emphasizes, it is Jesus who does the forgiving on their behalf, because Jesus "does not forget poor, dark, and despised bodies." He gave his body "in fidelity to the *baileia tou theou*, the reign of God, which opposes the reign of sin" And he gave his body "for these, for all, for us." But the understanding that Jesus does the forgiving is a selective reading.

Crucified, Jesus does not look down and forgive those who killed him; his death *itself* is the forgiveness. The forgiveness is enfleshed in the suffering victim, but the forgiveness must also come from a higher authority.

In this Me Too epoch, that higher authority might be God, but it might also be a slow, gradual shift in the structure of institutions that have smothered the voices of victims. And part of that shift might mean helping men to understand that their requests for forgiveness are a part of their patriarchal privilege. Those who have harassed and abused are allowed to be absolved, and to move on. Sometimes they even move on into positions of great power, as Cardinal Law's move to Rome after Boston, or the last presidential election, demonstrated.

But perhaps it is time that women stopped forgiving men. Maybe it is not our job to forgive them. While working on this essay, I thought of the work of Sister Helen Prejean. Her decades of work to end the death penalty in America might make one assume she believes death-row inmates should all be forgiven. But this is not the case. Rather, when Prejean describes looking into the eyes of killers and seeing their humanity, she is bringing them to a kind of reconciliation with themselves, with the "transcendental end for which human beings are created," as Copeland writes. Women do not have to forgive those who rape, abuse, and harass us, because in those acts, in their reduction of our humanity, they deny us a fully lived life. But we can see abusers as sinful, broken, and flawed—and as our fellow human beings.

I never wrote back to my former friend who asked for my forgiveness. But if I had, I would have said this. I do not forgive what he did, but I do not wish him ill: I hope he repairs what is broken about himself, if only so that no more women are hurt by him. I do not forgive the men who've grabbed me, pushed me around, groped me, leered at me, made suggestive comments, or demanded my body, attention, and time. Nor can I even remember at this point who all of them were; there have been so many over these decades of my life. I do not forgive them, but I do not want them to hurt as much as they hurt any woman, do not want them to feel the guilt, rage, self-blame and self-loathing that so many women feel. Maybe this lack of forgiveness makes me less Christlike. Maybe it makes me a bad Christian. Or maybe it makes me just as human as these men who hurt women. Just like them, I am capable of inflicting pain. I choose instead to bend my life to avoid doing that as often as possible. This is not forgiveness. But it is what most of us can do, if we try.

CHAPTER 12

A Welcoming Church No More

Sam Washington

I studied to become an evangelical pastor. Then I woke up on November 9, 2016, with the knowledge that my faith was now chained to the legacy of Donald Trump.

Many of my friends cheered. Polls showed that 81 percent of Americans who called themselves "evangelical" voted for a man who won office by disparaging, belittling, threatening, and dismissing people of color.

Now I'm no longer comfortable with the label of "evangelical" because I have become slack-jawed with disgust at friends who will defend Trump harder than they defend the gospel. They boisterously support a gleeful bully and a habitual liar who is hailed as God's instrument in these times. A pastor acquaintance told me he voted for Trump because he championed the antiabortion cause and was the lesser of two evils.

They gloss over the bigotry and insist they voted for Trump because of "other reasons," which amount to superficial buzzwords: crooked Hillary, draining the swamp, shaking things up, et cetera. They retreat into shells when you try to highlight the obvious cognitive dissonance it takes to cast a vote for what Trump really represents. They put their personal comfort above everything else.

I tried to listen to them. People I taught in my Bible study classes at church, people with whom I studied the Bible in seminary, people I considered my brothers and sisters in Christ, friends on Facebook. I gave it a massive amount of effort. But in the end Black Christians such as myself now have abundant reason to question our place at evangelical churches. We cringe when pastors and church members have no qualms about praying for law enforcement and hear deafening silence when it comes to victims of police brutality—or pointed accusations that it was the victims' fault. Our hearts break when people express jubilance that God "has finally moved back into the White House."

I had always been aware of Donald Trump as a pop culture figure. He was even on some of my hip-hop CDs (not rapping, thankfully). To me, he was a larger-than-life celebrity/media mogul who was nothing more than a cameo on some movie or a dude walking slowly from a helicopter as a '70s funk track played.

When Barack Obama became president, I observed with disturbed interest as Trump talked and tweeted about how Obama should not be president because he wasn't a US citizen. I shook my head as he appeared wherever anyone would have him and launched into his criticisms of the nationality of the nation's first Black president. It wasn't "fair" policy criticism, and people—Black people in particular—understood what he meant: Donald

Trump was saying that a person of African origin was incapable of being president of the United States.

And for eight years Trump ran with that flag. He waved it around and beaned people over the head with it. He tweeted he had detectives in Hawaii combing through birth records and leaving no stone unturned. In his hands, the birther movement took life and grew.

Trump's decision to enter the presidential campaign left me with a sense of foreboding that sadly was made manifest as the months went on. I noticed the obvious token smatterings of Black faces in the crowd. I saw his discomfort while he sat clapping in a Black church. I saw him talk at people who looked like me as opposed to talking with us. And most disturbingly, I saw bigots line up behind Trump. People who felt Obama was "other," people who swallowed the birther foolishness, people who felt that it was the victim's fault when they were shot by police, individuals who felt their skin color made them superior and somehow "oppressed" by social justice.

They flocked behind Trump. They screamed MAGA and called Black Lives Matter activists "terrorists." They shared mean-spirited memes, cheered Tomi Lahren, shouted "Lock her up," and pontificated on the state of things on 4chan and other internet bastions of hatred.

To my shock and chagrin, more than a few people in the evangelical pews started chanting MAGA as well. They became more vocal about their dislike for Obama and expressed no discomfort about rubbing shoulders with bigots. What we are now seeing is a break in the fragile alliance between Black and white evangelical Christians, which was always fraught with historical baggage. And all I could think was: "How did it come to this?"

My own story is relevant to this sense of personal betrayal.

I grew up attending the Pentecostal church my great-grandfather built and was the scion to his legacy of ministry. I have great uncles and cousins deeply involved in ministry, so naturally it was expected I would fall into the mold. But instead I rebelled.

After reading *The Autobiography of Malcolm X* during the summer of my fourteenth birthday, I become wholly invested in the cause of Black nationalism and subscribed to the beliefs of the Nation of Islam. I agreed wholeheartedly with their assessment that Christianity was the "white man's religion" and the cross had done nothing but bring slavery, suffering, and death to Black people. A blood-soaked legacy of slavery, lynching, segregation, and police brutality reinforced my ideals about the hypocrisy of Christianity. And I became well versed in debating such topics about how a so-called loving God could be used to justify such heinous acts. Even worse, I felt incensed at the tangible apathy that many white Christians displayed.

But my life was fueled by anger. It was righteous and justified anger to an extent, but anger nonetheless. It was rooted in a desire for justice, for freedom, for equality. It was coated in the betrayal of coming to understand that people who looked like me were singing praises to a person who looked like "them." It was a subconscious deference to white people, because we then put them closer to God.

It has been observed that Black men go into jails as "Christian" (i.e., raised in a Christian home and often identifying as Christian) but come out Muslim. In this transformation to Islam, they find a sense of self-worth and inner value. They develop a love for their communities, pride, and militancy for upliftment: factors the Christian Church tends to miss, with its focus on the hereafter while the oppressors enjoyed a heaven here on Earth.

These churches were on almost every corner in a community infested with squalor. Pastors were well dressed, decorated in jewelry, and escorted around in luxurious cars. But their parishioners were impoverished, fleeting lives surrounded by drugs, alcohol, and vice.

I donned my cloak of militancy and assailed what I felt was the element most damaging to my community; I began to wage war. My apathy to the Christian faith kept me hostile to church, and over the years to God. While I would eventually leave the Nation of Islam and settle into an atheist mindset, I soon found rest and contentment as a comfortable deist.

But God had other plans. My coming to faith was not a Hallmark movie of a "good boy gone rogue gone good again." It didn't involve a tearful heartfelt moment between me and my long-praying grandmother, who had borne the brunt of my rage at Christianity because she was so invested in it. I didn't run into church speaking tongues as powerful tears ran down my grandmother's cheeks and our stare was broken by an embrace as the choir reached its crescendo—she had passed away some twelve years before and would never smile in approval from the pews as she saw her defiant grandson take the pulpit, an action that nobody thought more unlikely than me.

In ways that only God could orchestrate, I came into my faith by way of the white evangelical church. The initial shock of seeing a pastor not dressed well, but in jeans and a T-shirt, gave way to a sense of peace. I enrolled at Fuller Theological Seminary in Pasadena, started leading Bible study, and worshipped next to people of all shades and hues. God helped me toward a broader definition of "brothers and sisters."

But something gave me pause.

I have learned that church has two diametrically opposite meanings within Black and white societies. For the Black community in America, since the early nineteenth century, church came to personify a refuge, a place of spiritual sustenance and succor. It was a foundation of perseverance that allowed Black men and women to face their days dealing with bigotry, discrimination, hatred, and injustice. The Black church also cultivated a robust demand for social change, which, even in my days of being an angry, young rebel, I could not deny.

For white America, church is seen differently. It is a place to celebrate the success of life. Church is a joyous reveling for the fortunate in what God has done for them. It seemed eager to embrace glib political jargon and to conflate the doctrines of Christianity with a vague Americanism. At a Southern Baptist church where I led Thursday Bible study, it wasn't uncommon to hear the word "socialist" precede or follow "Obama." Church isn't about injustice, because the people raising their hands to thank God for Donald Trump probably never had to face it.

The white evangelical church today now seems to me like a cruise ship with a mad captain at the helm. The passengers are dancing and partying as the band plays, totally oblivious to an oncoming catastrophe. The captain told them that the food would be exquisite, the help would be impeccable, the slot machines would ooze money even when you walked by them on your way to get drinks. But they don't see the holes in the ship. They miss the small ones, naturally, but even the bigger holes strangely elicit no cause for concern.

The evangelicals who voted for Trump effectively discarded the chapters of the Bible that extolled patience, love, forgiveness, peace, care for the poor and suffering, and replaced them with pamphlets for guided tours of the Wall, white nationalist jargon, and juvenile vitriol. They have gained the uncanny ability to campaign against "snowflakes," following up a heartless bigoted statement with a profession of faith or a selective biblical verse.

It looks and feels awful. So awful that I have effectively divorced myself from the evangelical church. I don't consider myself a part of it, because the 2016 election highlighted the fact that the people I considered my brothers and sisters in Christ truly never saw me as such.

I wonder if I should even go to church anymore. The unease I feel as heads are bowed to pray for the president that called neo-Nazis "fine people," used an obscenity to describe African and Caribbean nations, and has never objected to the backing of the KKK is just too much. Despite my absence and feelings of brokenheartedness, white evangelical churches across this country are gleeful with self-congratulated accomplishment as they thank God for Donald Trump, while people like me are excluded and the faith they hold dear is dragged through the mud in the eyes of the world.

A Scripture from the Gospel According to Mark keeps returning to me: "For what shall it profit a man, if he shall gain the whole world, and lose his own soul?"

CHAPTER 13

How Would Bonhoeffer Vote?

Joel Looper

Less than a month before the 2016 presidential election, evangelical journalist and biographer Eric Metaxas made the case in the *Wall Street Journal* that, though they might find his morals odious and his behavior unconscionable, American evangelicals had no choice but to vote for Donald Trump. Metaxas admitted that Trump's lecherous *Access Hollywood* hot-mic audio comments, which the *Washington Post* had made public five days before, might be a deal-breaker for some religious voters. But Trump's opponent, he argued, had "a whole deplorable basketful" of deal-breakers, and, purity be damned, Christians were obligated to stop her from reaching the Oval Office.

To make his point, Metaxas needed a weighty moral example, a name that had currency among churchgoers. Attentive observers of American Christianity could almost have predicted his choice. "The anti-Nazi martyr Dietrich Bonhoeffer also did things most

Christians of his day were disgusted by," Metaxas wrote, implying that pulling the lever for Trump was analogous to conspiring against Hitler's regime, while voting for Hillary Clinton was roughly equivalent to joining the brownshirts. As everyone knows, evangelicals bought what Metaxas was selling.

This was far from the first time the Berlin theologian and pastor's name was used to gain leverage in American politics. The Bonhoeffer of Metaxas's 2010 bestseller, *Bonhoeffer: Pastor, Martyr, Prophet, Spy*, had all the theological orthodoxy and manly grit an evangelical could want. Conversely, though, Charles Marsh's 2014 biography, *Strange Glory*, was exquisitely crafted and meticulously researched; his Bonhoeffer looked suspiciously like an American liberal Protestant with some inclination toward activism and progressive politics. He even spent the years he was incarcerated in the Nazi military prison at Tegel (1943–1945) suffering from unrequited love toward his best (male) friend, Eberhard Bethge, rather than pining for his fiancée, Maria von Wedemeyer.

More recently, both conservative and progressive journalists, pastors, and academics have entered the fray, claiming that either the *Obergefell v. Hodges* decision to legalize gay marriage (the Southern Baptist Convention's Ronnie Floyd) or the election of Donald Trump (*Sojourners* magazine) constitutes a "Bonhoeffer moment," one in which Christians must resist cultural or governmental authority in order to obey God. The debate about who has the right to claim Germany's most famous resistance figure has become so fierce that last year Rhodes College professor Stephen Haynes penned *The Battle for Bonhoeffer* to address the United States' recent reception of his theology.

With so many American Christians wielding his name in this cultural proxy war, one might assume Bonhoeffer's political commitments were common knowledge among college-educated believers. One would be wrong. Books on Operation Valkyrie and Bonhoeffer's association with the July 20, 1944, plot to assassinate Adolf Hitler are a dime a dozen. English-language studies that touch on Bonhoeffer's work on behalf of the Jews or his interest in the American Black church appear frequently enough. But if one sets out to peg Bonhoeffer as an ally of either American Democrats or Republicans, only a deep dive into current scholarship will offer any clarity.

That, of course, is because Bonhoeffer lived in a very different time and culture. He grew up among the Berlin *Bildungsbürgertum*—the city's cultural elite—in the western suburb of Grunewald. Many academics lived in this upscale neighborhood. Dietrich's childhood ambition to pursue a doctorate would not have seemed entirely abnormal in that environment. By his teenage years, his father, Karl Bonhoeffer, had become one of Germany's most famous psychiatrists; the eminent church historians Ernst Troeltsch and Adolf von Harnack were regulars at neighborhood gatherings.

However, these were hardly liberal, American-style academic circles. Most found themselves in agreement with their government's bellicosity when war broke out in 1914. In fact, many were passionate advocates of imperialism; Harnack even acted as a speechwriter for Kaiser Wilhelm II.

A different political mood prevailed in the Bonhoeffer family. Dietrich's older brother, Karl-Friedrich, joined the Social Democrats after a conversion to socialism during the war. The other siblings drifted toward the German People's Party and similar parties. Theirs was a bourgeois politics sympathetic with the more open and liberal atmosphere of the Weimar Republic of the

1920s, a stance that may help explain why so many in the Bonhoeffer family would later play active roles in the resistance.

Dietrich, however, stood mostly aloof from wranglings over political ideology. His friend Eberhard Bethge has written that in the 1932 elections Dietrich supported the moderate, lay Catholic Center Party because he thought their international ties—that is, partly ties to the Vatican—could provide "stability and independence" in a rather unstable time. This was an extraordinary step for a German Protestant minister, yet in one sense it fits Bonhoeffer perfectly. His foremost political concerns were never about economics, war and peace, or even the treatment of minorities, though obviously these things were not unimportant to him. Above all else, Bonhoeffer cared about the preservation of the gospel message and the freedom of the Christian Church from political and cultural entanglements that might obscure its message. The intricacies of politics, he firmly believed, were not the business of the Protestant pastor or theologian.

"There is no doubt that the church of the Reformation is not encouraged to get involved directly in specific political actions of the state," Bonhoeffer wrote in his 1933 essay "The Church and the Jewish Question." "The church has neither to praise nor to censure the laws of the state. Instead, it has to affirm the state as God's order of preservation in this godless world." There were rare exceptions to this rule of nonintervention, of course, and the plight of the Jews in Nazi Germany was clearly one of them. That was not, however, simply because the Nazi government was engaging in morally repugnant deeds and implementing unjust laws, but because those deeds and laws had driven the church into a *status confessionis*, a situation where the very truth of the gospel was at stake.

Republicans more anxious about safeguarding religious freedom than President Trump's peccadillos may read these lines and believe they have found a kindred spirit. When they encounter Bonhoeffer's conclusion in his *Ethics* that abortion is "nothing but murder" and discover his intense impatience with American liberal theology, they might feel themselves justified in christening the *Obergefell* decision a *status confessionis*—roughly what today might be called a "Bonhoeffer moment." Perhaps those who are potential targets of an antidiscrimination lawsuit feel especially justified in doing so.

Yet when Bonhoeffer came to Union Theological Seminary in New York for the 1930–1931 academic year and, again, for the summer of 1939, he had some harsh words for those obsessed with religious liberty. "The American praise of freedom is more a tribute to the world, the state, and society than it is a statement concerning the church," he wrote. "But where the gratitude for institutional freedom must be paid for through the sacrifice of the freedom of [gospel] proclamation, there the church is in chains, even if it believes itself to be free."

Bonhoeffer, it would seem, may have found the conservative panic over *Obergefell* more faithless than politically feckless. He may have thought their "Bonhoeffer moment" more about self-preservation and power politics than gospel proclamation.

American progressives might feel even more justified in appropriating Bonhoeffer's legacy. After all, the first thing most people learn about the Lutheran theologian is that he resisted a tyrannical government that systematically oppressed minorities. And, as many on the American left argue, the Trump administration has at least tried to do just that. These progressive believers might buttress their case by lauding Bonhoeffer's courageous philosemitic efforts or citing the Sundays in 1931 he spent with the Black community at Abyssinian Baptist Church in Harlem. And when they read the blistering criticisms of "otherworldly" faith in his essay "Thy Kingdom Come!" or discover his hope for the future development of a "religionless Christianity" in his final letters, enthused Democrats might be ready to enlist Bonhoeffer's help in the 2020 election. Those "Bonhoeffer moments," after all, will come in handy on the campaign trail.

Yet letters and documents from his year in the United States reveal a Bonhoeffer at odds with the progressive American version as well. The historical Bonhoeffer was sometimes appalled by the oppression of African Americans, but he spent much more of his time filling letters and essays with criticisms and even contempt for American liberal Protestantism and progressive politics.

"God is not the immanent progressive ethical principle of history; God is the Lord who judges the human being and his work, he is the absolute sovereign (God's kingdom is not a democracy!)," Bonhoeffer fumed in a memo about American Christianity. "The ideal of international, democratic, collectivist life together on the basis of the value of individuals (notice the inner contradiction!) is not identical with the kingdom of God."

For Bonhoeffer, American liberals had misunderstood an essential part of Christianity: no matter how hard we try, human beings cannot inaugurate the kingdom of God. The best believers can do before that bright day in which Christ returns is preserve human rights, political stability, and a modicum of justice and proclaim the gospel message whether or not they find it politically expedient.

So how would Dietrich Bonhoeffer vote in 2020? Which side would he back in the United States' vituperative, divided political landscape, and which would he think has the right to claim their political program as a righteous reaction to a "Bonhoeffer moment"?

Obviously, this is a speculative exercise, one that would be quite unhelpful if so many were not already claiming Bonhoeffer's record as a resistance figure and moral example for their cause. But since the desire among religious Americans to appropriate his name will doubtless only increase as we near the next presidential election, one may as well bring the political convictions he actually held into the conversation.

With chaos in the White House, human rights abuses happening on the border, and white supremacy on the rise, it seems hard to believe Bonhoeffer would not seize the opportunity to vote against Donald Trump. He may well have argued that the immigration crisis has all the earmarks of a *status confessionis*. Undocumented people who have never known a home other than the United States are being deported every day, and legitimate asylum claimants are being mistreated. Surely, this is a depravation of human rights that requires the church's intervention in the form of service and direct action. In this case, that intervention might mean voting Democrat.

On the other hand, Bonhoeffer might think that legalized abortion constitutes an even clearer *status confessionis*. If abortion is "nothing but murder" and "the preservation of bodily life is the very foundation of all natural rights," as Bonhoeffer argued, surely the church negates its own message if it does not intervene on behalf of the unborn. Would that intervention mean voting Republican?

Perhaps.

It would seem that Americans, particularly American Christians, are at an impasse with Bonhoeffer. Irreconcilable differences separate him from the values of both our political parties, and both liberal and conservative varieties of American Protestantism exasperated him. It would be very difficult for any American political movement to honestly appropriate his legacy. Perhaps the best thing believers can do as we approach the next election season is wait a bit before rushing to brand their political cause a "Bonhoeffer moment," look again into the Scriptures, and recall that, after all, Bonhoeffer was a German Lutheran theologian, not an American political operative.

CHAPTER 14

Zen and the Art
of a Higher Education

Jennifer Ratner-Rosenhagen

Within hours of Robert Pirsig's death at age eighty-eight in April 2017, newspapers and internet outlets began announcing the passing of a philosophical enigma and author of the surprise blockbuster *Zen and the Art of Motorcycle Maintenance: An Inquiry into Values* (1974). The obituaries were variations on the same theme: they described how Pirsig was initially blindsided when his book, after having been rejected by 121 publishers, became "one of history's unlikeliest bestsellers." Or they noted how the reclusive author reluctantly navigated his fame in the years after its publication. While a handful mentioned "Pirsig pilgrims" who still today retrace the motorcycle tour from Minnesota to San Francisco featured in his novel, most discussed the book's significance in the past tense. With its "do-it-yourself" mix of motorcycle repair and philosophical inquiry, Pirsig's book became the bible of the counterculture generation, many of whom were as disenchanted with technological progress as they were with their parents, political leaders, and professors. Pirsig had hoped that his book would also be taken seriously by professional philosophers. But the closest it came to the academy, according to the obituaries, was as a "dog-eared presence in many a college dorm room."

Beyond agreeing that *ZAMM* is a relic of the 1970s, the obituary writers struggled to characterize both the genre and the contents of the book that propelled Pirsig into global stardom. At its most basic, it is a first-person narrative of a father who takes a motorcycle trip with his eleven-year-old son and two friends, all the while journeying intellectually and existentially into his past, the philosophical questions that both enliven and torment him, and his fraught relationships with his boy, his friends, and the world. It is a thinly veiled autobiography, for it follows, in novelized form, Pirsig's own path from intellectual wunderkind to wayward drifter to technical writer to college rhetoric instructor and to doctoral student in philosophy before succumbing to—and nominally recovering from—a debilitating mental illness that landed him in a psychiatric hospital. How does one describe a book that works in different registers (narrative, expository, analytical), speaks in different idioms (mechanical, epistemological, experiential), and addresses such a wide range of themes, from the history of science, Eastern philosophies, and the Montana landscape to camping, valves, and values? The obituaries concurred with the assessment of one reviewer who marveled: "Anything you call it, it's also something else. They may seem silly, but these problems of nomenclature are symptomatic." Nevertheless, they all agreed that this inscrutable book—with this most improbable title, *Zen and the Art of Motorcycle Maintenance*—is utterly, profoundly, sometimes maddeningly sui generis.

Except that it isn't. While Pirsig's book is in many respects singular, he drew its title as well as insights on "Oriental philosophy" from Eugen Herrigel's *Zen in the Art of Archery* (1948). Herrigel was a German philosopher who took instruction in kyūdō ("the way of the bow") in Japan between 1924 and 1929 under Master Awa Kenzō, in order to penetrate what he considered to be the "pure introspective mysticism" of Zen Buddhism. Herrigel's book recounts his almost six-year-long struggle to experience first-hand the "mystery" of Zen's "primordial mystic phenomenon." This required fully submitting to his master, abnegating his "I," while trying to tap into the mysterious "It" of the "bottomless ground of Being." (When, in frustration with his bow and himself, Herrigel asked his master what exactly this "It" was, the latter answered, "Once you have understood that, you have no further need of me.") While the book was enthusiastically received by Western readers when it first appeared in English translation in 1953, Arthur Koestler, for one, was disturbed that it was saturated in "the more ponderous kind of Germanic mysticism," and manifested an "Eastern *guru*-father complex" that fetishized authoritarianism. Something was off. Gershom Scholem later confirmed what Koestler's antitotalitarian nose knew: if *Zen in the Art of Archery* seemed to reek of a disturbing "Zen-Nazism," it may very well be because Herrigel spent his "career as a convinced Nazi" and card-carrying member of the National Socialist Party, a fact "carefully hushed up by . . . his admirers."

Nazism, Mysticism, Zen, Archery, Motorcycles, Guru—this is the sort of word combination you might want to consider deleting from your computer's search history. Herrigel's and Pirsig's books share a portion of a title and an interest in using "Zen" for coming into right relationship with the world. But that's where the similarities end. While Herrigel's Zen is mystical, esoteric, and accessible to a chosen few, Pirsig's is plainspoken, unadorned, practical, and pragmatic.

Differences notwithstanding, the two books helped give birth to a new prolific "Zen-and-the-Art-of" title industry, and with it the convention of yoking "Zen" to an "art" of some task, craft, or field of knowledge. Alan Watts wasn't wrong when in 1957 he assured his Western readers that Zen "may be applied in any direction, to any conceivable human activity, and that wherever it is so applied it lends an unmistakable quality to the work." But even he might have been taken aback to learn that there are now "Zen-and-the-Art-of" guides for everything from knitting, running, dodgeball, changing diapers, diabetes maintenance, medical imaging, and statecraft to screenwriting, healthy eating, successful BBQing, the SAT exam, poker playing, getting rich, and committing murder.

No doubt, many authors simply use the formulation as a marketing hook. (Though few are as honest as Ray Bradbury, who, for his 1990 bestseller, *Zen in the Art of Writing*, admitted: "I selected the above title, quite obviously for its shock value.") Nevertheless, many of the works—like Pirsig's and Herrigel's before them—draw on "Zen" as an "art" to sharply rebuke received forms of wisdom, institutional learning, and familiar intellectual authorities. Their endorsement of an alternative "way of knowing" might be productive for readers if the authors actually provided some history of Mahayana Buddhism, distinguished Zazen from Zen, or perhaps even explained that while Zen emphasizes open experience, it is indeed an epistemology. Instead, as it crops up in this genre, Zen is typically a thin conceit. It can be many things, but even in all of its myriad interpretations and uses, Zen is not an admonition to, as Bradbury puts it, just "learn from instinct," and "Don't Think!" "Beginner's mind" isn't an exhortation to be stupid, naïve, or incurious. Rather, it is a powerful way of resetting one's approach to a knotty intellectual problem or an intractable moral dilemma; but it can also just be a way of finding the wonders and joys of prosaic tasks like housecleaning and dog walking.

While Pirsig's *ZAMM* did the most to establish the genre, his book is neither derivative of Herrigel's mystification and authoritarianism nor befuddled by the slack anti-intellectualism of the knockoffs that followed it. Too many of these books, however, followed Pirsig's title but not his book's erudition or earnest intellectual engagement. They used "Zen" only to mock expertise, evade thinking with evidence, or badmouth analytic thought.

Still we might ask of Pirsig's opus: What's Zen got to do with it? If we heed Pirsig's "Author's Note" on the first page of the book, the answer might be: nothing. "It should in no way be associated with that great body of factual information relating to orthodox Zen Buddhist practice." Note taken.

But despite this conscientious disclaimer, there is a lot of "Zen" talk in the book. It discusses concerns that should look familiar to any serious Zen practitioner. *ZAMM* explores the illusion of the self, all the ways in which our egos blinker, trick, and tangle us. It provides a vivid portrayal of impermanence—not only as the father and his companions ride their motorcycles from place to place, but also in his meditations on the "temporal condition" of ideas, beliefs, even scientific truths. The book offers an unmistakable critique of attachment and incessant striving, the kind of impassioned longings that characterized his earlier zeal for "Quality" and landed him in a psychiatric ward. In this regard, at least, the book is a challenge to the *elsewhereness* of truth:

Then, when you're no longer thinking ahead, each footstep
isn't just a means to an end but a unique event in itself. This
leaf has jagged edges. This rock looks loose. From this place
the snow is less visible. . . . To live only for some future goal
is shallow. It's the sides of the mountain which sustain life,
not the top. Here's where things grow.

Should Pirsig's *ZAMM* be read as a primer on Zen? No. But
neither should it be dismissed as a period piece of the '70s counterculture. To do so would be to miss how it subtly works with
some of the insights of Zen and Pirsig's own academic and para-
academic experiences as one long comment on higher learning,
which is still surprisingly resonant today. Pirsig's references to the
peculiarities, peccadilloes, and power of the university are frequent and unmistakable. *ZAMM* observes the tensions between
radical college professors and conservative state politics, reflects
on the euphemism of a "teaching college" (where "you teach and
you teach and you teach with no time for research, no time for
contemplation, no time for participation in outside affairs"), and
worries over a college education that encourages students' "cal-
culated mimicry." No doubt there's a now-clichéd petulance in
his characterization of the university as a cool and technocratic
"Church of Reason" (in which, at times, he desperately wanted to
worship, but which others rebuffed as a "blind . . . sinister, and
inhuman" citadel). Yet these are the warnings of a true believer in
the mission, if not methods, of the modern academy.

ZAMM may be critical of particular forms of intellectuality,
but it is in no way an anti-intellectual screed. Indeed, intellectual engagement happens all over the place—in the sun and in
the seminar, alone on dirt roads and together with students in

the classroom. Even though this is a travel narrative, most of the novel's episodes take place in the narrator's head. There are no crashes, no dramatic tire blowouts, no scenes with the father and son being chased by coyotes from their campgrounds. It's the narrator working through problems of philosophy, which he learned within and without the university, that drives the narrative. The thinking is the action.

ZAMM is in no way hostile to reason. Pirsig values "the Buddha that exists within analytic thought, and gives that analytic thought its direction." He explores how discursive thought, though insufficient for understanding the world, should not be silenced or ignored, but observed with curiosity and compassion. He recommends the Zen Buddhist "beginner's mind" as a powerful way of resetting one's approach to a complicated task, a painful memory, struggles with a loved one, and thinking itself. But rational inquiry has its role to play, too, though as a complement to—not a replacement of—book learning, scientific experimentation, and immediate experience.

Pirsig long regretted that the book's role in the life of the university was limited to students' extracurricular reading while flopped on a beanbag at the end of a long day of classes. Here, Pirsig was only partly right. Though it is rare to find *ZAMM* on a syllabus for a philosophy course, it has been a persistent presence in the academy as a resource for educators to reflect on the "art" of teaching. For decades now, professors and academic administrators have enlisted *ZAMM* to consider what it would mean for them to "teach the whole person" and to show students the "gumption traps" that keep them from studying. They have turned to it to ask where "Quality" can be found in the rankings of academic departments and to consider the perils of using grades for motivating students. And they have found it to be a way to demonstrate to scientifically illiterate humanities students the rewards of joining the "two cultures" by showing them that "the Buddha, the Godhead, resides quite as comfortably in the circuits of a digital computer or the gears of a cycle transmission as he does at the top of a mountain or in the petals of a flower."

Even Pirsig's use of chautauquas as a means of teaching, whether it be Zen, motorcycles, freshman English, or senior seminars, is worth a third look. I say "third," and not "second," because already in the 1970s, Pirsig's first generation of readers—those of a "counterculture" least likely to find anything in Victorian culture worthy of their appreciation—discovered in *ZAMM* a reason to reconsider the form. If ever there was a Victorian institution, it was the chautauqua, the traveling lecture circuit designed to—as Pirsig put it—"edify and entertain, improve the mind and bring culture and enlightenment" to mass audiences (and which William James famously derided as "tame," "second-rate," and the "quintessence of every mediocrity"). Surely, James would have agreed with Pirsig that learning should never be reduced to modeling good "table manners," nor should professors try to "sound like God talking for eternity, [as] that isn't the way it ever is." As Pirsig understood it, the true value of the chautauqua, as with any good form of instruction, is that "it's never been anything other than just one person talking from one place in time and space and circumstance. It's never been anything else, ever." Thus, with the use of chautauquas, Pirsig managed a most remarkable feat, one college students would surely appreciate today. Namely, to use education to cultivate what the Victorians called "self-culture": "The real cycle you're working on is a cycle called 'yourself.'"

It may seem odd for the university educated or even university educators to welcome a book that seems to view the academy as enemy territory. But properly understood, and more in keeping with Pirsig's original intentions, *Zen and the Art of Motorcycle Maintenance* shows how the learning in a lecture hall or seminar room should be preparation for a life of learning on the open road. His claim that the "real university is a state of mind" doesn't mean that there's no work for bricks-and-mortar higher education to do. Just the opposite: it's a reminder that awakening the appetite and practicing the skills for lifelong learning are what constitute a university education itself. The Zen and the art in a higher education would train students in these habits of mind and prepare them to take their learning with them, wherever they go, whatever roads they ride.

PART III

Natural Agon: Science & Technology

Introduction

Religion never lives by itself. It shapes or seeks to use other forms of intellectual life; it mingles and engages with them, to the point where it sometimes becomes difficult to tell one from the other. For all the supposed conflict between science and religion, from Galileo's trial to Thomas Huxley's defense of Darwinism, their relationship is complex and easy to reduce to mere questions of opposition. Fundamentally, both science and religion seek to address similar questions even if they follow rather different routes, employ different instruments, and expect different outcomes. In his *Aeon* essay "Why Religion Is Not Going Away and Science Will Not Destroy It," Peter Harrison addresses precisely this thorny issue of the relationship between science and religion and concludes that, for all the triumphalist reading of modern history as driven by secularism and an inevitable marginalization of religion, in today's society it is rather "science that is subject to increasing threats to its authority and social legitimacy."

In another piece originally published in *Aeon*, "Monuments to Unbelief," Leigh Eric Schmidt uses an atheistic perspective to complicate questions about the relationship between these two domains. He explores here the almost religious fervor with which atheists, especially in the United States, have traditionally pursued their unbelief. Yet the religion of irreligion is just one way of solving the tension. In his *Salon* piece "Amma's Cosmic Squeeze," Erik Davis suggests another approach: a syncretism of spiritual traditions (East and West, old and new, high-minded or down-to-earth) in response to social ills or to various human needs, such as the very human desire to touch and to be touched. Davis's collapsing into the arms of Amma, the "hugging saint," in a California ashram reminded him that humans are far more than "neurologically programmed DNA machines."

As well as a form of spiritual life, religion is something embedded in the texture of our everydayness—and that's where it meets technology, among other things. The notion that technological advances make us less spiritual and more religion-free is not only simplistic and prejudiced; it's factually wrong. We now use advanced technology not just to look for traces of a divine author in the world but also to pray, to find the direction of Mecca or the closest twelve-step meeting, and, increasingly, to livestream church services. We also use technology to try to discover our own personal narratives—at least genetically, as Daniel José Camacho shows in his *Sojourners* essay "Who Am I?" Camacho writes that "DNA tests can be meaningful, especially when combined with genealogy," and yet by learning more about the intimate fabric of our bodies, he concludes that we haven't really found out who we are. For that we need a different kind of testing.

We should not expect from technology more than it can deliver. In "Fake Meat," originally published in the *Paris Review*, Meghan O'Gieblyn uses her attempt to cook a vegetarian "beef" meal (the delicious, guilt-free, meat-free Impossible Burger, which technology has now made possible) as an excuse for thinking more broadly about how important such notions as flesh and blood have been for religion everywhere. As though to prove, if more proof were needed, that technology is neither good nor bad in itself, all depending on how we use it, Ann Neumann's piece "Opioids: A Crisis of Misplaced Morality," originally published in the *Revealer*, shows how drugs capable of alleviating suffering and significantly reducing human misery can also bring boundless pain and misery into the world. Technology and science thus come to be ethically understood as not so different from religion itself—neither good nor bad in themselves, but depending entirely on the "doing," as it were.

CHAPTER 15

Why Religion Is Not Going Away and Science Will Not Destroy It

Peter Harrison

Not only has secularism failed to continue its steady global march, but countries as varied as Iran, India, Israel, Algeria, and Turkey either have had their secular governments replaced by religious ones or have seen the rise of influential religious nationalist movements. Secularization, as predicted by the social sciences, has failed.

To be sure, this failure is not unqualified. Many Western countries continue to witness decline in religious belief and practice. The most recent census data released in Australia, for example, shows that 30 percent of the population identify as having "no religion," and that this percentage is increasing. International surveys confirm comparatively low levels of religious commitment in Western Europe and Australasia. Even the United States, a longtime source of embarrassment for the secularization thesis, has seen a rise in unbelief. The percentage of atheists in the United States now sits at an all-time high (if "high" is the right word) of around 3 percent. Yet, for all that, globally, the total number of people who consider themselves to be religious remains high, and demographic trends suggest that the overall pattern for the immediate future will be one of religious growth. But this isn't the only failure of the secularization thesis.

Scientists, intellectuals, and social scientists expected that the spread of modern science would drive secularization—that science would be a secularizing force. But that simply hasn't been the case. If we look at those societies where religion remains vibrant, their key common features are less to do with science and more to do with feelings of existential security and protection from some of the basic uncertainties of life in the form of public goods. A social safety net might be correlated with scientific advances, but only loosely, and again the case of the United States is instructive. The United States is arguably the most scientifically and technologically advanced society in the world, and yet at the same time the most religious of Western societies. As the British sociologist David Martin concluded in *The Future of Christianity* (2011): "There is no consistent relation between the degree of scientific advance and a reduced profile of religious influence, belief and practice."

The story of science and secularization becomes even more intriguing when we consider those societies that have witnessed significant reactions against secularist agendas. India's first prime minister, Jawaharlal Nehru, championed secular and scientific ideals, and enlisted scientific education in the project of modernization. Nehru was confident that Hindu visions of a Vedic past and Muslim dreams of an Islamic theocracy would both succumb to the inexorable historical march of secularization. "There is only one-way traffic in Time," he declared. But as the subsequent rise of Hindu and Islamic fundamentalism adequately attests, Nehru was wrong. Moreover, the association of science with a secularizing agenda has backfired, with science becoming a collateral casualty of resistance to secularism.

Turkey provides an even more revealing case. Like most pioneering nationalists, Mustafa Kemal Atatürk, the founder of the Turkish republic, was a committed secularist. Atatürk believed that science was destined to displace religion. In order to make sure that Turkey was on the right side of history, he gave science, in particular evolutionary biology, a central place in the state education system of the fledgling Turkish republic. As a result, evolution came to be associated with Atatürk's entire political program, including secularism. Islamist parties in Turkey, seeking to counter the secularist ideals of the nation's founders, have also attacked the teaching of evolution. For them, evolution is associated with secular materialism. This sentiment culminated in the decision this June to remove the teaching of evolution from the high school classroom. Again, science has become a victim of guilt by association.

The United States represents a different cultural context, where it might seem that the key issue is a conflict between literal readings of Genesis and key features of evolutionary history. But in fact, much of the creationist discourse centers on moral values. In the US case too, we see antievolutionism motivated at least in part by the assumption that evolutionary theory is a stalking horse for secular materialism and its attendant moral commitments. As in India and Turkey, secularism is actually hurting science.

In brief, global secularization is not inevitable, and, when it does happen, it is not caused by science. Further, when the attempt is made to use science to advance secularism, the results can damage science. The thesis that "science causes secularization" simply fails the empirical test, and enlisting science as an instrument of secularization turns out to be poor strategy. The science and secularism pairing is so awkward that it raises the question: Why did anyone think otherwise?

Historically, two related sources advanced the idea that science would displace religion. First, nineteenth-century progressivist conceptions of history, particularly associated with the French philosopher Auguste Comte, held to a theory of history in which societies pass through three stages—religious, metaphysical, and scientific (or "positive"). Comte coined the term *sociology*, and he wanted to diminish the social influence of religion and replace it with a new science of society. Comte's influence extended to the "young Turks" and Atatürk.

The nineteenth century also witnessed the inception of the "conflict model" of science and religion. This was the view that history can be understood in terms of a "conflict between two epochs in the evolution of human thought—the theological and the scientific." This description comes from Andrew Dickson White's influential *A History of the Warfare of Science with Theology in Christendom* (1896), the title of which nicely encapsulates its author's general theory. White's work, as well as John William Draper's earlier *History of the Conflict Between Religion and Science* (1874), firmly established the conflict thesis as the default way of thinking about the historical relations between science and religion. Both works were translated into multiple languages. Draper's *History* went through more than fifty printings in the

United States alone, was translated into twenty languages, and, notably, became a bestseller in the late Ottoman Empire, where it informed Atatürk's understanding that progress meant science superseding religion.

Today, people are less confident that history moves through a series of set stages toward a single destination. Nor, despite its popular persistence, do most historians of science support the idea of an enduring conflict between science and religion. Renowned collisions, such as the Galileo affair, turned on politics and personalities, not just science and religion. Darwin had significant religious supporters and scientific detractors, as well as vice versa. Many other alleged instances of science-religion conflict have now been exposed as pure inventions. In fact, contrary to conflict, the historical norm has more often been one of mutual support between science and religion. In its formative years in the seventeenth century, modern science relied on religious legitimation. During the eighteenth and nineteenth centuries, natural theology helped to popularize science.

The conflict model of science and religion offered a mistaken view of the past and, when combined with expectations of secularization, led to a flawed vision of the future. Secularization theory failed at both description and prediction. The real question is why we continue to encounter proponents of science-religion conflict. Many are prominent scientists. It would be superfluous to rehearse Richard Dawkins's musings on this topic, but he is by no means a solitary voice. Stephen Hawking thinks that "science will win because it works"; Sam Harris has declared that "science must destroy religion"; Steven Weinberg thinks that science has weakened religious certitude; Colin Blakemore predicts that science will eventually make religion unnecessary. Historical evidence simply does not support such contentions. Indeed, it suggests that they are misguided.

So why do they persist? The answers are political. Leaving aside any lingering fondness for quaint nineteenth-century understandings of history, we must look to the fear of Islamic fundamentalism, exasperation with creationism, an aversion to alliances between the religious right and climate-change denial, and worries about the erosion of scientific authority. While we might be sympathetic to these concerns, there is no disguising the fact that they arise out of an unhelpful intrusion of normative commitments into the discussion. Wishful thinking—hoping that science will vanquish religion—is no substitute for a sober assessment of present realities. Continuing with this advocacy is likely to have an effect opposite to that intended.

Religion is not going away any time soon, and science will not destroy it. If anything, it is science that is subject to increasing threats to its authority and social legitimacy. Given this, science needs all the friends it can get. Its advocates would be well advised to stop fabricating an enemy out of religion, or insisting that the only path to a secure future lies in a marriage of science and secularism.

CHAPTER 16

Monuments to Unbelief

Leigh Eric Schmidt

Christian Roman of Sidney, Ohio, found himself in the late 1940s in the hospital with severe heart problems and a grim prognosis. Told he was dying, Roman—a sometime teacher, traveling salesman, farmer, and lawyer—was counting up his final regrets, and the one that gnawed at him the most was that he had done nothing over his six-plus decades to advance the cause of freethinking secularism. Fearing the damage that an open avowal of unbelief would do locally to his business and reputation, he had long kept his irreligious views concealed from his neighbors. With various ministers visiting him uninvited in his infirmity—there were seventeen churches in town, and Roman cared for none of them—he decided that he would commission a glorious cemetery monument through which he would finally "speak my mind without reservation."

Roman's heart did not fail him this time—it would a few years later in 1951. Still, he wanted to make good on his hospital pledge and saw no need now to wait for a posthumous testimonial. Why not proactively erect his "Agnostic Monument" in Graceland Cemetery for all to see "regardless of public censure"? Investing much of his savings in the project, he wanted it to be the largest monument in the Sidney graveyard and pulled off the installation in August 1948. The result was imposing: a giant granite block heralding the freethinking triumvirate of deistic revolutionary Thomas Paine, infidel orator Robert Ingersoll, and Cornell president Andrew Dickson White. "READ THEIR WORKS," the megalith advised. Also, as his beloved Ingersoll was wont to do, Roman slipped in some bourgeois moralizing with his irreligious polemic: "EVILS OF MY DAY; USE OF TOBACCO, ALCO-HOLIC BEVERAGES AND RELIGIOUS SUPERSTITION." He wanted his neighbors to know that he could be good—and just as abstemious as a Methodist teetotaler—without God.

The monument certainly got the community talking. The pastor of the First Presbyterian Church, John W. Meister, devoted a whole sermon to the subject of "Christian Roman's Tombstone," which conjured to him a specter of infidelity weirdly out of place amid America's postwar religious upswing. "I never seriously thought that in my generation there would be cause for argument with a real, live agnostic," Meister preached to a crowded congregation. After two World Wars and the Great Depression, humanistic self-regard paled before the sterner stuff of neo-orthodox faith, and, with the dawning of the Cold War, there was little room for doubting God, Jesus, and the Bible without seeming to underwrite Soviet communism and atheism. No rabble-rouser, Meister framed the offense, "if not insult," of Roman's monument in careful theological terms. "Let the church never substitute dogma for intellect; let us never laugh off a questioning mind," the pastor advised those Christians who were "up in arms" over Roman's gravestone. The intellectual tenor of Meister's criticism was lost at least on some in town, particularly on those who talked glibly about "dynamiting it" right out of the cemetery. "For Shame," scrawled a vandal across the base of the marker. The indignation was still fresh enough two years later that Edwin H. Wilson, a national emissary for the American Humanist Association, called off a public dedication of the monument, much to Roman's chagrin.

Roman's desire to materialize his unbelief, to create a monument to secularism in a bucolic Ohio graveyard, was eccentric, but not—as it turns out—that eccentric. American freethinkers had long been preoccupied with the public memorializing of their incredulity and anticlericalism. They wanted to enshrine their commitment to scientific rationality over biblical revelation, their strict construction of church-state separation, and their worldly focus on human happiness in the here and now. They wanted their humanistic beliefs recognized in a nation that routinely pictured itself in godly, covenantal, and Christian terms. They wanted their secularism to be visible, out in the open rather than closeted away, celebrated rather than hidden. They wanted to render a secular public sphere tangible, to give it corporeality and granite-like solidity, so they strove to erect monuments, memorials, and museums. The commemorative landscape they hoped to enter was crowded, of course—with assorted tributes to the battles of the American Revolution, with Union shrines honoring Abraham Lincoln, with statues hallowing the Confederacy's Lost Cause, with Halls of Fame for every conceivable sport. Freethinkers wanted visibility in America's packed topography of memory.

As with so many things America's outnumbered secularists have tried to do, there was often a forlorn quality to their endeavors to concretize their irreligion. "The thought tides are in the direction of God," the Reverend John Meister was certain as he surveyed the religious landscape of the late 1940s, so much so that he found it easy to cast Roman's tombstone into the oblivion of the readily forgotten. "That monument, pretentious as it is," Meister averred, "will be mouldering dust when the [word] of Jesus will still be drawing men unto God." In the United States the promise of secularism always seemed to founder on the nation's next revival, awakening, or crusade—on religion's inevitable return, on Christianity's inescapable presence and power. That did not keep America's freethinkers from their building projects. The majoritarian odds against them only made them surer of the importance of materializing their politics and their doubts.

———

For freethinkers, the notion that temples of reason should replace churches was more than a figurative expression of science's supplanting of Christianity. The Enlightenment would require its own calendar of festivals and rites, its own pantheon of saints and apotheosized heroes, its own monuments and shrines. It was never enough for philosophes to dethrone Christianity; a positive civic faith had to supersede churches, sacraments, and Sabbaths. A new age of reason, science, liberty, and democratic citizenship would need its own religion of humanity—that proposition absorbed any number of nineteenth-century expositors from the French positivist Auguste Comte to the English theorist John Stuart Mill to the American radical Octavius Frothingham. Freethinkers recognized the functionality of rites, ceremonies, and monuments for the upholding of free inquiry, philanthropic benevolence, scientific knowledge, and social solidarity. Without Christianity or

Judaism to guide them, they had to become their own liturgists. Hence in 1877 America's leading freethought publisher, D. M. Bennett, issued "for the use of liberals," the *Truth Seeker Collection of Forms, Hymns, and Recitations*, a compendium of secular rites for public meetings, weddings, and funerals. Among the prescribed invocations was this one torn from the annals of the radical Enlightenment: "May churches and chapels be converted into Temples of Reason and Secular Institutions for the people."

No one exerted a more lasting influence on the ritual life of American freethinkers than Thomas Paine, whose *Age of Reason* attacking the Bible became the holy writ of nineteenth-century unbelief. It was no surprise that C. H. Roman had inscribed a familiar scrap of Paine's cosmopolitan sentiments on the face of his monument: "The world is my country and to do good is my religion." By the 1830s, America's resident deists had already turned Paine's birthday into their favorite annual festival, an occasion for banquets, odes, toasts, and orations—all dedicated to honoring Paine's contributions to forwarding religious and political liberty. In D. M. Bennett's ritual guide, George Washington and Thomas Jefferson shared a single toast as co-laborers in the cause of freedom; Benjamin Franklin and James Madison got nary a mention. "Immortal Paine," by contrast, was everywhere. "May he yet be placed upon a pedestal as high as ever erected to the memory of man;" a sample tribute proclaimed, "and may each returning anniversary witness the extension of the principles for which he contended, until the 'Rights of Man' shall be universally admitted, an 'Age of Reason' triumph over superstition, and priestcraft and kingcraft shall be known no more."

The pedestal was, again, a lot more than a rhetorical device. As early as 1839, the freethinker Gilbert Vale had led efforts to commemorate Paine with a monument in New Rochelle, New York, where Paine had lived for a time after his return to the United States in 1802. The growing fervor of Paine's evangelical critics had engendered a rude welcome for the old patriot, but those punishing attacks only made his admirers more committed to burnishing his reputation after his death. The solicitous upkeep of Paine's memorial in New Rochelle became part of the shared work of American secularists. Over the course of the century, they preserved it from vandals and souvenir seekers, raised money to refurbish and rededicate it, and made pilgrimages there for picnics and processions. They also conducted a dedicated hunt for Paine collectables, which was led by the roving American freethinker Moncure Conway, whose decades-long search spanned the Atlantic. Among the relics amassed by the turn of the twentieth century were a piece of Paine's lost gravestone, a chair he used for writing, two locks of his hair, and even supposedly a portion of his brain, which Conway had secured in London for £5. A decade after Paine's death, a British admirer had stolen the pamphleteer's remains from New Rochelle in order to repatriate them back in England, only to have the skeleton go missing. Conway tried to relocate and reclaim Paine's bones without success, but the artifacts he did secure for the Thomas Paine National Historical Association certainly made plain the corporeality of secularist memory.

Paine got most of the attention among American freethinkers as a founding father, but they were willing to push their calendar back for the heretic Giordano Bruno, burned at the stake in Rome by the Inquisition in 1600. Following the lead of historians like Cornell's Andrew Dickson White, one of the three guides whom Roman enshrined on his monument, liberal secularists saw a protracted war between science and religion as pivotal to the making of modernity. From Copernicus to Galileo to Darwin, Christianity was viewed as having continually tried to suppress new knowledge: Bruno, a dissident Italian cosmologist, was transformed into a martyr for free inquiry, a condensed symbol of the murderous violence and dark anti-intellectualism of the church against which modern science had courageously struggled. Thaddeus B. Wakeman, a Manhattan lawyer who sparred with the infamous vice crusader Anthony Comstock, was so taken with the heretic's emblematic power that he suggested recentering the entire calendar away from the birth of Christ to the death of Bruno. Time, he pronounced in 1881, properly began with Bruno's sacrifice in 1600, and a congress of freethinkers meeting the next year in Saint Louis heartily endorsed the proposal. So 1882 became the year 282, and many American freethinkers, for a decade and more thereafter, relished flaunting the revised dating system in their correspondence, journals, and tracts as a telltale sign of their emancipation from Christianity.

The veneration of Bruno peaked on June 9, 1889, with the grand unveiling of a statue in his honor in the very square in Rome where he had been executed. Unlike most of the memorial efforts in which American secularists participated, the Bruno monument was a global endeavor involving anticlerical, freethinking subscribers from Australia to Italy. More than thirty thousand people gathered for the event—a striking show of liberal solidarity in the very face of Catholic authority. With characteristic oratorical flourish, Robert Ingersoll had called Bruno "the first real martyr," an "atheist" who had died "neither frightened by perdition, nor bribed by heaven," whose murder would not be "perfectly avenged" until a monument was raised for him upon "the shapeless ruin of Saint Peter's, the crumbled Vatican and the fallen cross." By those standards, the redress freethinkers gained in 1889 was far from perfect. Pope Leo XIII, with the Vatican very much intact, excoriated Bruno anew as a deceitful apostate, decried the abomination of the holy city, and urged Catholics to keep fighting the infidelity of radical republicanism. That papal response hardly lessened the pride and satisfaction of freethinkers: they had bearded the lion in his own den and set up a monument to the "Herald of the Dawn."

The Bruno spectacle was a ceremonial high point for nineteenth-century secularists. No other commemoration could match the Eternal City as a staging ground for contesting religious authority and sanctifying free inquiry. Most freethinking monuments were necessarily more modest affairs, more Roman's Graceland Cemetery than Rome's Campo de' Fiori. When, for example, D. M. Bennett died in 1882, he was eulogized as a giant among American freethinkers, a valiant champion of a free press who had spent thirteen months in a New York prison for his blasphemous publications. His admirers immediately established a monument committee, and secularists from around the country contributed their mite. The result was a wordy memorial in a Brooklyn cemetery, dedicated with pomp and ceremony in June 1884. Bennett's irreligious enthusiasts pulled no punches in their engraved homage: "What is called revelation is a snare, a delusion, a falsehood," one side of the monument read. "Those who claim to speak for the gods simply speak their own thought. The gods do not speak; they are as dumb as the rocks." Bennett was not Bruno, but American freethinkers saw their widely separated lives as neatly paired monuments to the ideal of universal mental liberty.

The considerable labors of nineteenth-century freethinkers to materialize secularism carried forward into the next century. Memorial projects for the most celebrated American freethinker, Robert Ingersoll, who died in 1899, were particularly consuming to his twentieth-century heirs. One focal point was the erection of a lofty statue of him in a municipal park in Peoria, Illinois, in 1911, which became—like the Paine monument in New Rochelle—a ritual hub for humanists and atheists. From a centennial celebration of Ingersoll's birth in 1933 to a rededication ceremony in August 2016 led by the Freedom from Religion Foundation, American nonbelievers have maintained the Peoria bronze with reverential affection and used it as a public stage for dramatizing their own secularist commitments. The Philadelphia-based sculptor Zenos Frudakis, who oversaw the recent restoration of the hundred-plus-year-old statue, viewed the labor as expression of his own humanistic credo and as a counterpoint to the evangelical right. "Rational thinking" of the sort Ingersoll embodied, Frudakis suggests, is in short supply in a country where science-denying Christians hold all too much sway.

Peoria could claim Ingersoll as a longtime citizen, but Dresden, New York, was his actual birthplace. By 1921, freethinkers had opened a museum there in what had been the Presbyterian parsonage of Ingersoll's father. Still open for tours, it is a shrine of Ingersoll memorabilia—photographs, plaques, and posters, but also a silver spoon produced by an atheist jeweler with the great agnostic's likeness on the stem. Announcing an illustrious past, the Ingersoll Birthplace Museum—a modest house in a small town in the Finger Lakes—testifies as much to the limits of secularism's reach in the United States, to the spindly hold the heroes of freethought have on the nation's historical imagination: "Meet the most remarkable American most people never heard of," the museum beckons visitors. It was a sentiment of lost renown that echoed in the Peoria ceremony in the summer of 2016: Ingersoll is "the most famous Peorian you've never heard of," a local humanist told a reporter covering the event. Like Roman's "Agnostic Monument," the Ingersoll tributes of Dresden and Peoria stand as minority reports of infidelity in God's country.

Ingersoll's Birthplace Museum may have a quixotic air, but it seems an endeavor of restrained practicality by comparison to the founding of the American Atheist Museum in Petersburg, Indiana. Opened on the summer solstice in June 1978 with the notorious Madalyn Murray O'Hair on hand for the ribbon-cutting, the museum was the brainchild of Lloyd and Pam Thoren, both extremely lapsed Protestants. Part of a loose network of atheist activists whom O'Hair had organized from her base in Austin, Texas, the Thorens decided that the best way they could help the cause was to construct a godless exhibition on their rural property in a "small, religious community in the Bible Belt of the Midwest." With O'Hair's encouragement, the Thorens had an eye on the publicity possibilities of provoking Christian opposition and having the national media play up the controversy. The calculation worked. A UPI story, quickly wired across the country, quoted a pastor of a local Bible church who saw the new atheist museum in town as a sign of the last days and who repeated rumors about animal sacrifice and devil worship. Even when reporters did not resort to fundamentalist stereotypes, they found it hard to resist chronicling just how religiously out of place "the only atheist museum in the Western Hemisphere" appeared in small-town

Indiana. Not far away, a journalist for the *Indianapolis Star* noted, was a monument to major leaguer Gil Hodges, a beloved Hoosier and himself a graduate of Petersburg High School. "Above all [Hodges] was dedicated to God, family, country and the game of baseball," his monument read. An atheist museum—surely, that belonged behind the Iron Curtain, not in America's heartland.

To the Thorens, of course, the whole point was to materialize a secularist alternative to a nation resolutely under God. "In Reason We Trust" and "Born Again Atheist," announced a pair of buttons available in the museum's gift shop. The homemade exhibits—paeans to Darwinian evolution and the naturalistic study of religion—were the murals of grassroots atheism. The Thorens had even hauled in old church pews, so that visitors could sit down and contemplate everything from the Big Bang to the dangers of Christian indoctrination to a pioneer's log cabin. "A mentally tidy visitor," one reporter observed, might have trouble knowing "the proper cerebral slot" in which to file away many of the items on display. The museum, after all, sat in the shadow of a five-story wood tower that the couple had built as an enormous birdhouse in hopes of attracting purple martins. Taken all together, the compound represented the vernacular art of American atheism, a quirky pastiche of material secularism set against the headwinds of the Cold War and an awakened evangelical conservatism. "Most of the people around here wish we would pack up and leave," Lloyd told a reporter for the *Los Angeles Times* two-plus years into operating the museum. "But Pam and I have as much right to be here and express our views as anyone else." The Thorens carried on in their curatorial capacity for six more years but finally decided that they needed the anonymity of a big city, especially for their young daughter. When they left for San Francisco in 1987, they removed all but four letters from the large yellow rooftop sign announcing the American Atheist Museum. "MUSE" was the remaining remnant of their Indiana monument to unbelief.

Materializing secularism, giving it ritual shape and monumental expression, has continued apace in recent years. The most visible instance of such endeavors has been the Satanic Temple—a group of freethinking activists, led by the pseudonymous Lucien Greaves, that has puckishly deployed an occult statue of Baphomet to counter monuments devoted to the Ten Commandments at the state capitols in Oklahoma and Arkansas. For these "Satanists," the winged, goat-headed statue is a topsy-turvy symbol they use to forward the values of equal liberty, scientific rationality, and free expression and to question the singular privileges still accorded Christianity in American public life. The intentionally offensive statue becomes the material sign of enlightened revolt against oppressive religious authorities—a new American monument to blasphemy, free inquiry, and strict church-state separation. So it is that Baphomet, "the heretic who questions sacred laws and rejects all tyrannical impositions," stands in now for Paine, Bruno, Bennett, and Ingersoll. The mischievous architects of the Satanic Temple are the latest bearers of C. H. Roman's monumental impertinence.

CHAPTER 17

Amma's Cosmic Squeeze

Erik Davis

The Mata Amritanandamayi Center is a cluster of gardens, ponds, and institutional buildings nestled in the dry and rolling hills of Castro Valley, a rural area that lies about an hour east of San Francisco. For most of the year, it serves as the sleepy North American outpost for the empire of good works that surround the superstar Indian guru it's named after, who is best known as Amma. But twice a year, the Mother herself sweeps through, and the place is transformed. For a couple of weeks, thousands of devotees come to sing and meditate and stand in Disneyland-worthy lines to receive Amma's signature blessing: a great big bear hug.

I show up a little after noon, and Amma has already been at it for hours. Scores of devotees wait in line, while hundreds more mill about the center's large meeting hall. Charitable booths lie on one side of the space, with a well-stuffed shop of clothes, books, and geegaws on the other. Roughly two-thirds of the folks are white, with the rest largely South Asian; like Amma, most are wearing white. The hugging saint herself, a full-bodied woman as brown as the Virgin of Guadalupe, is plopped down in a comfy, low-key thronelike thing at the foot of the large stage that lies at the far end of the hall. Amma is embracing her flock, many of whom believe that she is literally a goddess.

Years of spiritual tourism have taught me that the magic often lies with the devotees rather than the object of devotion, and the scene before me is deeply charming—the spiritual equivalent of comfort food, like a sweet rice pudding scented with rose water. The endless flow of huggees are first asked to kneel, remove any glasses, and mop up their sweaty brows with a Kleenex before being guided into the enveloping embrace of the Mother. After half a minute or so, the devotees are plucked out of Amma's arms, and the guru hands them flower petals, sacred ashes, or maybe a foil-wrapped Hershey's Kiss.

While I am waiting for an audience with Amma herself, I speak with Swami Dayamrita, the orange-robed manager of the Castro Valley ashram. We stand crammed together just to the side of Amma's nest. A sober, no-nonsense fellow, Dayamrita hails from the southern Indian state of Kerala, where Amma was born to a Dalit fisherman's family in 1954 and where her principal Indian ashram now lies. Kerala is a traditional center of tantra and goddess worship, but it is also a progressive and well-educated state with a strong, if waning, left-wing culture. As a young man, Dayamrita was an atheist and a filmmaker, and he decided to shoot a damning exposé about his region's most famous god-person.

While following Amma about he witnessed an event that has since become central to Amma lore. When her village ashram was just starting out, a local leper came in for a hug. Amma embraced him and, in her mad compassion, licked his sores and sucked the pus out of his wounds, which she then covered with sacred ash. "That changed my whole life," the swami says. "Poor or sick, it doesn't matter, she embraces them. Shingles, chicken pox, infectious diseases—she does not get them. Only love is exchanged."

Dayamrita gets a call on his cell and departs. Then another fellow in orange robes squeezes through, his hippie glasses and windblown black hair calling to mind a mid-'70s Jerry Garcia. He is Swami Amritaswarupananda Puri, aka "Big Swami," Amma's most senior disciple and her main translator, and he collects my questions with an amusingly world-weary, businesslike air.

I ask Amma what she's doing with all this hugging stuff. Big Swami puts the question into Malayalam for his guru, who is in the midst of double-hugging two Indian teens wearing Izod shirts. Amma launches into her response immediately, with twinkling eyes and a toothy, infectious smile. As she speaks I realize that, Kali or not, she is definitely a firecracker.

"What's happening here cannot be described," she says. "It is true communion, pure love that flows, flows like a river. It is pure subjective experience. It's like somebody trying to explain about drumming. You cannot explain with words. In order to really understand, you have to play a drum or listen to it. It's a direct experience, a real meeting between hearts. It's like looking in a mirror and cleaning your face."

The guru-speak continues. "I'm trying to awaken true motherhood in people, in men and women, because that is lacking in today's world. Today there are two types of poverty. The first is a lack of basic necessities. The second is a lack of love and compassion. As far as I am concerned, the second is more important because if there is love and compassion then the first kind can be taken care of."

Though she'll play the role of the divine goddess, Amma's own vibe is informal, earthy, and rather spunky. The shoulders on her plain white sari are smudged with the sweat and tears of thousands of strangers, but she seems completely comfortable soaking up the effluence of emotions and desires swimming her way.

"Today people are willing to die for religion, but no one lives in the central truth of religion," she goes on. "Religion is just the outer shell. The fruit is spirituality. People look at the outer shell and don't realize the spiritual essence. Spirituality is not different from a worldly life. Spirituality shows how to lead a happy life in the world, to minimize problems and maximize happiness. It is like an instruction manual. What is wrong if you get more happiness from spirituality than worldly pleasures?"

It's a great question, one that today's increasingly arrogant atheists have yet to answer. If humans are nothing more than neurologically programmed DNA machines, why not run sacred applications that bring happiness and meaning and active compassion? I start to ask another question, but Big Swami is through. "Okay, that's all," he says and departs.

Then it's my turn for some subjective experience. I'm a Californian, so I'm down with hugs, but it is rare to meet a master. As a VIP for the day, I get an E ticket that enables me to skip the hours-long line. I feel kind of lame about taking cuts, and I have a sneaking suspicion that the wait, as is so often the case in this world of desire, amplifies the fun. But there I am, a minute later, headlocked by a perfumed lady who maybe, just maybe, is the mother of the universe.

She rubs my back with her hand as she mumbles into my right ear, a string of syllables I first take to be some esoteric mantra but that gradually reveal themselves to be the homeliest of addresses: "Darling, darling, darling, darling . . ." I receive no shivering blasts of Shakti, the feminine energy cultivated by yogis and sought by devotees. But a warm, childlike nostalgia seeps into my heart, and I have some vague sense of being in the middle of the ocean at night. Then I'm back in the light of the day with a smiling Indian lady handing me a chocolate. I almost immediately reach for my pad to take notes, but Rob Sidon, Amma's press person, sees me and suggests I "turn off my computer." So I do.

Innocuous and intimate, the hug is a brilliant gesture for a reputed saint to make—a cosmic download about compassion and connection delivered in a package that's about as challenging and exotic as a Hershey's Kiss. Amma is not the only one to have embraced the activist power of the hug—last year, Juan Mann's "Free Hugs" campaign rode the viral spread of a YouTube video into the hearts of millions, while peace organizers recently staged a "Jerusalem Hug" that surrounded the walls of the benighted old city with thousands of people holding hands.

But Amma hugs on a truly global scale, exhibiting a spiritual athleticism that boggles the mind. As the loudspeakers that surround the main meeting hall of the M. A. Center are happy to announce, Amma has hugged more than twenty-six million people. During her massive fiftieth birthday celebration in 2003, which was inaugurated by the Indian president Dr. A. P. J. Abdul Kalam, Amma cranked through a stadium full of devotees for twenty-one hours straight while a scoreboard racked up numbers well into the five figures.

Though all this can be seen as some kind of bizarre mass performance art, Amma's trademark gesture is also a brilliant and quietly subversive transformation of traditional South Asian worship. Hindus, and especially followers of the devotional path of bhakti, have long placed a special emphasis on being in the physical presence of holy beings, whether living saints or revered icons or sacred mountains and rivers. This practice of presence is called "darshan" and is usually considered a visual or visionary experience (the word means "sight"). But after having a number of powerful goddess visions of her own in the 1970s, a young Amma broke the fourth wall of darshan and started physically embracing those who came to her for succor, spiritual or otherwise.

In India, where traditional mores limit physical contact between women and strangers, Amma's embrace also announced a liberating and almost feminist activism. As well it should. Amma's mission, the Mata Amritanandamayi Math, is now one of India's major humanitarian nongovernmental organizations. In the late 1990s, the Math was already the second-largest Indian recipient of foreign contributions, totaling $11 million, and her organization has grown dramatically since then. Though its books are closed, materials provided by the Math trumpet scores of large and successful feats, including mass housing projects, disaster relief, food programs, schools, a university, and hospitals, one of which is the best research hospital in southern India. The Math contributed $46 million to souls weathering the aftereffects of the Southeast Asian tsunami, while the American M. A. Center gave a million bucks to the Bush-Clinton Katrina Fund. While the university and hospital services are not generally free, and the extent of good works may certainly be exaggerated, Amma's mission has developed the international reputation of actually delivering the goods, and tons of folks have had their lives materially transformed by the organization.

Of course, with abundance comes power, and power means politics. Amma's flock certainly includes individuals and organizations associated with right-wing Hindu nationalism, or Hindutva. Many Hindutva ministers of state are Amma devotees, including former prime minister Atal Bihari Vajpayee, and her ranks swell with members of the RSS and VHP, nationalist organizations that have been accused of, among other things, helping foment the bloody Gujarat riots in 2002. These are complex issues, of course, and Amma is the very opposite of fascist demagogue. But many of the liberal Westerners lining up for their hug have no understanding of how their guru plays in reactionary or "fundamentalist" circles in a modern India with a large Muslim population. And the global managers of her brand are perfectly happy to keep it that way.

And Amma is a brand; her organization has a cute registered trademark, good PR, a snappy slogan ("Embrace the world"), a TV station, and an ad campaign that recently plastered the Mother's mug on billboards and buses across the world. The video shown before her evening gathering at the M. A. Center was essentially an infomercial, though its sentiment was no more manipulative than your average junk letter from the Sierra Club or Amnesty International. What's amazing, however, is that this juggernaut is sustained by Amma's own personal example of ceaseless and exhausting activity; even cynics cannot doubt her industry. Eating and resting little, giving out thousands of hugs a day for most of the year, Amma is moving at a supernatural pace.

Amma's example also creates a culture of self-abnegating service, as followers are encouraged not only to hand over cash, but to sacrifice themselves on the altar of volunteer labor. This is great news for the NGO's bean counters, but not always so great for the young devotees who are offering "seva," or service. One ex-devotee, who is wary enough of the organization that she asked me to simply call her Lakshmi, describes the Amma scene as a competitive, backbiting, and self-righteous culture where volunteers are encouraged to work beyond the point of exhaustion in order to please Mother. "There is a very strong focus on selfless service," she wrote in an email. "However, much of the 'selfless service' in the West involves assisting people who have enough money to pay for retreats so that there is no paid labor during these programs." Lakshmi left the organization partly because she "realized that *seva* might be short for slave labor."

Another reason that Lakshmi and others have soured on the Amma scene is the growing materialism that feeds the empire. A good quarter of the meditation hall at the M. A. Center, for example, was given over to the Amma Shop, where volunteers in bright orange safety vests oversee a brisk trade in books, mugs, jewelry, clothes, calendars, decals, CDs, unguents, oils, and Ayurvedic medicines. Photography and videotaping are forbidden in the hall, but devotees can buy DVDs and photographs of Amma; in some she looks like Queen Latifah. Many objects are advertised as having been blessed—touched—by Amma; I heard one story of a woman who offered a priceless heirloom to Amma, only to see it reappear hours later in the shop. But the most incredible commodity fetishes are the handmade Amma dolls, which were being lugged around by a surprisingly large number of adult women in the hall. These cute and pudgy figures fetched a decent price—$180 for the Cabbage Patch–size ones—and they could be accessorized with colorful silk outfits (blessed by Amma, natch) associated with Durga, Kali, and other goddesses.

As a fan of alt-dolls and vinyl figures, I'd have to say the Amma dolls are pretty cool. But for some observers of the spiritual scene, they incarnate nothing so much as spiritual infantilism. Jody Radzik, a forty-eight-year-old graphic designer who writes the muckraking and funny Guruphiliac blog, calls Amma a "space mommy," which he defines as a guru who fulfills "the function of a cosmic parent for insecure, self-loathing devotees." A "spiritually informed skeptic," Radzik nonetheless considers himself a devotee of Kali and a follower of Vedanta, the nondualist summa of Hindu thought. "Vivekananda described Vedanta very simply. Everyone is God. That means that a single person can't be more god than any other person. Gurus like Amma pay lip service to the Vedanta while also presenting themselves as special beings who wield magic powers because of their divinity. But self-realization is the opposite of magic—it's the most mundane thing in their world. It's always right there right on the end of your nose. These gurus have people looking everywhere but the tip of their nose."

Amma herself seems to wear her robes lightly; she is a cheery woman of little education who makes no divine claims and carries an air of good-humored humility. But the lore that surrounds her—much of which derives directly from her tight-knit group of core disciples—is redolent with the miraculous. Many devotees, East and West, believe that Amma's divine Shakti can give them children, or fix their marriages, or make them money. One of the first Amma videos that comes up on YouTube shows a reenactment of a young Amma miraculously transforming water into pudding. No one less than Big Swami narrates the clip.

The guru game has many levels. Devotion to divine beings can certainly generate something like miracles in people's hearts and lives—even if that devotion is nothing more than a placebo effect conjured through a kind of sacred theater. To do their job, gurus must take on all manner of popular projections, but the great teachers also create situations that open up to deeper truths. "Amma's ability to meet people exactly where they're at is actually a profound statement of nondualism," says Greg Wendt, a longtime devotee who lives in a plush Hindufied bachelor pad in Santa Monica, California. "It's really the long view of recognizing people's journey, and not trying to give people the whole enchilada all the time. Amma has said on a number of occasions, 'Why teach people Vedanta when all they want is something to eat?'"

Wendt was initially turned off by people "mommy-izing" Amma, but he has since come around. "The whole guru yoga thing is to meditate on the form of your teacher. That's a core teaching of tantric Buddhism and tantric Hinduism." From that perspective, Wendt says, even the dolls make sense. "If Amma's really embodying that path, then she's not going to stop people from their bhakti ways. There's a doll there, and you can buy it if you want. She doesn't care."

As a successful investment advisor specializing in sustainable and socially responsible capitalism, Wendt has no problems with Amma's marketing and fundraising machine. Wendt was staying at the Math in Kerala when the tsunami destroyed scores of fishing villages nearby, and he worked on the temporary structures while Amma went toe-to-toe with local officials jockeying for part of the disaster relief pie. Wendt has also been around big-time guru scenes that were far more rapacious. "I don't even notice that Amma is asking for money," he says. "But her flow is far more abundant. She's taking money from crazy housewives and giving it to widows and disaster victims in India. These Westerners are actually having dramatic benefits in their lives, and they in turn are actually housing and feeding the people in India who need it. What a great, compassionate way to take from the rich and give to the poor. Even if it were shallow and false, it's still beautiful."

———————

Every guru needs his or her rock stars, and Amma seems to attract guitar gods. The first that came to my attention is J Mascis, the guitarist and singer for Dinosaur Jr., the awesome indie-rock band from the 1980s and '90s that recently completed a reunion tour. Despite his long hair and transcendent slashing solos, the younger Mascis was the polar opposite of the starry-eyed peak experience junkies that fell for Eastern gurus during the golden age of rock. I profiled him a couple of times, and the impression I had already gleaned from his songs—that he was a mopey and kind of disconnected guy—seemed right on the money. This was no bliss bunny.

Last year, around the time that his album with the Black Sabbath style hard rock band Witch came out, Mascis released *J + Friends Sing + Chant for AMMA*. An excellent collection of American neokirtans, the record blends Mascis's whiny indie drawl with dholek and Sanskrit and the occasional monster lead. Unlike the neokirtans you might hear in yoga class—those slick call-and-response hymns to Krishna with the funky bass lines and electronic twaddle—Mascis's god songs sound like the yearning product of, well, a mopey and kind of disconnected guy, "nursing wounds that never end." I hear you, J: sometimes only a space momma will do.

Amma's other fret-board devotee also happens to be the most remarkable person I met during my long day at the M. A. Center. Jason Becker is, or was, what they call a shredder—a master of technically ferocious superfast neoclassical heavy metal guitar. As a young player, Becker had the honor of replacing Steve Vai in David Lee Roth's band. But Becker soon came down with amyotrophic lateral sclerosis—aka Lou Gehrig's disease—and his sweep-picking days were done. These days his body is a withered husk strapped down, gaunt head and all, to an elaborate reclined wheelchair replete with tubes and respirators. The thirty-seven-year-old Becker cannot speak, but converses using a system of eye movements developed by his father and interpreted by his helper Marilyn, who, like him, is robed in white.

Becker has been following Amma for years, and stickers of her cover the contraption, which is scattered with sacred ash. "She's always new and inspiring," he explains. "Love never gets boring." Becker mentions Amma on his CDs (he continues to compose by computer), and occasionally metal-heads show up at Amma gatherings, curious to check out the guru of their guru. Becker's forthcoming collection will feature an Indian-inspired tune with Sanskrit and Mayalam lyrics, as well as shred guitar supplied by Joe Satriani.

We chat for a spell about God and guitars, and I cannot relate the peace and impish friendliness that came through this man, who was essentially confined, like all of us, I suppose, to a corpse. I ask him what the best thing was about getting the disease. "That's easy," he says. "I got to know God closer, and I got to meet Amma." He pauses. "I guess I might also be more mature too, but Marilyn would probably disagree." He laughs with his eyes.

I am reminded of those laughing eyes a few hours later, when Amma once again takes the stage. The curtains part, and she is sitting in an elaborate throne beneath a parasol bedecked with flowers. The plain white sari is gone, replaced with crimson robes, carnations, and a crown. This is Devi Bhava, a popular ceremony where Amma visibly performs the presence of the goddess. The devotees are lined up to the sides of the stage, the front lines of a battalion of devotees whose assault on this plump fisherwoman would last all night. As they surge toward Amma, her face blooms into a radiant, unrestrained glee, and for a spell she looks much less like a cosmic matriarch than a great big kid.

CHAPTER 18

On the Threshing Floor

Daniel José Camacho

I'm highly suspicious of the growing obsession with genetic ancestry tests. 23andMe. AncestryDNA. People can now scrape their inner cheek with a swab, mail it to a company for $99, and brag to you about a cultural or racial epiphany they've had based on being 4.7 percent of something. Who knows how this personal genetic information might be used. I suspect these companies respect people's privacy as much as Facebook does. I've heard that governments and police departments are already using this information to track people.

And yet, I would be lying if I said I haven't thought about purchasing a DNA kit for myself. Yes, I know that such tests provide limited and potentially misleading information. Yes, I understand that they fuel problematic framings of race that tie race to genetics when race is actually something socially and politically constructed. But I'm still curious!

I don't know if I will ever take a test. I ask myself: Should I be contributing to this system? Could I convince *Sojourners* to pay for my test if I were to write an article about it, thus shifting some of the ethical burden away from me as an individual?

Thankfully, I was able to cheat. Sort of. My brother recently took a test through AncestryDNA. He sent a link to the results in our siblings group text saying that we should have the exact same results. While what he said was inaccurate—because siblings who share the same two parents can still vary in the percentage of DNA taken from each parent—I did not fact-check his text. I simply replied "thank you" and happily clicked.

An elaborate breakdown pops up: 26 percent Spain; 18 percent Native American from North and Central America; 14 percent Cameroon, Congo, and Southern Bantu peoples; 12 percent Portugal; 8 percent Andean Native American; 5 percent France; 4 percent Benin/Togo; 3 percent Mali; 2 percent Basque; 2 percent Middle East; 1 percent Senegal; 1 percent European Jewish; 1 percent Ivory Coast/Ghana.

Upon seeing these results, the first thing that came to mind is that there's a high probability that I have significantly more Native American ancestry than Elizabeth Warren. The next thing is what this test does and doesn't reveal. It shows the obvious: behind categories such as Latino and Colombian exists a highly mixed heritage stretching back to the period of conquest and slavery, and to the Iberian Peninsula. But at the same time, the test can't tell me how I see myself. And it certainly can't control how others see me.

So what if I do have a significant amount of Native American ancestry or African ancestry? Does that mean I should identify as Native or African? That would be absurd. I lack continuity with such communities. But erasing that part of my heritage also seems wrong. I want to honor my ancestry but not exploit it. I can hear an agent or publicist saying, "Daniel, if you lean into X part of your identity, you can increase your market share and increase the number of topics and venues in which you are perceived as an expert."

Or I could play the game of identity overcompensation. Having been negligent of certain parts of my heritage, I could—later in life—come to a dramatic awakening in which all of my social media posts become me sharing Bantu proverbs and burning sage. But this would feel cheap, like a projection, a shallow performance. It wouldn't be the real me. It would be a certain packaging of me.

Still, I don't want to erase my Black and Indigenous roots in some North American melting pot of whiteness. I don't want to only privilege my European heritage. There is something true and subversive about refusing to forget one's ancestry while living in a vast sea of assimilating forgetfulness. But how to do this? My brother's DNA test doesn't tell me. It doesn't tell me how to relate to this information.

The test just says "26 percent Spain." But what does "Spain" mean? The territory that we now know as Spain was previously known as al-Andalus when it was ruled by Muslims for centuries, and by other names when it was ruled by the Visigoths and the Roman Empire before that. During the medieval period, southern Spain was a site of great cultural exchange. Christians. Jews. Muslims. Europeans. North Africans. Arabs. Without figures such as Córdoba's Ibn Rushd (Averroes), the Christian West might have never recovered Aristotle's writings and Thomas Aquinas might have lacked a large chunk of his inspiration.

But we're often stuck with the whitewashed history of Spain, from the vantage point of the Christian Reconquista, the conquest of Muslim Iberia led by Catholic monarchs Ferdinand II and Isabella. In January, I traveled to southern Spain for the first time and saw this complicated legacy on display. The city of Córdoba has a Catholic cathedral that is built into a mosque, which itself was built on top of a Visigothic basilica. From one spot I could see faded early Christian mosaics; bold, red, double-horseshoe arches; elaborate geometric patterns; and Arabic calligraphy. It's a beautiful site, but it's also the exception.

After the Reconquista, most churches ended up like the Gothic cathedral of Sevilla, which was built to completely replace the mosque that came before. Sevilla's cathedral is an imposing structure. I lost my breath as I climbed steps for what seemed like half an hour to get to the top of the cathedral's tower. As I walked on the ground floor, through what felt like six churches in one, I noticed the site where Christopher Columbus is allegedly buried. Both Spain and the Dominican Republic claim to have his remains. In 2006, Spanish researchers announced that a DNA test proved that Columbus was in Sevilla; Dominicans dismissed the findings and argued that they had the real body of Columbus. Either way, the casket I saw played into a narrative. This Gothic cathedral, the biggest in the world, was meant to tell a new story, even if the remaining orange-tree courtyard continues to betray its intentions of purity.

The Reconquista culminated in 1492 with the final defeat of the Moors in Granada and with the official expulsion of unconverted Jews. In the emerging nation of Spain, remaining Jews and Muslims were either killed or forcibly converted. And even after conversion, there was an extreme anxiety about whether the conversions were genuine. Known as *conversos* and *moriscos*, Jewish and Muslim converts to the Catholic faith were deemed suspicious. The Spanish Inquisition emerged to purify Spain of these foreign influences, and any former Jews or Muslims suspected of "lapsing in the faith" were put to the death.

In this process, the Spanish obsession with religious purity spilled over into an obsession with a purity of blood, a purity of descent. Conversion wasn't enough. One needed to prove pure Christian descent, which meant pure European, non-Jewish descent.

Spain was, arguably, the first modern nation that believed itself to be white. It believed itself to be white and violently made it so. Christian supremacy gave way to purity of blood. The history of Spain itself seems to be a projection of identity.

When a DNA test says "26 percent Spain," what does "Spain" mean? The test can't say. It can't say because DNA tests are inconclusive when it comes to proving identity. They're inconclusive because they provide information that still needs to be interpreted.

Nevertheless, I can understand why individuals latch onto such information, however inconclusive it may be. Colorful graphs, dotted maps, and percentage pies provide some solace in what is otherwise a cold, nebulous search for meaning. Something as fluid as identity is given back to us, quantified, with metrics. We want to understand who we are. We're looking for anything that can help. One test. Anything. Some type of sign.

These struggles of deciphering identity make me think about Jesus and the moment that his identity was made absolutely clear.

According to the gospels, Jesus is baptized. In seminary, I learned that historical Jesus scholars disagree on virtually everything about the life of Jesus except for a few things. This is one of those few things. Almost all agree that Jesus was, in fact, baptized by a man named John. Why? Because in the ancient context, this was the kind of embarrassing fact that a religious group would not invent about their leader, their divine figure. Why would God need to go through a purity ritual? Why would God need to be told who they are? This is the scandal of the incarnation. God in human flesh. The life of Jesus is about showing us what it truly means to be human.

Before Jesus enters public ministry, before he declares that the spirit of the Lord is upon him to proclaim good news to the poor, Jesus is baptized. Before Jesus engages in any activism, God calls him "beloved." Before Jesus's prophetic activity sweeps across the land, this identity is tested. Jesus's baptism reminds us that before we go out, before we act, before we change the world, we must change ourselves.

Jesus's mission begins with a humble cleansing. A voice from heaven tells him who he really is. The Christian contemplative tradition describes this dynamic as the true self versus the false self. We all have a true self that is one with the love of God. But we all are also shadowed by false selves that want to exist outside of this reality. In *Seeds of Contemplation*, Thomas Merton writes: "The secret of my identity is hidden in the love and mercy of God. . . . Therefore there is only one problem on which all my existence, my peace, and my happiness depend: to discover myself in discovering God. If I find God, I will find myself, and if I find my true self I will find God."

The baptism that is greater than John's goes to the very core of who we are. As the text says, "His winnowing fork is in his hand, to clear his threshing floor and to gather the wheat into his granary; but the chaff he will burn with unquenchable fire" (Luke 3:17). The winnowing fork and threshing floor refers to the site of our souls. The wheat is our true self; the chaff is our false self. The process of separating these can be painful.

The text continues: "And the Holy Spirit descended upon him in bodily form like a dove. And a voice came from heaven, 'You are my Son, the Beloved; with you I am well pleased.'" The true self is relational, is greatly loved, is inherently pleasing. The true self is peaceful and does not build itself through domination of others. The false self is violent and formed through domination. The false self eschews relationality and pretends to be utterly independent. The false self is hatred, is internalized self-hatred, is a child of God vandalized. The false self is always depleted, in need of greater approval, greater success, greater results.

Jesus's baptism points to the inward reality that we struggle with every day, for our entire lives: Realizing who we really are. Realizing who we are not. Spotting the dangerous counterfeits.

To change the world, you must change yourself. What this platitude entails is actually scary. If we want injustice in the world to die, parts of us have to die too.

Lately, I have been struck by the meditations of Howard Thurman, a mystic who lived at the height of Jim Crow America. His central concern was this: What does the religion of Jesus have to say to those with their backs against the wall? Although he supported civil rights activists and influenced major figures such as Martin Luther King Jr., Thurman emphasized the importance of the inward life to help people live in the present with dignity. I come away from reading him with a sense of freedom. In a world with such heartless conditions, there is still so much I can do.

This message runs counter to the lie that some of us internalize. The lie that presents us as powerless, helpless, voiceless. The tension is how to be honest about our suffering without being reduced to it.

Chicana writer Gloria Anzaldúa wrote about the US-Mexico border as an open wound. But her radical spirituality also compelled her to look deeper. The border exists within us, within how we see others and see ourselves. Liberation begins with defining the self. In her book *Borderlands*, she writes: "I seek an exoneration, a seeing through the fictions of white supremacy, a seeing of ourselves in our true guises and not as the false racial personality that has been given to us and that we have given to ourselves."

What is white supremacy but a systemic false self? It is violent, formed through domination, defaces children of God, and exhibits great fragility through it all. Whiteness is a false self that has formed all of us. But it's unsustainable. It's chaff that God will burn, hubris that will burn down the planet.

Whiteness is a fiction that will go down in flames, one way or another.

In the gospel passage, the voice from heaven tells Jesus that he is beloved not because that's what God needs to hear. It's what we need to hear. "Beloved" is the true self that the powers and principalities of this world write countless fictions against.

One of the strongest scenes to ever capture this truth is found in Toni Morrison's novel *Beloved*. The character of Baby Suggs preaches a kind of sermon and officiates a kind of baptism for a group of people that recently escaped slavery. In a place called "the clearing," she reintroduces men, women, and children to their own flesh as something to love.

DNA tests can be meaningful, especially when combined with genealogy. They can teach us about family and ancestors. They can correct false stories. When histories of forced separations lead to dead ends, they can provide small clues about what's on the other side.

But a test can't get you to love the you that is the culmination of this entire legacy. That requires a type of baptism.

Our own work to build beloved community must begin here, where Jesus begins, grounded in the true beloved self. And what these mystics understand, perhaps better than some others, is that this work takes on a bodily form. Finding our true self is not some purely disembodied act of contemplation. It involves seeing through the lies that have attached themselves to our skin, the fictions that others have written—and sometimes we ourselves have written—onto our bodies.

I don't know about you, but the skies have never parted for me with a voice telling me I'm beloved. I've never found that one indisputable sign that proves my identity. But my grandmother, who is one hundred years old and doesn't remember much, still recognizes my name and smiles when she realizes who I am.

And maybe these are small signs that add up to something, if I observe.

I'm afraid what makes the search for our true self difficult is that it won't always be pleasant. It'll be like separating us from the versions of us we are addicted to. It'll be like finding ourselves with our backs on the threshing floor.

CHAPTER 19

Fake Meat

Meghan O'Gieblyn

Science lifted us out of nature. It tamed the wilderness; it gave us tools to transcend our lousy, fallen bodies; and it shot us to the moon. Now it has produced a hamburger made entirely of vegetables that bleeds like real beef. The packaging of the aptly named Impossible Burger instructs you, as if daring you, to cook the patties medium rare. Three minutes on each side, and the center will remain the fleshly pink color of raw sirloin. This effect is the result of heme, the protein that carries oxygen through our blood and gives it its crimson color, and which food scientists have discovered how to ferment in a lab using genetically engineered yeast. (Pedantic foodies will point out that the red in beef is not blood but myoglobin, but this is beside the point. We call burgers "bloody" to acknowledge a truth that modernity has long tried to obscure: that meat was once, like us, a living thing.) Heme, which is abundant in animal muscle, is also what lends beef its distinctive flavor. The first time I prepared the Impossible Burger at home, the skillet erupted into a fatty sizzle (the patty contains emulsified coconut oil, which melts like tallow), and within seconds the air filled with the iron aroma of singed flesh. But the most uncanny moment arrived when I finished eating and there remained on the plate a stain of pinkish-brown drippings. In that moment, when I should have been marveling at the wonders of food science, I confess I was thinking of the weeping Madonna of Civitavecchia, a wooden statue that was said to shed tears of real blood—the signs of flesh where there is none.

Religion, of course, was our original method of transcending nature. Asceticism, in its efforts to overcome carnality, has always rested on the renunciation of *carnis*. (Beyond Meat, a popular vegetarian brand, evokes this transcendental promise.) The earliest meat analogues favored by Buddhist monks bear little resemblance to animal flesh. Is it possible to envision a more notional form of sustenance than tofu? Colorless, odorless, it recalls nothing in nature—certainly not the soybean from which it is derived. This, coupled with its lack of any definitive origin story, seems to confirm that tofu is an otherworldly substance, dropped from heaven like those UFO alloys that have been found in the Nevada desert. But what makes tofu the ideal ascetic food is its consistency: even vegetables require the brutish baring of teeth, but bean curd is soft enough that it can be consumed practically by osmosis. (In China, it is brought to the graves of relatives whose ghosts have long ago lost their chins and jaws.) Seitan, another ancient substitute, is more versatile: it can pass as duck or goose, but this verisimilitude has inspired its own brand of spiritual anxiety. In the Ming dynasty novel *Journey to the West*, demons attempt to trick a monk by serving him a meal of human flesh and human brains stewed as if it were wheat gluten.

It is odd that we have invested so much ingenuity into putting "blood" into fake meat when the oldest Abrahamic religion has fixated, for millennia, on its removal. In addition to its painstaking lists of clean and unclean animals, the foremost prohibition in the Hebrew Bible, reiterated again and again, warns against eating meat "that has its lifeblood still in it." Historians have speculated about the psychological motivations behind the elaborate process of salting, rinsing, and—in some Orthodox communities—blanching that ensures kosher products maintain no trace of blood (hygiene has been proposed, unconvincingly). But the reason is stated by God himself in the book of Leviticus: blood was to be reserved for ritual atonement. The animal's life was ransom for your own and its blood could not be consumed like a common food. As barbaric as this ritual appears today, it did rely on a rigorous spiritual algebra. Like the Eastern ascetics, the rabbis understood that nature was a scrupulous accountant who could not be cheated. If you wanted transcendence, you had to pay the price—if not by abstention, then by finding a living thing to take your place.

Christ was the final lamb led to slaughter, spilling enough heme to cover the sins of the world. His death inaugurated a new covenant of food ethics—one that arrives, with dramatic flourish, in the book of Acts. The apostle Peter has gone up to the roof to pray, but while doing so, he becomes hungry and falls into a trance. When he looks up, he sees an enormous sheet descending from heaven, containing every kind of animal: mammals, reptiles, and birds. A voice commands him to kill and eat the animals, but Peter recoils—"Surely not, Lord!"—since many of them are unclean. The voice bellows in reply: "Do not call anything impure that God has made clean." The message could hardly be more blunt: there would be no more abstention, no more substitution; everything was fair game. But it is a dreary scene of liberation. It's impossible not to hear in Peter's protest the vague dread that always accompanies the abolition of a long-standing limit.

We in the modern, secular West are still living under this new covenant of abundance and are rapidly approaching its logical end. We have killed and eaten all animals, then bred more. We have surfeited the earth's arable land with cattle farms and slaughterhouses, which collectively emit more greenhouse gases than all forms of global transportation combined. The new bleeding veggie burgers are billed as a solution to our ecological crisis. They are not marketed to vegetarians and vegans; their corporate mission is evangelical: to convert carnivores at a moment when the taste and means for meat is spreading, like a zombie virus, across the globe. These companies have attracted the same billionaire investors (Bill Gates, Li Ka-shing) who back biofuels and nuclear energy, and, like all forms of green growth, they stand to profit on a bleak—though perhaps not inaccurate—view of human nature. It is now simply assumed that we will cling to our burgers and SUVs even as the ozone vanishes and the polar bears die—unless, that is, the laboratory manages to produce from plants something identical: not a substitute but the thing itself.

Today, it is not Christ but science that declares all things clean. Most of us have by now come to dread its never-ending factory of miracles: bacon conjured from tempeh and wheat gluten; meat lover's pizza topped with soy sausage and cashew cheese. Ours is the dispensation of meatless buffalo wings and vegan philly cheesesteaks (surely not, Lord!); of chick'n nuggets and White Castle veggie sliders. In the beginning, many meat analogues consisted of soy and gluten, foods that likewise came under scrutiny and were eagerly forfeited—until we discovered that there existed still more, fully permissible, substances. Cakes could be concocted out of amaranth and sorghum. Gumdrops could be summoned from agave. Hemp and oats could be milked and enriched with calcium, and the finished product was passable as—and, in some cases, better than—what it claimed to imitate. In America, the ascetic impulse is thwarted by the engine of consumer choice and limitless growth.

But the blood in vegetarian burgers is too richly symbolic to be dismissed as a gesture of verisimilitude. Should we take it as a sign of atonement, an acknowledgment that we have repented and been granted forgiveness? Or is it a gothic reminder of our ecological sins—an indelible stain, like the blood Lady Macbeth cannot wash from her hands? Early coverage of these products routinely declared them "eerie," "creepy," and—in the words of one food critic—"a dark sorcery." Such derision reveals something more than aesthetic revulsion, something approaching spiritual unease. It's possible that fake meat is beginning its shadowy descent into the uncanny valley. This is true, at least, of the "clean meat" in development at West Coast start-ups—beef, chicken, and salmon grown in vats from stem cells. Despite few people having yet tried them (one brand of clean meatball costs $18,000 per pound), these products have been widely spurned as "Frankenmeat." The allusion to Shelley reveals a counter-Enlightenment ethos that still, occasionally, rears its head—or perhaps an older, more primitive knowledge that nature cannot be coerced into performing wonders, that miracles are always tricks. (As for the weeping and bleeding virgins: One such icon was taken to a laboratory, where scientists discovered that it had been coated with pork and beef fat. When the statue was placed in a slightly warmed room, the fat would liquefy into droplets that resembled tears.)

A good portion of the UN's most recent report on climate change addressed the problem of land scarcity due to animal industries. Technological solutions alone, the UN argued, could not be relied on to solve this problem; instead, the crisis demanded "diet shifts" on a massive scale. What it called for was—in a word—asceticism (or, in the jargon of the IPCC scientists, "demand reduction"). If we wish to survive on this planet, economies must be restrained; we must learn how to live on less. It's possible that mock meat, with its uncanny verisimilitude, may help avert, or at least delay, total catastrophe. Or perhaps it will merely confirm our secret hope that human ingenuity will outwit all our creditors, that, in the end, we will be made to relinquish nothing.

For now, the sacrificial ethic persists—at least superficially— in the language of "substitution," which still appears on restaurant menus, where meat analogues are accompanied by an up-charge of a dollar or two. In raw financial terms, the new and improved fake meats are still more expensive than the lives of animals. And perhaps it is this fact—even more than the symbolism of blood— that reminds us that absolution always comes at a cost. Every dispensation of grace demands its pound of flesh.

CHAPTER 20

Opioids: A Crisis of Misplaced Morality

Ann Neumann

"What does spirituality or morality or a good feeling toward others have to do with addiction? Zero. Addiction isn't about that. Addiction is a psychological symptom to help you get through feelings of being overwhelmed." —Dr. Lance Dodes, Boston Psychoanalytic Institute

Heroin, hydrocodone, OxyContin, morphine, fentanyl. "Everyone keeps talking about awareness. We're aware there is an opiate epidemic," Jessica Hall, director of judicial programs at the McShin Foundation, an addiction and recovery program in Henrico County, Virginia, told AOL News in July. There are more women in Henrico County's jail than there have ever been. "Where's recovery at in this?" Hall asked.

Yes, we're aware of the opioid epidemic. It's been hard to miss in the media—or our personal lives—for the past decade. But there's a kind of conundrum effect to our current reactions to the opioid crisis. Wade into studies and articles about the unprecedented rate of opioid overdoses in the country and you're likely to come away confused about how drug epidemics happen and about how to stop what is killing so many right now across the nation.

Yes, people are dying in mass numbers; our prison, health care, education, financial, social support systems—and every other system you can think of—are overwhelmed. And no, nothing is being done. "There's been a lack of policy action to end the opioid epidemic," German Lopez wrote at Vox in August, "The only major bill passed by Congress on the crisis appropriated $1 billion to drug treatment over two years—far from the tens of billions a year that studies suggest the crisis actually costs."

Trump stated on August 10 of 2017 that he would address opioid addiction, but waited until the end of October to take any action. Trump's declaration of a public health emergency, rather than a national emergency, prevents the necessary funding and resources—trained people on the ground—from being committed to the epidemic.

"What we need is for the president to seek an appropriation from Congress, I believe in the billions, so that we can rapidly expand access for effective outpatient opioid addiction treatments," Andrew Kolodny, the codirector of opioid policy research at the Heller School for Social Policy and Management at Brandeis University, told the *New York Times* after the president's announcement. "Until those treatments are easier to access than heroin or fentanyl, overdose deaths will remain at record-high levels."

What is clear from endless reporting is the horrifying starkness of the numbers. If nothing is done, half a million more people will die over the next decade. Morgues in Ohio are full.

So are prisons in Virginia. Scores of people are dying of opioid withdrawal in jail. Distraught parents are using their children's obituaries to speak out about opioid use. Children are flooding foster homes.

All of which also makes it clear that opioid addiction is a moral crisis. The *moral* part in this moral crisis, however, isn't the habits and behaviors of those addicted or the sellers or makers of those drugs. It is our lack of moral action—our immoral inaction. It is the failure of our legislators to do the right thing, it is our misplaced moral judgment. It's the application of the entrenched moralizing frame we use to talk about mass addiction: The frame which says that addicts have made bad decisions, have failed to get help, have failed to love themselves, to love God. The dominant perspective which claims that addicts have put their drug before all things, they have robbed their mother blind, they have lost their job, their wife, their kids, and their dignity. The fact is, it is precisely because we have characterized addicts as immoral actors enslaved to evil substances—for, like, ever—that we've failed to prevent the destructive cycle of drug epidemics, past and present.

———————

When we do bother to address this moral crisis, we address it as a problem of national purity. I have written before about how our country uses laws regulating sexual purity to express anxieties about the condition of our nation-state, conflating them into stories we tell ourselves about national purity. To preserve the nation, we must be "pure" in all respects. It is especially important to mind the ways in which ideas about national purity carry a particular racially charged weight when applied to public health. Health care and other social support programs are under attack—not least because they serve minorities. The "Us and Them" narrative Trump and his predecessors have employed regarding "entitlements," education, and immigration shows that a growing faction of "us" define "American" by an ever-decreasing number of demographic traits: white, Christian, suburban or rural, in a hetero-nuclear family, gainfully employed, gun owning, *healthy*.

The number of "us" fitting this profile is vastly smaller than we imagine or publicly acknowledge. Yet, a nation can dream. So the American dream has been winnowed to the sole task of maintaining systemic white supremacy in our politics and our government. When Obamacare reasserted the government's role in health care, efforts to redefine deserving Americans were reinvigorated.

Even those of "us" who live in (blue) cities are getting pushed out of the national family. Throughout the campaign, Trump used the term "inner city" to dog whistle to MAGA Americans his racial, economic, political, and religious exclusions.

Trump is no saint, but his personal foibles are forgiven because he continues to pursue the religious right's unforgiving agenda. The Trump administration and party are stacked with constituents who see poor health as a moral failing. In October of 2017, Betty Price, a Georgia state representative and the wife of the former secretary of Health and Human Services, Tom Price, felt comfortable enough to ask on video if quarantining people who are HIV positive was an option to address Atlanta's high number of predominantly young, African American HIV patients. "It seems to me it's almost frightening the number of people who are living that are potentially carriers, well they are carriers, with the potential to spread, whereas in the past they died more readily and then at that point they are not posing a risk," she said.

Later, under national criticism, she walked back her comments. But the point remains clear: those who fall outside a strict definition of America are not worthy of protection or even basic human rights. (It's worth noting, while we're on the subject of morality, that Tom Price resigned from HHS after he was criticized for his exorbitant use of private jets for government work. Tax dollars are, apparently, only for the deserving, like Price.)

Our white Christian nation is under threat, so the narrative goes, from those brown, needy, gay drug users in the inner city. Betty Price's construction of Americanness is clear. She's not asking how we care for ourselves and our public health, but how we protect "ourselves" from "them." Yet, we should know from the past what happens when we let a nationalistic politics of purity and prejudice determine public health policy.

Race clearly played a role in the 1980s, when the term "crack baby" was coined. Vann R. Newkirk II wrote in the *Atlantic* in 2017, "'Crack baby' brings to mind hopeless, damaged children with birth defects and intellectual disabilities who would inevitably grow into criminals . . . unthinking black mothers who'd knowingly exposed their children to the ravages of cocaine." Blame the addict, science and our politicians told us. "The term made brutes out of people of color who were living through wave after wave of what were *then* the deadliest drug epidemics in history," Newkirk writes.

As *On the Media*'s Brooke Gladstone has noted, you can fix the date of the nation's modern war on drugs to Nixon's declaration in 1971, when he designated drug abuse as America's enemy number one. The Nixon administration set the tone for future epidemics by using addiction to target and "disrupt" communities the administration saw as opponents.

As Nixon's chief of domestic policy, John Erlichman, told writer Dan Baum, "We knew we couldn't make it illegal to be either against the [Vietnam] war or black [*sic*], but by getting the public to associate the hippies with marijuana and blacks with heroin, and then criminalizing both heavily, we could disrupt those communities," Ehrlichman said. "We could arrest their leaders, raid their homes, break up their meetings, and vilify them night after night on the evening news. Did we know we were lying about the drugs? Of course we did."

Gladstone notes that subsequent administrations have all consistently spent more on enforcement than treatment. As a result, wrote the *Chicago Tribune*'s Dahleen Glanton in August of 2017, during the 1980s crack epidemic, "Hundreds of thousands of African-Americans across the country ended up with prison records because of minor drug violations . . . a legacy that continues to contribute to the decay of poor, urban communities."

Today, with the opioid epidemic, we see a stark contrast to the racialized and sexualized reactions during the crack and AIDS epidemics. According to a 2015 Kaiser Family Foundation study, twenty-seven thousand of the thirty-three thousand who died the previous year from opioid overdose were white.

What's different about today's opioid epidemic is that, instead of blaming white people the way we blamed Black people in the past, we've found ourselves a new devil: Big Pharma. It took an epidemic striking the white Christian heartland for the dominant narrative to redirect blame and turn against, of all Republican-heralded things, profitable corporations.

In a recent blockbuster for *Esquire* magazine, Christopher Glazek went after the Sackler family, who amassed billions of dollars by manufacturing and selling OxyContin. In the piece, Glazek writes, attacking what he calls "the chronic pain movement":

> As the decade wore on, these organizations, which critics have characterized as front groups for the pharmaceutical industry, began pressuring health regulators to make pain "the fifth vital sign"—a number, measured on a subjective ten-point scale, to be asked and recorded at every doctor's visit. As an internal strategy document put it, Purdue's ambition was to "attach an emotional aspect to noncancer pain" so that doctors would feel pressure to "treat it more seriously and aggressively." The company rebranded pain relief as a sacred right: a universal narcotic entitlement available not only to the terminally ill but to every American.

I have no interest in defending the Sacklers or the pharmaceutical industry, but jeopardizing the lives and health of pain sufferers to do so is a dark and immoral path for journalists and politicians. Not least because tighter restrictions on Pharma and doctors won't solve the problem. In fact it's already making it worse, and not just for those who legitimately need pain relief. Now that prescription pain medications are becoming scarcer, some addicts are going straight to heroin. Addiction is no more the product of easy-access pills than national impurity is the product of easy-access women.

The government's crackdown on prescription painkillers has dried up the surplus, but now doctors who fear the CDC's strict new guidelines are cutting off patients with chronic pain. People are suffering. But we continue to turn a deaf ear to pain and suffering because our political system is still committed to the feeling of moral superiority that such judgment gives us. In September of 2016 I wrote about our nation's already muted response to pain treatment, particularly in women. Suffering is a part of our national—and Christian—narrative: it makes us great, it teaches us lessons, brings us back to God and moral behavior. Which in turn should make our nation healthy, whole, and great again. Except it doesn't.

Which brings us to October 2017's fracas over Trump's appointee for drug czar, Pennsylvania representative Tom Marino. A *Washington Post*/*60 Minutes* report fingered Marino for supporting the Ensuring Patient Access and Effective Drug Enforcement Act, passed under Obama. The report claims that the bill curtailed the DEA's drug enforcement efforts and therefore "helped pump more painkillers into parts of the country that were already in the middle of the opioid crisis."

Democrats were left to rail against Marino as soft on drug enforcement, never a good stance for them, however common. "I was horrified when I read the *Washington Post* piece and cannot believe the last administration did not sound the alarm on how harmful that bill would be for our efforts to effectively fight the opioid epidemic," Senator Joe Manchin, a Democrat from West Virginia, said. Senator Claire McCaskill, a Democrat from Missouri, has promised to repeal the law, passed in 2016 under President Obama. (To the growing list of lessons the Democratic Party refuses to learn, add the debilitating and ineffectual impact of increased drug enforcement.)

The default, then, on how to address the opioid epidemic is the same as it ever was—with a twist: increase DEA and drug enforcement power. The only difference this round is where the blame is placed; not on the predominantly white users, as Black addicts were blamed and penalized during the crack epidemic, but on pharmaceutical companies and doctors who manufacture and prescribe opioids. Nicholas Kristof's recent *New York Times* column, "Drug Dealers in Lab Coats," is a perfect case in reactionary point. He writes: "The opioid crisis unfolded because greedy people—Latin drug lords and American pharma executives alike—lost their humanity when they saw the astounding profits that could be made."

However little sympathy doctors and Pharma deserve, like Manchin and McCaskill, Kristof is barking up the wrong tree. Here's how Maia Szalavitz, a neuroscience journalist and author of *Unbroken Brain: A Revolutionary New Way of Understanding Addiction*, described Pharma's role in the opioid crisis to me in an email exchange last month: the epidemic was originally driven by the "diversion" of liberally prescribed pain medication. Studies show that "70 percent of those who misuse these drugs were getting them from friends, family, dealers." Pain patients weren't misusing their liberally prescribed pain medications; they were letting them get into other people's hands. Think, perhaps, of a grandfather who gets seventy-five "oxys" after surgery and takes only three of them; the rest are left on a shelf where an experimental teenage grandchild could easily find them. The problem isn't the doctor, the grandfather, anyone's morals, the pills, or even the company producing and advertising them: the problem is our willful misunderstanding and mistreatment of addiction.

"Most 'addicted pain patients' are people with a past or current history of addiction," Szalavitz told me, "many of whom deliberately sought doctors for the purpose of getting drugs;

others got readdicted after having alcohol or other drug problems in their youth." Szalavitz added that "90 percent of all addictions start with recreational use in the teens or early twenties." Addiction will find a drug, whether it's alcohol, crack, or opioids. It is a medical condition, one that requires and deserves medical treatment, not punishment, and certainly not self-righteous promises of redemption.

———————

Addiction is the cause of opioid use, not personal character, not the drug, and not the drug maker or prescriber. "The real roots of addiction lie in child trauma, mental illness, and despair and we've done nothing about them," Maia Szalavitz told me. We've been getting this wrong for centuries.

Citing Szalavitz's work in an article I wrote about Prince's death for the *Guardian* in 2016, I wrote:

> American history is rife with "drug panics," from opium in the 1700s to alcohol in the early 1900s, from coke in the 1970s and crack in the late '80s to methamphetamines in the early aughts. From the beginning, the way that users have been viewed has affected drug regulation and treatment, often with disastrous results.

Those disastrous results are continued addiction epidemics. The drugs are ever changing, but the problem, as we address it, sadly remains the same: an issue of misplaced morality. We'd rather blame anything other than our own failure to address the causes of addiction. So we give moral jurisdiction to law enforcement, to drug makers, to Donald Trump, to God.

Churches across the country are stepping up to support addicts, either by giving over their basements to AA and Al-Anon meetings or by giving over their pews to moral lessons for addicts. As Deborah Becker wrote at WBUR in April:

> The issue of spirituality and addiction treatment is complicated and controversial. The vast majority—by some estimates more than 85 percent—of substance use disorder treatment in the U.S. is based on the 12 steps. Among other things, the steps ask adherents to believe that a "power greater than ourselves can restore us to sanity."

Some faith leaders are realizing that support can't come from a place of moral judgment. But the shaming of individual choice and the emphasis on "personal responsibility" that has long been applied to addiction often prevails. Becker observes Tom Thelin, a former Catholic priest who now runs a treatment center in Massachusetts, telling a group of recovering addicts, "In many of our groups we talk about: What is the purpose of our life? And I know it's not to suffer and die miserable. Our purpose in life is literally to live a life of purpose. That is, in giving we receive. This addiction is the exact opposite—it's all about getting for ourselves."

Yet, if addiction is a disease, why don't we treat it as we do other diseases? With science rather than spiritualized self-help? As Szalavitz wrote at *Huffington Post* in March, there are two reasons: the existing mobilization of law enforcement against use and possession and the prevalence of a spiritual and moral failing model of treatment and recovery. These are ineffectual approaches, yet we have no better solutions because most of the population still doesn't see addiction as a medical problem. And thus addiction—wave after wave of heartbreaking drug epidemics—continues.

So, again we ask, just as Hall in Henrico County, Virginia, asked, "Where is recovery at in all this?" Nowhere. In past drug epidemic iterations, the white, Christian, hetero powers that be had an easier time blaming the victims—the evils were starker thanks to differences in race and class. Today we've only managed to find a new and false cause. As long as we continue in this way, so too will addiction, regardless of the drug du jour or the race of the person addicted.

PART IV

Divine Agon: Theology & Philosophy

Introduction

If religion, at its core, is a quest for all-encompassing meaning (personal and collective, social and cosmic, in this world and the next), what makes it philosophically fascinating is the multitude of paths that people are willing to undertake. One can choose the highway of an established world religion, just as one can opt for the winding country road of heresy or the narrow path of a demanding spiritual discipline. The paths offered are overwhelming—we can join churches, sects, heresies, informal groups, new-age clubs, apocalyptic movements, and fundamentalisms of all varieties. And yet whatever choice we end up making, it will be motivated by the same fundamental quest for meaning. The final section of this volume seeks to examine a small sample of the disconcerting diversity of ways (including doctrines, schools, and interpretations) we have at our disposal when it comes to approaching the divine.

In "Christ's Rabble," originally published in *Commonweal Magazine*, David Bentley Hart recounts how while translating the New Testament, he came to seriously question the idea that there are, or can be, any Christians in our world today. After spending some time among the early adherents to Christianity, he

225

finds it reasonable to ask "not whether we *are* Christians (by that standard, all fall short), but whether in our wildest imaginings we could ever desire to be the kind of persons that the New Testament describes as fitting the pattern of life in Christ."

One of the indirect implications of Hart's piece is that Christian identity is a fluid, evolving thing. Marcus Rediker, in his *Aeon* piece "The Forgotten Prophet," illustrates precisely this point. The radical, colorful Quaker Benjamin Lay (the "Forgotten Prophet" in the title) found slave ownership absolutely incompatible with being a Christian at a time when most of his fellow Christians wouldn't find any problem with it at all. That the meaning of Christianity is always evolving is further illustrated by Jim Hinch in his piece "Evangelicals Are Losing the Battle for the Bible. And They're Just Fine with That," originally published in the *Los Angeles Review of Books*.

To complicate matters, space can alter faith as much time does, particularly when considering interactions with local cultures. When Christianity grew roots in Mexico, it was no longer the same religion that left Spain. We get some of its local flavor in Daisy Vargas's piece "La Llorona Visits the American Academy of Religion: A Tribute to Luís de León," originally published in the *Revealer*. Obviously, such considerations do not apply just to Christianity. Other major religions also change in time and space, and according to local cultures and politics. In his *Aeon* essay "Against Muslim Unity," Faisal Devji makes a case for the significant internal diversity of Islam. There is not one type of Muslim in the world but many, Devji concludes, and imposing some kind of artificial unity upon them would be not only impractical but also undesirable.

In "Their Bloods Cry Out from the Ground," originally published in *Tablet*, Shira Telushkin recounts the mass shooting that took place at the Tree of Life synagogue in Pittsburgh in October 2018. Telushkin places the attack in a long, blooded history of persecution and intolerance: "For millennia, Jews have been collecting and burying the blood of our martyrs. This week, the Jews of Pittsburgh have joined that history." We celebrate and praise diversity, easily taking it for granted. There is an agon in making sure that such diversity is cherished and celebrated against those who would wish it ill, for all of our theological speculation is for naught if at its core it doesn't engender love of our neighbor.

CHAPTER 21

Christ's Rabble

David Bentley Hart

For two and a half years I have been working on a translation of the New Testament for Yale University Press, which I recently completed. It should not have taken me that long, but an extended spell of ill health disrupted my life just as the project was getting under way. The only good result of this is that the delay forced me to take an even more reflective and deliberate approach to the task than I might otherwise have done; this, in turn, caused me to absorb certain conclusions about the world of the early church at a deeper level than I could have anticipated. Most of them I already knew, admittedly, if often as little more than shadows glimpsed through a veil of conventional theological habits of thought—for instance, how stark the dualism really is, in Paul's letters and elsewhere in the New Testament, between "flesh" and "spirit," or how greatly formulations that seem to imply universal salvation outnumber those that appear to threaten an ultimate damnation for the wicked. Still, none of that *surprised* me; it merely roused me from my complacent assumption that, simply by virtue of having read the text in Greek for many years, I had a natural feel for its tone.

What did surprise me, however, was the degree to which the whole experience left me with a deeply melancholy, almost Kierkegaardian sense that most of us who go by the name of "Christians" ought to give up the pretense of wanting to be *Christian*—at least, if by that word one means not simply someone who is baptized or who adheres to a particular set of religious observances and beliefs, but more or less what Nietzsche meant when he said that there has been only one Christian in human history and that he had died on the cross. In that sense, I think it reasonable to ask not whether we *are* Christians (by that standard, all fall short), but whether in our wildest imaginings we could ever desire to be the kind of persons that the New Testament describes as fitting the pattern of life in Christ. And I think the fairly obvious answer is that we could not. I do not mean merely that most of us find the moral requirements laid out in Christian Scripture a little onerous, though of course we do. Therein lies the deep comfort provided by the magisterial Protestant fantasy that the apostle Paul inveighed against something called "works righteousness" in favor of a purely extrinsic "justification" by grace—which, alas, he did not. He rejected only the notion that one might be "shown righteous" by works of the law—ritual observances like circumcision or keeping kosher—but he also quite clearly insisted, as did Christ, that all will be judged in the end according their deeds (Romans 2:1–16 and 4:10–12, 1 Corinthians 3:12–15, 2 Corinthians 5:10, Philippians 2:16, and so on). Rather, I mean that most of us would find Christians truly cast in the New Testament mold fairly obnoxious: civically reprobate, ideologically unsound, economically destructive, politically irresponsible, socially discreditable, and really just a bit indecent.

Perhaps my melancholy was deepened by an accident of timing. The final stage of my work on the translation coincided with my involvement in a series of public debates that I initiated by writing a short column for First Things praising Pope Francis and his recent encyclical *Laudato si'*, and that I prolonged when I contributed another article to the same journal arguing for the essential incompatibility of Christianity and capitalist culture. My basic argument was that a capitalist culture is, of necessity, a secularist culture, no matter how long the quaint customs and intuitions of folk piety may persist among some of its citizens; that secularism simply is capitalism in its full cultural manifestation; that late capitalist "consumerism"—with its attendant ethos of voluntarism, exuberant and interminable acquisitiveness, self-absorption, "lust of the eyes," and moral relativism—is not an accidental accretion upon an essentially benign economic system, but the inevitable result of the most fundamental capitalist values. Not everyone concurred. The most representative statements of the contrary position were two earnest articles in the *Public Discourse* by Samuel Gregg, neither of which addressed my actual arguments, but both of which correctly identified my hostility to libertarian apologetics. And on at least one point Gregg did have me dead to rights: I did indeed say that the New Testament, alarmingly enough, condemns great personal wealth not merely as a moral danger, but as an *intrinsic* evil. No, he rejoined with calm certainty, it is not wealth as such that the New Testament condemns, but only a spiritually unhealthy preoccupation with it (the idolatry of riches, wealth misused, wealth immorally gained);

riches in and of themselves, he insisted, are neither good nor bad. This seems an eminently reasonable argument, I suppose. Certainly we have all heard it before, almost as a truism.

Here, however, my more than two years laboring in the vineyards of the Koine Greek had rendered me immune to the reasonable view of things. For, while Gregg had common sense on his side, I had the actual biblical texts on mine, and they are so unambiguous that it is almost comical that anyone can doubt their import. Admittedly, many translations down the centuries have had an emollient effect on a few of the New Testament's severer pronouncements. But this is an old story. Clement of Alexandria may have been the first—back when the faith had just begun to spread widely among the more comfortably situated classes in the empire—to apply a reassuring gloss to the raw rhetoric of Scripture on wealth and poverty. He distinguished the poverty that matters (humility, renunciation, spiritual purity, generosity) from the poverty that does not (actual material indigence) and assured propertied Christians that, so long as they cultivated the former, they need never submit to the latter. And throughout Christian history, even among the few who bothered to consult Scripture on the matter, this has generally been the tacit interpretation of Christ's (and Paul's and James's) condemnations of the wealthy and acquisitive. In the early modern period came the Reformation, and this—whatever else it may have been—was a movement toward a form of Christianity well suited to the needs of the emerging middle class, and to the spiritual complacency that a culture of increasing material security dearly required of its religion. Now all moral anxiety became a kind of spiritual pathology, the heresy of "works righteousness," sheer Pelagianism. Grace set us free not only from works of the law, but from the spiritual agony of seeking to become holy by our deeds. In a sense, the good news announced by Scripture was that Christ had come to save us from the burden of Christianity.

Perhaps that is a bit unfair. It is, at any rate, impossible not to be moved by the Protestant sanctification of the ordinary. There is something delightful in discovering, as Kierkegaard did, the figure of the "Knight of Faith" in a plump, contented burgher happily strolling home, his mind set upon nothing but the roast beef awaiting him there. This spiritual heroism of the everyday is so attractive an idea that it may constitute Protestantism's single greatest imaginative contribution to Christian culture as a whole. Even for a modern Catholic like G. K. Chesterton, one of the greatest spiritual advantages of "the faith" over the creeds of other peoples was its robust appetite for "beef and beer"—a sentiment that, on the surface, has a kind of merry medievalism about it, but that few medieval Christians would have found intelligible. I certainly find it deeply appealing. But if, as its proponents insist, it is indeed a genuine unfolding of some logic implicit in the gospel, it was a logic utterly invisible to those who wrote the Christian Scriptures. Because one thing in remarkably short supply in the New Testament is common sense. The gospels, the epistles, Acts, Revelation—all of them are relentless torrents of exorbitance and extremism: commands to become as perfect as God in his heaven and to live as insouciantly as lilies in their field; condemnations of a roving eye as equivalent to adultery and of evil thoughts toward another as equivalent to murder; injunctions to sell all one's possessions and to give the proceeds to the poor; and demands that one hate one's parents for the kingdom's sake and leave the dead to bury the dead. This extremism is not merely an occasional hyperbolic presence in the texts; it is their entire cultural and spiritual atmosphere. The New Testament emerges from a cosmos ruled by malign celestial principalities (conquered by Christ but powerful to the end) and torn between spirit and flesh (the one, according to Paul, longing for God, the other opposing him utterly). There are no comfortable medians in these latitudes, no areas of shade. Everything is cast in the harsh light of final judgment, and that judgment is absolute. In regard to all these texts, the qualified, moderate, commonsense interpretation is always false.

———

It is undeniably true that there are texts that condemn an idolatrous obsession with wealth, and that might be taken as saying nothing more than that. At least, 1 Timothy 6:17–19 is often cited as an example of this—though (see below) it probably should not be. Perhaps, to avoid trying to serve both God and mammon, one need only have the right *attitude* toward riches. But if this were all the New Testament had to say on the matter, then one would expect those texts to be balanced out by others affirming the essential benignity of riches honestly procured and well used. Yet this is precisely what we do not find. Instead, they are balanced out by still more uncompromising comminations of wealth *in and of itself.* Certainly Christ condemned not only an unhealthy preoccupation with riches, but the getting and keeping of riches as such. The most obvious citation from all three synoptic gospels would be the story of the rich young ruler who could not bring himself to part with his fortune for the sake of the kingdom, and of Christ's astonishing remark about camels passing through needles' eyes more easily than rich men through the kingdom's gate. As for the question the disciples then put to Christ, it should probably be translated not as "Who then can be saved?" or "Can anyone be saved?" but rather "Then can any [of them, the rich] be saved?" To which the sobering reply is that it is humanly impossible, but that by divine power *even* a rich man might be spared.

But one can look everywhere in the gospels for confirmation of the message. Christ clearly means what he says when quoting the prophet: he has been anointed by God's spirit to preach good tidings *to the poor* (Luke 4:18). To the prosperous, the tidings he bears are decidedly grim: "Woe to you who are rich, for you are receiving your comfort in full; woe to you who are full fed, for you shall hunger; woe to you who are now laughing, for you shall mourn and weep" (Luke 6:24–25). Again, perhaps many of the practices Christ condemns in the rulers of his time are merely misuses of power and property, but that does not begin to exhaust the rhetorical force of his teachings as a whole. He not only demands that we give freely to all who ask from us (Matthew 5:42), and to do so with such prodigality that one hand is ignorant of the other's largesse (Matthew 6:3); he explicitly *forbids* storing up earthly wealth—not merely storing it up too obsessively—and allows instead only the hoarding of the treasures of heaven (Matthew 6:19–20). It is truly amazing how rarely Christians seem to notice that these counsels are stated, quite decidedly, as commands. After all, as Mary says, part of the saving promise of the gospel is that the Lord "has filled the hungry with good things and sent the rich away starving" (Luke 1:53).

Of the compilation of pericopes, however, there is no end. What is most important to recognize is that all these pronouncements on wealth and poverty belong to a moral sensibility that saturates the pages of the New Testament. It is there, for instance, in Paul's condemnations of *pleonektia* (often translated as "greed," but really meaning all acquisitive desire), or in the pastoral epistles' condemnation of *aischrokerdes* (often translated as "greed for base gain," but really referring to the sordidness of seeking financial profit for oneself). James perhaps states the matter most clearly:

> Come now, you who are rich, weep, howling at the miseries coming upon you; your riches are corrupted and moths have consumed your clothes; your gold and silver have corroded, and their rust will be a witness against you and will consume your flesh like fire. You have stored up treasure in the Last Days! See, the wages you have given so late to the laborers who have harvested your fields cry aloud, and the cries of those who have harvested your fields have entered the ear of the Lord Sabaoth. You have lived in luxury, and lived upon the earth in self-indulgence. You have fattened your hearts on a day of slaughter. You have condemned— have murdered—the upright; he did not stand against you. (James 5:1–6)

Now, we can read this, if we wish, as a dire warning issued only to those wealthy persons who have acted unjustly toward their employees, and who live too self-indulgently. But if we do so, we are in fact inverting the text. Earlier in the epistle, James has already asserted that, while the "poor brother" should exult in how God has lifted him up, the "rich man" (who, it seems, scarcely merits the name of "brother") should rejoice in being "made low" or "impoverished," as otherwise he will wither and vanish away like a wildflower scorched by the sun (1:9–11). He has also gone on to remind his readers that "God has chosen the poor to be rich in faith and to inherit the Kingdom," and that the rich, by contrast, must be recognized as oppressors and persecutors and blasphemers of Christ's holy name (2:5–7). James even warns his readers against the presumptuousness of planning to gain profits from business ventures in the city (4:13–14). And this whole leitmotif merely reaches its crescendo in those later verses quoted above, which plainly condemn not only those whose wealth is gotten unjustly, but *all* who are rich as oppressors of workers and lovers of luxury. Property is theft, it seems. Fair or not, the text does not distinguish good wealth from bad—any more than Christ did.

I imagine this is why the early Christians were communists, as the book of Acts quite explicitly states. If these are indeed the last days, as James says—if everything is now seen in the light of final judgment—then storing up possessions for ourselves is the height of imprudence. And I imagine this is also why subsequent generations of Christians have not, as a rule, been communists: the last days seem to be taking quite some time to elapse, and we have families to raise in the meantime. But at the dawn of the faith little thought was given to providing a decent life in this world for the long term. Thus the first converts in Jerusalem after the resurrection, as the price of becoming Christians, sold all their property and possessions and distributed the proceeds to those in need, and then fed themselves by sharing their resources in common meals (Acts 2:43–46). To be a follower of the Way was to renounce every claim to private property and to consent to communal ownership of everything (Acts 4:32). Barnabas, on becoming a Christian, sold his field and handed over all the money to the apostles (Acts 4:35)—though Ananias and Sapphira did not, with somewhat unfortunate consequences.

Even those verses from 1 Timothy 6 that I mentioned are not nearly as mild and moderate as we tend to think they are. Earlier in the chapter, the text reminds us that we bring nothing into this world and can take nothing with us when we leave it, and tells us to content ourselves with having enough food and clothing. It also tells us that all who seek wealth—not simply all who procure it unjustly—have ensnared themselves in desires that will lead to their ruin: because "a fondness for money is a root of all evils," and those who reach out for wealth have gone astray (*apeplanēthēsan*) from the faith and girdled themselves about with piercing pains (6:7–10). True, verse 17 merely advises the rich not to be "arrogant" or "in high spirits" (depending on how one interprets it), and not to put their trust in wealth's "uncertainty" (or, better, in "the hiddenness" of their riches) rather than in the lavishness of God's providence. But verse 18 goes further and tells them not only to make themselves rich in good works, but also to become—well, here the customary translations are along the lines of "generous" (*eumetadotous*) and "sharing" (*koinōnikous*), but the better renderings would be something like "persons readily distributing" their goods, in the former case, and something like "communalists" or "communists" or "persons having all their possessions in common," in the latter. (A property that is *koinōnikon* is something held in common or corporately, and therefore a person who is *koinōnikos* is certainly not just someone who occasionally makes donations at his own discretion.) Only thus, says verse 19, can the wealthy now "store up" a good foundation for the age that is coming, and reach out to take hold of "the life that is real." And this would seem to have been the social philosophy of the early church in general. When Christianity arrived in Edessa, for instance, its adherents promptly became a kind of mendicant order, apparently owning nothing much at all. In the words of that very early manual of Christian life, the *Didache*, a Christian must never claim that anything is his own property, but must own all things *communally* with his brethren (4:9–12).

Which brings me back to where I began. I confess I do not really know what to make of these observations, or how to deal with the more onerous prescriptions and harsher judgments of the New Testament. Most of us in the modern West, by comparison to other peoples and times, might well think of ourselves as rich. Nor can I pretend ever to have embraced poverty myself—except in the sense that an unguarded jaw might be said to embrace the fist that strikes it. I do know, however, that I have no good grounds for treating those prescriptions and judgments as mere hortatory hyperbole.

Throughout the history of the church, Christians have keenly desired to believe that the New Testament affirms the kind of people we are, rather than—as is actually the case—the kind of people we are not and really would not want to be. The first, perhaps most crucial thing to understand about the earliest generations of Christians is that they were a company of extremists, radical in their rejection of the values and priorities of society not only at its most degenerate, but often at its most reasonable and decent. They were rabble. They lightly cast off all their prior loyalties and attachments: religion, empire, nation, tribe, even family. In fact, far from teaching "family values," Christ was remarkably dismissive of the family. And decent civic order, like social respectability, was apparently of no importance to him. Not only did he not promise his followers worldly success (even success in making things better for others), he told them to hope for a kingdom not of this world and promised them that in this world they would win only rejection, persecution, tribulation, and failure. Yet he instructed them also to take no thought for the morrow.

This was the pattern of life the early Christians believed had been given them by Christ. As I say, I doubt we would think highly of their kind if we met them today. Fortunately for us, those who have tried to be like them have always been few. Clement of Alexandria may have been making an honest attempt to accommodate the gospel to the realities of a Christian empire, but it was those other Egyptians, the Desert Fathers, who took the gospel at its word. But how many of us can live like that? Who can imitate that obstinacy and perversity? To live as the New Testament requires, we should have to become strangers and sojourners on the earth, to have here no enduring city, to belong to a kingdom truly not of this world.

And we surely cannot do that, can we?

CHAPTER 22

The Forgotten Prophet

Marcus Rediker

In September 1738, Benjamin Lay, a radical Quaker barely four feet tall, filled an animal bladder with bright red pokeberry juice, then tucked it into the secret compartment of a book. He donned a military uniform and a sword, covered himself in an overcoat, hid the book, and set off from his home in Abington, Pennsylvania, for Burlington, New Jersey, where the Yearly Meeting of Philadelphia Quakers was being held, a gathering of the colony's most powerful Quakers. Lay had a message for them.

Quakers have no formal ministers, so congregants speak as the spirit moves them. Lay was a man of large and unruly spirit. In a thundering voice that belied his stature, he announced that slaveholding was the greatest sin in the world. He threw off his overcoat to reveal his military uniform. The crowd gasped. He raised the book above his head, unsheathed his sword, and declared: "God will take vengeance on those who oppress their fellow creatures." He ran his sword through the book. The bladder exploded in a gush of blood, spattering the slaveholders sitting nearby. A group of Quaker men grabbed up Lay—he did not resist—and threw him out of the meetinghouse into the street. The soldier of God had delivered a chilling prophecy: slave owning would destroy the Quaker faith.

Three weeks earlier, Lay had published his first and only book, *All Slave-Keepers That Keep the Innocent in Bondage, Apostates.* Here he detailed his struggle against wealthy and powerful Quaker slaveowners to abolish what he considered an evil institution. Two full generations before a robust antislavery movement would emerge in America and Great Britain in the 1780s, he demanded an immediate, uncompromising, and unconditional end to slavery all around the world, joining his protest to the resistance of hundreds of thousands of enslaved Africans in the New World, who were always the first abolitionists. Lay imagined not only an end to slavery, but a way of living outside the marketplace of capitalism, without violence to any living creature. He lived in a cave, made his own food and clothes, and practiced vegetarianism. How did this man of common means and ordinary background arrive at the conclusion that slavery must be abolished at a time when so few others did? How did he break through to this very unusual position for his day and age? How did he become a revolutionary?

Lay's radicalism can be thought of as a rope of four tightly braided strands. The first strand is a radical variant of Quakerism; this was the core of his very being. The second was seafaring, and the culture of the sea that he discovered during his working life as a sailor for a dozen years. Third was his direct contact with the enslaved people of Barbados in his time on that island during 1718–1720. Fourth was a kind of "commoning" radicalism that he took up later in life, in the 1730s, based in part on his reading of ancient philosophy, especially the Cynic philosophers of Greece and Rome and their founder, Diogenes. These four strands combined to make Lay a determined radical who against all odds helped to forge the world's first modern social movement: abolitionism.

Lay was born in 1682 in Copford, a village near Colchester in England; he was a third-generation Quaker. His grandfather and grandmother had joined the Quakers during their formative years, in 1655, and his parents followed in the faith. His father, William, was especially active. Like many children born to humble rural families in this sheep-farming and textile region, he worked as a shepherd. He loved the gentle hills of pastoral Essex and the animals he cared for there. It was, he later noted, the best work that a human being could do.

Even though Lay was born more than two decades after the conclusion of the English Civil War, that grand convulsion shaped his life in profound ways. As parliamentary forces led by Oliver Cromwell clashed with the royalist followers of King Charles I, censorship collapsed and radical Protestant groups such as the Levellers, Diggers, Ranters, Seekers, and Quakers rushed into print proposing their own solutions to the problems of the day. They preached radical messages of equality and millenarianism, sometimes urging that the world itself be turned upside down. And they articulated democratic principles, arguing for their broad adoption throughout English society. Theirs were the first real critiques of slavery, which at the time was not yet fully racialized. These radicals attacked the press gang, the loss of the commons, forced labor, indentured servitude, and African slavery. This was the bubbling cauldron of revolutionary thought from which Lay's Quakerism was born, the first strand of his radicalism.

The early Quakers formed an intense and egalitarian religious community based on the notion of a shared "inward light," the spark of divinity that resides in each and every person. Led by James Nayler and George Fox, the latter now remembered as the founding father of Quakerism, they challenged the class order of their times, insisting on spiritual equality and subversively refusing to remove their hats to their so-called social superiors.

The more radical Nayler was the movement's leading theologian, more sophisticated than Fox, and more given to direct action and elaborate street theater, which became a Quaker staple. In 1656, Nayler reenacted the return of Jesus Christ to Jerusalem as women sang hosannas and lay flowers in his path. Parliament saw this as an opportunity to get rid of a dangerously charismatic preacher who stirred up both religious and political resistance from below. They decided that his theater constituted blasphemy and ordered that his forehead be branded with a *B*, his tongue be drilled through with a hot metal rod, and the flesh of his back be torn away by repeated floggings in both Bristol and London. Nayler never recovered from these vicious punishments and died a broken man in 1660.

Years later, Lay carried on his tradition of radical street theater. He also drew on the practice of John Perrot, who advised fellow Quakers not to take off their hats even when praying to God, who was, after all, within them; he was simply their equal.

In 1660, Charles II ascended to power, and England became a monarchy again. The pendulum swung the other way: censorship returned, and many Quakers were persecuted and banished. Fox responded by implementing a series of reforms in the Quaker community during the 1660s and '70s that would root out the radicals, increase group cohesion, and turn a small revolutionary group into a robust, long-living Christian sect. Even though Lay was born twenty-two years later, he was a throwback to that early, radical phase of Quaker history. In some ways, he was the last radical of the English revolution as he channeled the militant ideas and practices of Nayler and Perrot throughout his revolutionary life.

The second strand of Lay's radicalism took shape in 1703, when the twenty-one-year-old was set to inherit his father's farmstead in Copford. Ever the rebel, he turned his back on the farm and the animals that he loved and set off for London—and from there for the high seas, where he became a sailor. His diminutive stature made him a valuable member of a ship's crew: being smaller and more agile, he could do many things a sailor of average size could not do, such as scampering around in the top of the ship or getting into otherwise unreachable corners.

Lay lived on tall ships amid a motley crew for twelve years, and this is likely how he got his education, as literate sailors often taught their illiterate brothers how to read. He sailed around the world and acquired a rich cosmopolitan experience and an initiation into a longstanding tradition of multiethnic radicalism at sea. He understood the fundamental truth of seafaring: every day, your life is in the hands of your fellow sailors. The occupation requires strict solidarity, regardless of who your fellow worker might be—brown, Black, or white; English Protestant or Irish Catholic. A common sailors' phrase of the era was "One and all, we are one and all together." Lay became a citizen of the world and learned to transfer his seafaring solidarity to oppressed people around the globe.

He learned much about slavery through the stories of his fellow seamen. The sailor's yarn was an important international means of communication. Sailors sat in a circle on the main deck, picking oakum and spinning yarns, knitting themselves together as a cohesive group as they told the stories of their lives, which for several included the horrors of slavery. A couple of Lay's shipmates had been slaves themselves in Turkey or North Africa—this was not uncommon for European sailors who braved the waters of the Mediterranean. Other sailors had sailed on slavers, transporting human cargo from Africa to the Americas. What Lay remembered most vividly about these tales was the extreme violence committed against African women on the Middle Passage.

He related his seafaring experiences in his book *All Slave-Keepers . . . Apostates*, but tellingly he never talked about "race," even though this idea and its associated practices were rapidly dividing up humanity at the very moment that he wrote. Throughout the Americas, slaveowners legislated slave codes to criminalize cooperation between Black and white workers. Sensing the division inherent in the term, Lay used more neutral words to express human difference: "colour," "nation," and "people." He refused the standard trope of the day to refer to Africans as "savage" or "barbarian"; on the contrary, he reserved those descriptions for slave traders and owners of European descent. Even more importantly, in his eyes, he used biblical passages to resist the racial division of the world, emphasizing Acts 17:26: God "made of one blood all nations of men for to dwell on all the face of the earth." In other words, he said we are not different people; we are all the same people, deeply and divinely connected. This antiracializing rhetoric reflected his experience at sea, where he worked with a variety of people who were all "of one blood." Maritime solidarity was the second strand in his rope.

Lay ended his sailing days in 1718 when he decided to marry Sarah Smith, a Quaker from Deptford on the River Thames. She too was a little person. Lay had begun to quarrel with his fellow London Quakers, who were now under the sway of Fox's reforms. With his wife, Lay left for Bridgetown, a bustling port city in what was then the world's leading slave society—Barbados. There they opened up a little shop selling general merchandise on the waterfront. Lay would now see the workings of slavery with his own eyes. His contact with the brutality of the slave system and the struggles of Afro-Barbadian people produced the third strand in his rope of radicalism.

Lay watched in horror as enslaved people staggered into his shop and collapsed on the floor. Some actually died of overwork and hunger. He saw people being tortured, a common sight in Bridgetown. He saw grisly executions of slave rebels. He witnessed workers lose limbs to the machinery of the sugar factories. He got to know an enslaved cooper who committed suicide on a Sunday night, rather than endure the whippings his master administered every Monday morning. The tenderhearted Sarah was also affected by the pervasive atmosphere of violence. On her way to visit Quakers in Speightstown, ten miles north of Bridgetown, she came upon an African man hanging by a chain, trembling as he was suspended above a pool of blood. She was struck dumb by the horror of the scene. Once she recovered, she went into the Quaker home where the slave owners explained that the man had run away from the plantation and must now be taught a lesson for all of the enslaved to see. The Lays were deeply shaken by the cruelty they saw all around them.

They responded to the situation by feeding the hungry: they invited slaves to their home on Sundays, the day of rest, for meals and fellowship. Word of this kindness spread, and the Lay home became a kind of meetinghouse for hundreds of enslaved people, who not only partook of the food but listened to the couple denounce the slave system that was the source of their misery. The wealthy slave-owning master class of Barbados got wind of the meetings and immediately applied pressure to the Lays to leave the island. Their antislavery ideas and even their basic human kindness made them enemies of the country. As the elite moved to banish them from Barbados, the Lays decided on their own to leave. Neither had the stomach to live among such violent depravity as all other whites on the island chose to do.

The couple returned to Colchester for a few years, and then left England for the last time. They sailed to Philadelphia in 1732. When Lay discovered slavery in the Quaker city of Philadelphia, where at the time about one in eleven was enslaved, and when he realized that many of these slaves were owned by wealthy Quakers, he flew into a rage. He redoubled his antislavery commitment and confronted Quaker slave owners in meeting after meeting, eventually getting himself disowned from the Quaker community for the ardor and direct action of his protests involving the symbolic spattering of blood on the heads and bodies of slave owners in 1738.

In *All Slave-Keepers . . . Apostates*, he spoke directly to Quaker merchants involved in the slave trade, charging them with the deaths of many innocent Africans. Warming to the fight, he added that, for all he knew, the merchants might have killed "many Hundreds of Thousands." The Trans-Atlantic Slave Trade Database shows that in 1738, the very year that Lay wrote these words, more than five hundred thousand Africans had already died as a result of transoceanic slaving. Lay drew on his background in seafaring to denounce slave traders as murderers. He was probably the first person to make a chilling allegation that would later be commonplace among abolitionists.

In Philadelphia and especially in the town of Abington, where the couple moved in 1734 (Sarah died only a year later), Lay not only carried out his militant actions against slaveowners, he added a final and distinctive strand to his rope of radicalism: he withdrew from the capitalist economy, adopted a radical lifestyle, and lived off the land as a commoner. In one sense, Lay returned to his rural roots in Copford, and in another he not only embraced but expanded the Quaker commitment to a simple, unpretentious life, the "plain style" as it was called. He lived in a cave, grew his own food, and made his own clothes. His goal was to be a living example of equality with all living things, subsisting on "the innocent fruits of the earth"—that is, without exploiting any human beings or animals. He refused complicity with any form of oppression.

Lay was thus the first to articulate a modern politics of consumption. He boycotted all slave-produced commodities, which always disguised the horrific conditions under which they were produced. Anyone who dropped a cube of sugar into a cup of tea was thereby complicit with the sugar planters of Barbados and the tea-plantation owners in East Asia, with their violent means of creating wealth. To refuse sugar, in turn, was to express solidarity with oppressed enslaved workers in the Caribbean, and to acknowledge that sugar was made with their blood. The modern global movement against sweatshops is based on the same idea.

An avid reader, Lay followed two writers on his path to commoning radicalism. He so dearly loved Thomas Tryon's early argument for vegetarianism, *A Way to Health, Long Life and*

Happiness (1683), that he carried the heavy tome with him on his travels. Tryon believed that war and violence grew from the way that human beings treated animals. Lay agreed. He saw the Quaker "inward light" in all living creatures, and therefore thought it sinful to kill and eat them. His pacifist pantheism became a source of all ethics. He even refused to use wool for clothes as this would require the violent shearing of sheep. He therefore used flax, spinning it himself in his cave and making his own clothes of tow linen.

Lay also found antecedents and inspirations for his commoning radicalism in ancient philosophy, which he read avidly. Called a "Pythagorean-Christian-Cynic philosopher" by Benjamin Franklin, Lay had a special interest in Diogenes, the founder of Cynic philosophy and a vegetarian who chose to live life in accordance with nature. Diogenes lived for a time in a *pithos*, a large jar used for storage, not unlike the small cave where Lay made his home. Both men conceived of philosophy as public action. Ideas must be acted out in visible, confrontational ways. Principles must be lived and expressed in everything one does. Lay also embraced the most fundamental idea of Cynicism: *parrhesia*, or "speaking truth to power." He repeated the Cynic saying "The love of money is the root of all evil," which had likely been spread among the early Christians by Cynic philosophers in the first place. Lay used Diogenes and other thinkers of antiquity to twist into place the last strand of his rope of radicalism, incorporating a militant, outspoken philosophy based on respect for nature.

In the end we must ask, Why is Lay unknown to us? Most members of the general public have never heard of him. Historians are little better. Even specialists on abolition have rarely read his book. How did this happen to a man who must properly be regarded as a pioneer of abolitionism, the world's first great social movement?

Quakers in the eighteenth century, led by their wealthy slave-owning elite, bear the original blame because of their unrelenting attacks on Lay. They denounced him, vilified him, and laughed at him. Worse, they cast him out, four times. He was probably the most disowned Quaker in the eighteenth century. His marginal-ization began in his own lifetime.

Historians—including eminent historians of abolition—have also played a major part in erasing Lay from our historical mem-ory. He never really fit the story they told about the abolitionist movement: "enlightened" middle- and upper-class men arrived at the rational conclusion that slavery was wrong, and hence they abolished it. Lay was from the wrong class. He was not properly educated and therefore could not be considered enlightened. His ideas were too radical, and his methods were too extreme. He must have been out of his mind. In *The Problem of Slavery in West-ern Culture* (1966), the renowned historian David Brion Davis called Lay a mentally deranged "little hunchback," which draws attention to his dwarfism and disability. These too were causes of dismissal, when in fact they should have been seen as a source of empathy for others who made up the wretched of the earth.

In the end, radical Quakerism, the solidarity of seafaring cul-ture, firsthand knowledge of the struggles of enslaved people, and a pantheistic commitment to animals and nature, all shaped by his understanding of subversive Greek philosophy, made Lay a revolutionary far ahead of his time. He deserves a central place in our history. As Americans debate who is a proper historical hero, Lay should be remembered as someone who, against all odds, stood for the highest and most humane ideals.

CHAPTER 23

Evangelicals Are Losing the Battle for the Bible. And They're Just Fine with That.

Jim Hinch

Like many evangelical Christians, AJ Zimmermann tells his conversion story with near-pointillistic detail. A twenty-five-year-old recent divinity school graduate from Southern California, Zimmermann grew up in a nonreligious household near Los Angeles with what he called "a lot of divorce" and an abusive stepfather. During his freshman year of high school, he writes:

> There was this really cute girl in my Spanish 1 class. We started talking and she invited me to go to youth group. I had no idea what that was, but I thought, "She's cute, maybe this will work out." I'd never been in that context before—guitars and music and teaching about the Bible. I just kind of sat there and I was like, "Okay, I'm open to whatever's here." And I had this sense of love and peace come out of

nowhere, and I was crying and crying, and I was just really curious about what this was.

Two days later, after learning "about Jesus and the cross and this whole salvation thing" at a second youth group meeting, Zimmermann committed his life to Christ. He became a regular churchgoer and went on to attend Azusa Pacific University, an evangelical Christian college east of Los Angeles. (The cute girl in Spanish class wound up dating his best friend.) Zimmermann graduated with a degree in biblical studies, enrolled in Azusa Pacific's seminary program, married a fellow student (they struck up a conversation in a café after eyeing each other reading theology books), and began working part-time as a youth pastor at a local church. He now directs a training program for prospective pastors at Life Pacific College, a Pentecostal seminary in San Dimas, California.

Zimmermann's prototypical evangelical experience is emblematic in one additional, unexpected way. Since graduating from high school, Zimmermann has undergone a revolution in his thinking about evangelicals' foundational text, the Bible, to the extent that he no longer regards the Bible as inerrant, dictated by God, historically accurate in all of its claims, or even internally consistent with itself. "The Bible holds high authority in my life," Zimmermann told me recently. And yet, he added,

> I think it's important to remember the intent and purpose of the biblical texts. These texts were not intending to portray exact historical fact but to show how God is moving with history, alongside people. . . . If we understand the

term inerrancy to be "without error" then no, I don't view the Bible as inerrant. . . . The Scripture is not trying to be without error. It is trying to communicate the love God has for His creation.

I was introduced to Zimmermann by one of his seminary teachers, an Azusa Pacific biblical studies professor named Karen Strand Winslow, who put me in touch with several of her students after I asked her what young evangelicals think about the Bible these days. In addition to his dismissal of biblical inerrancy, Zimmermann told me he no longer believes the biblical book of Genesis is "concerned . . . with young-versus-old-earth, literal days of creation stuff." He said biblical passages appearing to condemn homosexuality are products of their time and do not necessarily apply to present-day same-sex couples "committed in a consensual relationship." The same goes for New Testament prohibitions against women in church leadership. "We often forget that Jesus's ministry was founded by women and that the first evangelists were women," he added. Overall, Zimmermann said, the days when evangelicals defined themselves by their uncompromising style of biblical interpretation are over. "Before my generation . . . it was like, if you don't believe this doctrine, you're undermining the work of Christ on the cross. [My generation is] not as okay with the simplified answers."

Evangelical Christianity in America is in the midst of a wholesale generational, cultural, and doctrinal transformation. Confronted by a secularizing and diversifying society, evangelicals are abandoning long-held political allegiances, softening their views on sexuality, grappling with the racial divide in their churches,

and rethinking their entire approach to ministry and evangeliza-
tion. Underlying all of these developments is a more fundamental change in the way evangelicals understand and interpret their
most cherished text, the Bible. Though evangelicals proclaim
themselves—and are portrayed in most media accounts—to be
univocal followers of an inerrant, plainly interpreted Bible, in fact
there is widening diversity in their approach to Scripture. Like
Zimmermann, a growing number of evangelicals are abandoning "the simplified answers" and seeking a richer, more nuanced,
more challenging engagement with Scripture, one grounded not
in aphorisms or political ideology, but in what Zimmermann
called the deeper "truth of who God is."

This quest has led many evangelicals to revise their interpretation of key biblical passages (especially those addressing sexual or
social justice themes), downgrade parts of Scripture as historical
anachronisms, and reject the political call to arms still sounded
by a dwindling generation of conservative elders. A new evangelical theology is taking shape, one that retains the Bible as its
centerpiece, but understands it very differently. Evangelicals once
summarized their approach to Scripture with a staccato catch-
phrase: "The Bible says it. I believe it. That settles it." Today, especially among younger evangelicals, each part of that formula is
undergoing revision. "I've never been in the camp of wanting to
draw these hard lines," Zimmermann told me. He went on:

> My hard lines are sort of, "Just go with the basic statements
> of the faith." Yes, I believe in Jesus, and if people don't believe
> in Jesus, alright, there's room for conversation there. I never
> want to be the one to count someone out. I don't think that's

my job. What I've seen in the Scriptures is to love, and love, and love, and keep on loving until they kill you.

This is a big, variegated change, with profound consequences for evangelicals' distinct religiosity and their often combative relationship with mainstream American society. So far, no single observer has captured the change, or its ramifications, in its entirety. But the picture is coming into focus as journalists, scholars, and evangelical leaders grapple with increasing sophistication and candor with evangelicalism's uncertain future in a secularizing America. An array of recent publications, both online and off, portray a church taking determined steps to survive by rethinking some of its basic approaches to faith.

One of the sharpest and most recent of those accounts is a book-length immersion into the hitherto underreported world of progressive evangelicalism by Deborah Jian Lee, a religion journalist and visiting scholar at Cornell University. In *Rescuing Jesus: How People of Color, Women, and Queer Christians Are Reclaiming Evangelicalism*, Lee tells interlocking stories of gay, Black, Asian, and female Christians agitating for change in a faith tradition characterized by its doctrinal and cultural conservatism. Combining immersive reporting with brief forays into historical research, Lee profiles key activists and cites an array of sociological data showing that evangelical churches are diversifying ethnically and stratifying generationally as younger evangelicals cast aside hostility to gays and seek to end their faith's alienation from mainstream America.

"For a long time, whatever white evangelical leaders said was theology was theology with a capital T," Lee said when I spoke with her recently.

Today, because of the demographic shifts and because of where young evangelicals are theologically and the influx of people of color, we're seeing that theology can come from many different places. . . . Theology is becoming more inclusive of the people who are within the church.

Evangelical observers do not dispute such claims. "There's a shift as older generations are passing away and new generations are coming of age," said Jonathan Merritt, an evangelical author and columnist for Religion News Service, whose coverage has closely tracked evangelicals' evolving attitudes toward Scripture. He added:

You've seen a fracturing of the movement. You've got an approach now where when people want to know what the truth is about something, young Christians are still consulting the Bible. But oftentimes they're bringing the Bible into conversations with other forms and sources of knowledge. . . . To see the Bible as a one-stop shop for everything, science, history, every matter of faith, and anything and everything you need to know is contained there—that's been a perspective that's shifted.

Thanks to America's recent about-face toward same-sex relationships, that shift is now observable in real time, both in print and online. "I'm opening a can of worms," writes Ken Wilson, a prominent Michigan pastor, at the start of his 2014 book, *A Letter to My Congregation: An Evangelical Pastor's Path to Embracing People Who Are Gay, Lesbian and Transgender into the Company of Jesus.* In over two hundred densely argued pages, Wilson tells how what began as a "fleeting unease" grew into a wholesale reevaluation not only of what the Bible says about sexuality, but of basic assumptions about biblical truth long considered sacrosanct within evangelicalism.

"We become understandably concerned when we think the authority, value, or trustworthiness of Scripture might be at stake," Wilson writes. Nevertheless, he concludes that overinterpretation of a handful of biblical prohibitions against homosexuality has obscured a deeper biblical message:

> We are called to practice the gospel discipline, the gospel glory, the gospel *enactment*, of mutual acceptance. . . . It seems to me that this ethic is emphasized so strongly because the Jesus movement knew all too well the danger of overzealous or harmful application of the Bible.

Sexuality figures prominently, too, in megachurch pastor Adam Hamilton's recent book-length effort to persuade evangelicals that many of their most cherished biblical views are the product of convention, not timeless truths. "There are statements on [the Bible's] pages that I don't believe capture the character and will of God," Hamilton writes at the beginning of *Making Sense of the Bible: Rediscovering the Power of Scripture Today*. Hamilton, named a Distinguished Evangelist by the United Methodist Church, goes on to dismiss many totems of conservative Christianity—the six-day creation of the world, subordination of women, opposition to homosexuality—replacing them with what he calls "an attempt to honestly wrestle with the difficult questions often raised by thoughtful Christians and non-Christians concerning things taught in the Bible." One thing his book does not contain: claims of biblical inerrancy or scientific accuracy, which he calls "flawed. . . . When the Bible is read while holding these assumptions the reader will, at some point, become confused, misguided or profoundly disappointed."

To the dismay of conservative leaders, views like Hamilton's are gaining ground. Just one in five of all Americans—and only 13 percent of those under age thirty—currently believes that "the Bible is the actual word of God and should be taken literally, word for word," according to the American Bible Society, which each year conducts what it calls a national "State of the Bible" survey, measuring American attitudes toward Scripture. Most Americans hold a more nuanced opinion of the Bible, viewing it as either an inspired text with historical errors or "just another book of teachings written by men." Close to a majority believes "the Bible, the Koran and the book of Mormon are all different expressions of the same spiritual truths." In a 2009 study by the Barna Group, an evangelical research organization, more than 20 percent of self-proclaimed "born-again" Christians disagreed that the Bible "is totally accurate in all of the principles it teaches." Sixty percent of born-agains denied that Satan is real, and nearly 40 percent said they did not believe "Jesus lived a sinless life."

Conservative evangelicals have tried to counter such trends with their own publishing efforts—salvos in what a recent *Christianity Today* editorial called "the New Battle for the Bible." Two years ago, Kevin DeYoung, a prominent Michigan pastor and co-leader of a national network of theologically conservative churches, published *Taking God at His Word: Why the Bible Is Knowable, Necessary, and Enough, and What That Means for You and Me*, a book expressly intended, as he put it to me, "to help reassert for a new generation the divine inspiration and total trustworthiness of the Scriptures." DeYoung said he "often hear[s] from older Christian leaders that they've never seen more hunger for the Bible, more of a willingness to learn, and a more of commitment to sound theology in younger generations than they see today." But he acknowledged that preserving traditional biblical interpretation in contemporary evangelicalism has become a challenge. "I think we are seeing the beginning of a big sort in American Christianity, and among evangelicals in particular," he said,

I have no doubt many young people are more flexible and less traditional in their understanding of the faith, especially when it comes to sexual ethics. . . . I don't think there is less formal allegiance to Scripture in evangelical churches. But practically, the authority of the Bible can be neutered when churches don't think it's clear, it's sufficient, or it's all that understandable.

DeYoung's careful distinction between evangelicals' "*formal allegiance to Scripture*" and their actual adherence to biblical principles is on point. Though evangelicals continue to portray themselves in public—especially to their opponents in political debates—as unwavering upholders of biblical orthodoxy, in practice even many high-profile evangelical leaders appear increasingly comfortable jettisoning those parts of the Bible that might interfere with their ministry to contemporary America. "I believe the Scripture is without error in its original autographs, as I tweeted the other day," California megachurch pastor Rick Warren said in a 2011 online interview. Nevertheless, despite Jesus's unambiguous prohibition of divorce in three different New Testament gospels, Warren's Saddleback Church not only welcomes America's sizable population of divorced evangelicals, it offers them a special ministry led by Saddleback members who, according to the church's website, "have healed from the impact of divorce and can minister to those who have just completed the walk." The divorce ministry is not unique to Saddleback. It is a video-based program called DivorceCare developed by Church Initiative, a North Carolina para-church organization that crafts ministry products for Christian single parents, divorcés, and the grief-stricken. "How can God produce something good out of something as bad as divorce?" the DivorceCare website asks. "This segment [of the twelve-part DivorceCare program] will show you how to grow closer to God as you go through your divorce experience."

Similarly, Willow Creek Community Church in suburban Chicago, flagship of a global network of thousands of evangelical congregations, employs women pastors and elders despite clear biblical prohibitions against women leading in church. "A few isolated scriptural texts appear to restrict the full ministry freedom of women," a statement on Willow Creek's website explains.

> The interpretation of those passages must take into account their relation to the broader teaching of Scripture and their specific contexts. We believe that, when the Bible is interpreted comprehensively, it teaches the full equality of men and women in status, giftedness, and opportunity for ministry.

"I don't know of anybody who's a biblical literalist," New York City megachurch pastor Tim Keller says in a 2009 online video tutorial about biblical interpretation. Keller, founder of Redeemer Presbyterian Church in Manhattan and cofounder of the national conservative church network where Kevin DeYoung serves on the governing council, is widely hailed by evangelicals for successfully ministering in a secular city without compromising biblical integrity. Keller's official position on the Bible is that "Scripture is our final authority" for all matters of faith. Nevertheless, he carves out room in his tutorial for skeptical New Yorkers to rein-terpret individual biblical passages that conflict too discordantly with modern life. Keller says he himself doesn't take the creation story in the first chapter of the biblical book of Genesis literally because it is not written "as historical prose."

> Obviously, Genesis 1 has a big impact on how you under-stand evolution and so forth. So, I would consider myself a person who believes in the full authority of the Bible, and yet even if you believe that, there's room for debate about what parts of the Bible you take literally or not.

At a recent Sunday morning service at Redeemer, I spoke with Aaron Link, a twenty-eight-year-old software engineer for Google who teaches first graders in the church's Sunday School. He told me he was, like most Redeemer members, theologically conserva-tive, believing the Bible to be "the Word of God, therefore it's inerrant, it's trustworthy, it's authoritative." Yet Link was flexible when it came to particulars. The creation narrative in Genesis? "I've heard different things from people here . . . I'm still trying to figure it out." Should women be allowed to lead in churches? "It's not something I've looked into. If a person argued that it's scrip-turally based, I'd go with that." Should all parts of the Bible be taken literally? "Just because you believe a part of the Bible is met-aphorical, you're not compromising the inerrancy of Scripture."

What remains unclear is whether evangelicals' gradual loos-ening of biblical strictness will enable them to overcome the sig-nificant demographic challenges coinciding with their change of course. Last year's most important religion-related publication might well turn out to have been the Pew Forum's 2015 Reli-gious Landscape Study, a comprehensive survey of the nation's religiosity that found a startling five-million drop in the number of American Christians since 2007. The number of evangelicals rose by 2.4 million, but the increase was not enough to keep pace with overall population growth. If current trends continue, evangelicals will be outnumbered by nonreligious Americans in just a few years. A closer look at the Pew numbers suggests even the growth evangelicals experienced was powered largely by mainline Protestants and Catholics fleeing their own declining congregations. More than a quarter of all evangelicals were raised either as mainline Protestants or as Catholics, according to Pew, compared to just 9 percent converted from outside Christianity. Among millennials, the youngest age cohort surveyed by Pew, just one-fifth are evangelical, compared to 35 percent professing no religion at all.

"Most teens will walk away from faith when they graduate from high school," said Guy Wasko, an evangelical pastor in New York City with whom I spoke about the challenges of sustaining Christianity in a secularizing America. He was referring to an emerging body of research showing that up to 80 percent of Christian young adults turn their back on faith. Two-thirds of those dropouts eventually find their way back to church later in life. But that remains a high rate of attrition—roughly a quarter of children raised as Christians walking away from their faith. Among those who depart, according to the Barna Group, close to a majority—41 percent—said they left because their church seemed "judgmental," "hypocritical," "unfriendly," or "unwelcoming."

Wasko said his church, Trinity Grace, a nine-year-old megachurch headquartered in the Chelsea neighborhood of Manhattan with ten satellite branches throughout the city, has succeeded in luring back young church dropouts by replacing the "vehemently opposed to gay marriage fire and brimstone guy on Sunday morning" approach to Christianity with what he described "a current, more relevant expression of the faith." "More relevant" includes Wasko's earrings and tattoos, "Philosophy and Faith" nights with atheist guest speakers, "artist salons" featuring "drinks and wine and cheese," and sermons about the irony of irreligious Manhattanites worshipping at the altar of work and success.

Most importantly, said Wasko, Trinity Grace does not insist that its members adhere to a strict, literal interpretation of Scripture. "A lot of damage has been done by the preacher on a soapbox shouting out hellfire and brimstone," he said. Trinity Grace offers a different form of Christianity:

> We invite people into community. We invite them into groups exploring the Scripture, and no question is taboo. Let's look at the text and read it together and ask for wisdom from those who have gone before us and the spirit itself. . . . I would make a lot of enemies in the evangelical world if I was quoted saying that parts of the Scriptures are parabolic, that there wasn't a six-day creation. . . . [But] let's argue that the Scriptures as a whole are parabolic in nature. Does that make them less true? Sheep don't cry wolf, but the parable still delivers a truth. At a thirty-thousand-foot level, if we can agree with that, then maybe we can get past some of the hang-ups people have toward the text.

Trinity Grace's online statement of faith begins with the declaration—standard in evangelical churches—"We believe the Bible to be the inspired, the infallible, authoritative Word of God." In practice, said Wasko, church members do not read all Bible passages with the same interpretive lens:

If my whole faith is ruined because all of a sudden creation wasn't six days or Jesus didn't walk on water, that's not really faith. I still believe lots of crazy-sounding things, like Jesus's resurrection from the dead. If you reject that, you're moving away from orthodox Christianity. . . . I'm just saying that if my God of the Scriptures is not bigger than my ability to make sense of them, that's not God. If I can figure everything out, then that's pretty pathetic. A lot of people like to work with bricks, not rubber bands and springs. But I think life is more dynamic than bricks.

Zimmermann told me his own evolution away from biblical literalism began with his first Bible class at Azusa Pacific. Though the college's official statement of faith also begins with the words "We believe the Bible to be the inspired, the only infallible, authoritative word of God," professors nevertheless introduce their students to the basics of biblical scholarship, and to what Karen Strand Winslow, Zimmermann's seminary teacher, called "the human side" of the text's origins and meaning. Zimmermann said he instantly realized the "aphorisms" he was taught in church youth groups were woefully simplistic. "We were given these answers that worked for our parents but didn't work for us," he said.

Zimmermann said his goal as a Christian, what he called his "capstone project," was to win back disenchanted young evangelicals by showing them a richer, more open-ended way to read the Bible. "How do we bring alive these texts we've heard over and over again? How do we address our generation?" he said. He concluded:

There are some people who come into faith through logic and seeing that God is the only way. But we're people of feelings, and we just want to know that we're loved. [. . .] I think it's a lot easier to create doctrinal statements and say, "These are true, and if you don't believe them, you're out," than it is to say there's room for ambiguity and relationship, and we're all just different people trying to figure this thing out together.

CHAPTER 24

La Llorona Visits the American Academy of Religion: A Tribute to Luís D. León

Daisy Vargas

One of my first memories of Luís D. León, a renowned scholar of Latinx religious practices, is helping him construct a Days of the Dead altar for one of his undergraduate classes. He asked each student to bring an object that represented a dead loved one to place on the makeshift altar. I'd only met Luís three months before, when I arrived at the University of Denver from Southern California to begin my master's program in religious studies. I was touched by the invitation and the opportunity to participate in an activity that reminded me of my family and community. As a first-generation Chicana graduate student, I was happy to join a celebration that connected me to my home. I don't remember what object I took to the event, only that Luís pulled a small plastic lion out of his pocket—"*Un león*, for my father." Luís set it on the table with pride for his dad, the deceased Reverend Daniel León.

Luís died of natural causes on October 16, 2018. He was fifty-three years old. After the initial shock wore off, his close friends and colleagues wanted to do something for him the next month during the annual American Academy of Religion (AAR) meeting, a gathering of religion scholars from around the world, in the city he'd called home for over a decade, Denver, Colorado.

A group of five of us video conferenced to brainstorm and plan an event, but the usual recommendations of panel presentations fell flat. The memory of Luís was still too fresh, our pain still immediate, and the conference approaching fast. We wondered aloud to each other: How would we honor and remember Luís in a way that reflected his playfulness, his clever and biting wit, and the critical contributions of his academic work?

One of us mentioned an altar. Someone else added that it should be a moving altar. Eventually someone joked, "We should have La Llorona haunt the AAR." We all laughed and then nodded in agreement. It was the perfect suggestion, as Luís used the Mexican legend of La Llorona, the wailing female spirit, as the namesake of his first book. We decided to construct an image of La Llorona and wheel her throughout the conference for the duration of the annual meeting.

Luís published *La Llorona's Children: Religion, Life, and Death in the US–Mexican Borderlands* in 2004. A study of the religious diversity of Chicanx and Mexicans in Mexico and the United States, the book title is based on the Mexican folk legend of La Llorona.

La Llorona, a cautionary and tragic tale of the apparition who is condemned to roam the world in search of her murdered children, is also a story of the Mexican–United States borderlands. The legend of La Llorona is ubiquitous among Mexican and Mexican American communities. Some trace the story to pre-Hispanic mythologies of the serpent goddess, Cihuacoatl, the first mother, who can be heard weeping as she wanders the night dressed in white. Others understand her through the framework of colonialism, as the ghost of La Malinche (first known by the name Malintzin, and later Doña Marina), the infamous Indigenous translator and consort of Hernán Cortés, who has been subject to various historical narratives as a traitor who helped the Spanish conquer the Aztec empire and the symbolic mother of modern Mexicans. The significance in her part of La Llorona myth derives from a tradition of vilifying La Malinche, the woman who betrayed her nation and her people, and folk stories of her killing her son to prevent Cortés from taking him. Both La Llorona and La Malinche have been imagined as condemned to search for their dead children, lost in grief and regret.

Luís's portrayal of La Llorona uses Chicanx feminist ideas to reinterpret this mythological tale. Luis describes La Llorona's children as the descendants of Mexicans in the postcolonial diaspora to include those who live in the United States. Luís uses the tale as a metaphor for his academic pursuits—like La Llorona, he searches for children across the borderlands and identifies them through local forms of religious practices that provide meaning to marginalized communities. In Luis's scholarship of Mexican and Chicanx practices of Roman Catholicism and Pentecostalism, he recognizes ancestral ties to pre-Hispanic Indigenous traditions amidst contemporary religious innovations. Like the wandering mourning mother, Luís followed narratives of transnational migration and religion. He searched for her children across the borderlands and found them (alive!) and embodying religion and identity in temples, botánicas, and storefront churches in spite of institutional forces that rendered them invisible. Luís worked continuously to construct an ethical position within postcolonial violence, just as La Llorona searched for her family, for forgiveness, and for justice.

———

On Saturday night, November 17, 2018, in the lobby of a Denver conference hotel, Luís's friends and colleagues gathered to create a set of *ofrendas,* offerings. Family and friends constructed a table altar with objects and art from his home. Upstairs, another group of us constructed a less conventional offering: La Llorona, veiled in black to cover her crystal tears, resting on a mobile catering cart decorated with white votive candles and a scattering of the same orange flowers that we used to make her crown. With hands outstretched, she held small buttons printed with an image of "*El León,*" beckoning people to approach her, to leave an offering, or take a button. The front of the cart was decorated with the Mexican pride flag, secured with large paper flowers. The tribute reflected Luís's multiple identities—queer, Latinx, and scholar of religion—identities he fought hard to maintain and make present. He made it his life's work to create spaces for Latinx women and queer people of color.

We wheeled La Llorona downstairs, and together the group of us completed the largest of the *ofrendas*—in community, Luís's friends, colleagues, mentees, and family celebrating his memory.

Carting La Llorona through the halls of the Denver Convention Center, at panel presentations, and receptions, created an alternative mode for experiencing the event—it imbued the conference with our memories of Luís and our shared connection through those memories. As La Llorona interacted with people putting on their *León* pins, we began to see a visual representation of how many lives Luís touched. This network invoked his memory through nods of mutual recognition, smiles, and waves. There were also moments of disgust and confusion—La Llorona was an aesthetic and spatial disruption to the conventional conference atmosphere of business casual outfits and long sterile hallways.

Sometimes we introduced La Llorona when she arrived at a panel; often she simply sat in the corner of conference rooms, her black veil hiding her face as academics read their papers and discussed their scholarship. She was invited to sit in on the emergency session on the Catholic Church sexual abuse crisis, and she sat next to the podium during the Religion in Latina/o Americas panels that Luís helped create. La Llorona represented our mourning and loss of Luís, but she also beckoned to the possibilities for future scholarship following his example. La Llorona bore witness to the loss of one of our own, but also to the possibilities that Luís's work created for the future.

———

I think about Luís often—in my teaching, scholarship, and personal life. I left the University of Denver in 2012, but my relationship with Luís grew stronger as I pursued a PhD at the University of California, Riverside. We were reflections of each other's choices to be academics—scholars of religion, unmarried, and child-free. Between conferences, Luís visited Riverside and the Los Angeles area. His colleagues soon became my colleagues—he gave me the gift of community. Luís was my academic father, quick to take me under his wing and provide rigorous critique. His scholarship continued to inform my doctoral work, and his comments and advice were formative as I continued my research among Latinx communities in the US-Mexico borderlands. In the last year of his life, we corresponded regularly about applying to tenure-track positions and research opportunities. Luís was proud of my appointment as assistant professor in religious studies and classics at the University of Arizona. His last email to me was a reminder to apply to the Young Scholars of American Religion Program— advice that I am eternally grateful to have received.

While I remember Luís as an academic mentor, my favorite memories are much more personal. I remember his sunglass-clad face riding in the passenger seat of my car when he'd visit Southern California, his emails signed "*El León*," the club lights in his dark hair, his laughter at introducing me to strangers as his daughter. I can imagine him watching academics pose with La Llorona at the AAR, laughing with joy even amidst the tragedy.

In haste, we packed La Llorona into a cardboard box with her flowers and her votive candles at the end of the conference. When I collected her from the baggage carousel in the Tucson airport, rattling sounds of broken glass warned me against removing her from the box. I'm unsure about whether she'll make another appearance; I imagine the shards of glass have formed thorns on the orange flowers. La Llorona won't journey to San Diego for this year's American Academy of Religion conference, but we will participate in another *ofrenda* instead.

Last year, La Llorona's specter haunted the conference with memories of Luís; this year, we answer her call as we gather to remember Luís in a panel presentation that imagines the future of religious studies from the perspectives of his mentors, colleagues, and mentees. Many of us will be wearing the Léon button with pride, as members of Luís's pride. I'll be sitting there too, with a small plastic lion on the panel table.

CHAPTER 25

Against Muslim Unity

Faisal Devji

Even sophisticated people speak of Islam as if it is one thing. The devout, the haters, and the indifferent often share this belief in Muslim unity. And for them all there is no greater display of Muslim unity than the hajj.

The hajj, the pilgrimage to Mecca, is a grand and dramatic display of Islamic brotherhood without racial or national bounds. Or so it appears from the outside. But this way of seeing the pilgrimage is relatively new. It seems to have originated in accounts by nineteenth-century European travelers. The most active and best proponents of the myth of the hajj have always been notable Western converts, such as the Galician Jew Leopold Weiss, who became the Islamic thinker and Pakistani politician Muhammad Asad, or Malcolm X, the activist for equality in the United States, who wrote about the hajj in rapturous terms. Given that Saudi Arabia had abolished slavery only a few years before Malcolm X's pilgrimage, his view of the hajj as the embodiment of a long-standing and more just alternative society might have been a bit naïve.

Muslims themselves have also taken up the claim that the hajj represents a kind of ideal society, free of the prejudices and divisions that dominate the profane world.

Proponents of the hajj as a social ideal speak of the brotherhood it enacts. Brotherhood is a common and powerful metaphor of closeness. As all brothers know, however, brotherhood is rarely if ever about equality.

Muslim teaching has much to say about brotherhood, and about equality. Clearly, they are not the same thing, and can even contradict one another. Families, after all, tend to be hierarchical and harbor various kinds of violence. They often sacrifice some members for others. The newly fashionable term *Abrahamic religions* tries to mask such unhappiness. In the past generation, this term has grown in popularity as an alternative to "Christian" or "Judeo-Christian."

By emphasizing the patriarch Abraham—the common ancestor—"Abrahamic religions" is meant to express the familial relationship between Judaism, Christianity, and Islam. The patriarch Abraham's sacrifice, according to the metaphor, makes him foundational for all three religions. Proponents of the "Abrahamic religions" want to emphasize closeness and deemphasize conflict.

But Abraham was ready to sacrifice one son and abandon another. This is not a simple and happy family. Nor is it necessarily a close one.

The historical experience of Abraham's metaphorical descendants is simply very different. Only a minority of Muslims, those living around the Mediterranean Basin or the Caucasus, have grown up with Christians and Jews as interlocutors and neighbors.

Historically, Islam's primary siblings have been not Jews or Christians but Hindus, Buddhists, and Zoroastrians. Unlike their Jewish and Christian "brothers," Muslims are part of a polytheistic and non-Semitic world. The poor "Abrahamic religions" metaphor tears away the historical experience of the majority of the world's Muslims.

Like the idea of the three monotheistic brothers, the idea of Muslim unity is recent, well-meaning, and highly misleading. At a deep level, both ideals—Muslim unity and Abrahamic religions—are based on violence. But what does it really mean to describe as violent such a seemingly benign ideal as Muslim unity?

Last August, I was in Riyadh for a conference. It's not so easy to get into Saudi Arabia, and, while there, I thought I might visit the sacred cities of Mecca and Medina. The hajj was about to begin, so the opportunity was a rare one. Thanks to the Indian consulate in Jeddah, I managed to secure the services of guides in both cities. And so I found myself travelling to Mecca with an Indian driver and companion. He turned out to be a Muslim divine from the city of Deoband, one of the great seminaries of the subcontinent.

In its magnificently craggy desert setting, Mecca is a redeveloped place, devoid of any historical or aesthetic character. The black-draped Kaaba, standing at Islam's ritual center, lay within a corset-like framework of stairs and floors that allow pilgrims to circumambulate it on three levels. Many circled the Kaaba while filming themselves with mobile phones, adding a new gesture to the ceremonies of pilgrimage. Two disasters marred last year's hajj: a crane collapsed in the Great Mosque, and a stampede occurred at Mina. Both involved hundreds of fatalities. But the only discomfort I suffered was when a pilgrim in a wheelchair ran over my foot as I trudged my seven circles around the Kaaba.

On the road back to Jeddah, the driver got into an argument with the Deobandi divine. Our driver was a fan of the Mumbai-based television preacher Zakir Naik. Naik's satellite TV show has made him a global Muslim celebrity. He is a conservative televangelist whose sermons are in the model of American media figures such as the Southern Baptist pastor Jerry Falwell, as were the orations of his predecessor, the South African Muslim preacher Ahmed Deedat. Like Deedat, Naik preaches in English, and his popular show espouses highly conservative views. He wears a Western suit and a skullcap. The driver also wore Western clothes, and clearly saw himself, like Naik, as a modern man, yet one who prized social and religious harmony above all else. The driver said he disapproved of the sectarian disputes among Muslims and religious conflict in India, too. He praised the peaceable nature of the hajj.

The Deobandi cleric pointed out that the order and harmony of the hajj derived from Saudi Arabia's monarchical form of government. The Saudis, he observed, support one form of Islam and prohibit the public manifestation of all others. The nature of Saudi government ensured many different kinds of believers could mingle without open dispute. Indian democracy, the Deobandi divine noted, entailed the absence of a state religion. Sectarian disagreement and disputes, he observed, resulted naturally from the freedoms of a republican form of government. Republics, he insisted, maintain their democratic character through disagreement. They would lose it by favoring any one religion—by which of course he meant Hinduism—even if it was to promote social harmony. Consensus, he was saying, was not a mark of freedom but its opposite.

Liberal Muslims commonly make this argument about the good of religious difference. When they do, they often cite scriptural passages about the virtue of difference and the competition in goodness it makes possible. The Deobandi divine, however, drew his justification not from theology, but politics construed as a realm autonomous of it. He was not interested in tolerance or pluralism as inherently good things. Instead, the divine made a case that conflict and contestation must be part of political life. Democracy, he was saying, was not afraid of disagreement. On the contrary, democracy and freedom depended not on some false consensus, but on institutional mechanisms that helped prevent dispute from turning into violence or oppression. In other words, democracy made living with disagreement possible.

The channels and institutions of disagreement in India and other democracies might not always prevent violence. During elections they can even foment it. Nevertheless, their ideal is meant to stand as a guarantor of freedom for all citizens, not just members of one religion or sect. By focusing on disagreement in the political life of a democracy, my Deobandi guide was criticizing the driver's liberal pleas for harmony and unity as antipolitical and illusory in nature. The cleric left scripture to the side. He focused on the state, and its essential role as the guarantor of this freedom. Indeed, there is no group in India—Muslims chief among them—that does not advocate for a secular state. What exactly secularism means, however, constitutes one of the great subjects of disagreement in India.

Importantly, there is nothing peculiarly Indian about the cleric's turn to the state and its politics. The nation-state is inescapable when it comes to matters of establishing and governing matters within and between religious communities. People often see the hajj as an example of Islam's global, transnational community. However, even the possibility and experience of the hajj is shaped entirely by nationality. It is not a melting away of national distinctions in transcendental unity. Rather, the hajj is a carefully managed, entirely conventional instance of internationalism. First, quotas for pilgrims are set by their national citizenship: 1 percent of a country's Muslim population are given visas. Throughout the hajj, pilgrims are marked by national identity. They are provided name tags, backpacks, sun visors, and other paraphernalia by tour companies. All are embossed with national flags or printed in their colors. Guides have national flags attached to their clothing.

National languages play a crucial role in the hajj. Housing and services provided to Indian pilgrims are identified in Hindi, whose script is also that of Hinduism's sacred language. Because of the large numbers of Keralans settled in Gulf countries, one also saw housing and other services identified in Malayalam, the language of Kerala, in southern India. Sometimes, a dormitory in Mecca becomes full, and a pilgrim from one part of the country must be housed with pilgrims from another region. I am told that loud complaints about inedible food and strange tongues always follow—as they would among the pilgrims' Hindu compatriots similarly housed in the holy city of Benares.

In Mecca, pilgrims' native tongues vary at least as much as their nationality. As a result, very few pilgrims can communicate with those from other countries in any language but English or French: which it is depends on their particular history of colonization. Thus even the experience of Muslim global unity supposedly exemplified by the hajj is facilitated by the languages of the Western European colonizer.

Arabic, English, and Urdu are the languages most conspicuous at the hajj, visible on signs and notices all over Mecca and Medina. Arabic is there largely for symbolic reasons, given that there are relatively few Arab pilgrims. My guide and I conversed in Urdu, which is both a north Indian language and the national language of Pakistan. We often came across Pakistani pilgrims speaking the same language. But because my guide and I were marked as Indian, never once did they acknowledge us, nor us them. We exchanged no words of greeting at this most sacred site of Muslim brotherhood and unity. We remained identified by our nation-states, which defined our experiences.

The multilingual signs of Mecca proliferate at important sites and monuments. Illustrated with citations from Muhammad's sayings, these notices warn pilgrims against touching or kissing structures that the Saudis haven't torn down, and warn against taking back sand from the holy places as a souvenir. The Saudi government fears that such souvenirs could engender idolatrous, un-Islamic attachment. As a result, authorities have fenced off the areas that once held the tombs belonging to the Prophet's relatives and Islam's early martyrs. Such monuments would surely become objects of idolatry. The historic battlefield of Uhud outside Medina, for instance, had been walled with opaque glass, but pilgrims broke holes to peer at the wilderness within.

The hajj is also replete with small acts of insubordination. Signs bearing images of forbidden practices, each crossed out by a red X, serve only to highlight these instances of minor rebellion. The pillar outside Mecca at the site of Muhammad's last sermon, for example, has its top plastered with signs warning pilgrims against paying it any devotion. But the bottom of the pillar is

covered with graffiti, which in the circumstances is not a deface-
ment, but the only way to recognize the site's sacredness. In effect,
the signs speak of a city under occupation, apparent prescriptions
for order imposed from above by a foreign ruler. The Saudi royal
family and its Wahhabi form of Islam, after all, took the holy cities by force only in the twentieth century, in the wake of the First
World War.

The harmony of the hajj is simply not based on any kind of
Muslim unity of any significance. Its order and concord derive
from, on the one hand, the dominance of Saudi monarchy and
Wahhabi establishment and, on the other, mutual indifference
among Muslims.

My Indian driver told me of a rumor about the Barelvis, great
rivals of the Deobandis in India and Pakistan. He accused the
Barelvis of praying privately in their hotel rooms. They feared,
he alleged, that standing behind Wahhabi imams in the mosque
would imperil their salvation. It is true that Saudi control con-
fers on the Wahhabi denomination some exclusive prerogatives
in the holy cities. But the shuffling, inelegant rows of pilgrims
at prayer in Mecca, each with his or her own slightly divergent
ritual tradition, are subtle demonstrations that Islam, even in the
heart of Wahhabism, even during the hajj, can never be brought
completely under any sect's control.

Today, calls for Muslim unity come from so-called militants
and moderates alike. Such calls for Muslim unity do not date
back much before the twentieth century. To be sure, the ideal of
universal agreement in Islam might have existed before. But it sel-
dom constituted a political or even religious project beyond fairly
circumscribed arenas of debate. On the contrary, the internal

schisms and conflicts of Muslim societies demonstrated a sense of confidence and comfort with disagreement as a political necessity. This recognition of disunity is illustrated by an oft-cited saying attributed to Muhammad; in it, the Prophet pronounced that his community would be divided into seventy-two sects until the end of time, with only a single crucially unspecified one bound for salvation.

With the rise of European empires in the eighteenth and nineteenth centuries, Muslim unity emerged as a significant theme. In other words, this unity served as a defensive strategy to counter the loss of Muslims' control over their own political life. Still, the desire remained largely theoretical, even during the heyday of Pan-Islamism in the early twentieth century. It took the rise of new global movements and identities following the end of the Cold War for the current visions of Muslim unity to arise.

One of the earliest moments in the new, and now explicitly global rather than merely international, project of Muslim unity came with mobilizations that followed the outcry over Salman Rushdie's allegedly blasphemous novel, *The Satanic Verses* (1988). The demonstrations were not and could not be confined to a particular country, movement, revolution, or terrorist group. Made possible by television and the sense of simultaneity and collective identification that it offered, these reactions to a perceived affront catalyzed new calls for a global form of Muslim unity that, unlike Pan-Islamism, didn't take a coalition of states as its model.

This global mobilization presented novel opportunities and challenges for Muslim leaders. Initially, this "Muslim unity" appeared in the form of declarations signed by a motley crew of divines, politicians, and ideologues for or against the Iranian fatwa calling for Rushdie's murder. Some of these attempts at generating agreement sought to corral global forms of Muslim mobilization in opposing ideological directions. The initial calls came in response to supposedly insulting depictions of the Prophet. More recently, such calls are made both in support and to counter the much less popular cause of recruiting Muslims to al-Qaeda or ISIS.

In some ways, these declarations resemble the long history of Christian ecumenical councils. But since Islam lacks an institutional basis comparable to the Vatican, the results are even less coherent. The calls for Muslim unity are no less, and no more, than the collective expression of a pious wish by a random assortment of dignitaries. If pressed or asked to take any actual measures signifying unity, even the signatories of these declarations would immediately find themselves in disagreement about "Muslim unity."

At root, however, the problem is not the details of these calls for unity. It is the essence, the very ideal of consensus. As a matter of course, calls for Muslim unity customarily violate the spirit of their claims by anathematizing their Muslim opponents. Calls for unity are not high-minded but, in a word, disingenuous, a seemingly noble pretext for anathematizing or demonizing opponents.

Even more deeply, however, the ideal of unity is inherently antipolitical. The Deobandi cleric was right in identifying the political as the sphere offering the only real potential for peaceful accommodation of differences and disputes. Posturing about an illusory "Muslim unity" tends only to alienate Muslims from the political world of nation-states that govern their societies. From this perspective, Muslim militancy, too, is actually a consequence of depoliticization and not, as is commonly presumed, the reverse.

Whether by Western or Middle Eastern governments, condemnations of terrorism in religious language, in the name of Islam, are losing causes. Real problems will not be solved on theological terrain. When liberals and advocates of tolerance too celebrate or promote moderate Islam, it is another step away from the world of politics and institutions, the world of progress and solutions. The quest for harmony, for unity, is a siren song, and is to be resisted.

CHAPTER 26

Their Bloods Cry Out
from the Ground

Shira Telushkin

The dead have been accounted for, but their blood has not.

Under Jewish law, every remnant of human material contains the life force of a person—and, as such, is sanctified. At the Tree of Life synagogue, the bodies of the eleven Jews murdered on Saturday morning have all been removed, first to be examined as part of the criminal investigation, and now to be buried. But their blood cannot be forgotten, simply scrubbed away and disposed of. It must be honored, collected, and buried.

On Tuesday morning, eight members of the local Pittsburgh *chevra kadisha*, the Jewish burial society, prepared to enter the building and begin this final task of collecting the blood. There were three rabbis, two medics, a painter, and a doctor. They are all local, all from Squirrel Hill, all veteran members of the *chevra kadisha*—the most junior one among them has been a volunteer for over five years. All of these men—and they were all men, though other female volunteers will join in the coming weeks as well—are professionals with day jobs who have taken off from work to be here, as a sacred obligation to their community. Many of them have full gray beards. One is in his twenties. Their work inside the synagogue is physically laborious, involving scrubbing and bending and kneeling for many hours. They feel honored to serve the dead in this way.

Most of the men here have been doing this work for fifteen or twenty years and are familiar with the process of scraping blood and collecting remains—though never at a crime scene like this.

They are not the only Jewish burial society in town, but as Orthodox Jews they knew the victims of this synagogue less personally than the other Pittsburgh *chevra kadisha*, and so offered to take on the task for now. Other volunteer burial societies—including Chesed Shel Emet, which specializes in graphic tragedies—came in from elsewhere but were sent back home: Pittsburgh Jews are prepared to bury their own dead.

The men are soft-spoken, subdued, moved by the respect for privacy that categorizes Jewish burial societies across the world. One older man explained to me that when he is working with a dead body, he can feel the soul still hovering, watching as he does his work. He sees it as his job, he told me, to ease its journey on to the next world.

———

Throughout Jewish history, the blood of the Jewish martyr has served as an active witness against the horror of the crime they endured. In accordance with historical law, when someone is murdered for being Jewish—for dying *al kiddush hashem*, for the sanctification of God's name—there is the tradition to bury the individual in the clothing in which they were murdered. The individual is not washed or dressed in the typical shrouds, or *tachrichim*, of the Jewish dead; their own blood is understood to recommend them far more than any purification ritual ever could. They need no further purification; they have been made holy in their death, and their clothing itself engenders God's mercy, and demand God's justice on Earth. The blood is supposed to outrage those who witness it, and stir the Jewish people from any complacency to such an act.

Here in Pittsburgh, where the dead are also part of a modern crime scene, many of the victims' bodies had undergone autopsies and other preparations that precluded the possibility of being buried in the shrouds of their martyrdom. But not all. As one of the members of the burial society explained about the situation here, "if the bodies are being buried in their original condition, then there is no *taharah*," the word for preparation for burial. "They are buried in the clothes in which they died," because those are their holiest shrouds; but for those bodies which had to be examined, and therefore undressed, there will be a regular *taharah* and preparation, if the family desires it, and carried out by either of the burial societies. Their clothing, with their blood, is to be included in the grave.

On Saturday afternoon, after he heard about the shooting, Rabbi Daniel Wasserman, rabbi of the local Shaare Torah synagogue and one of the heads of the *chevra kadisha*, and his colleague Rabbi Elisar Admon, a local rabbi who moved to Pittsburgh from Israel and is involved in ZAKA, the Israeli organization founded to identify and collect human remains in the aftermath of bombings, walked over to Tree of Life and gave their names to the security forces there, letting them know they would want to come back and oversee the process of caring for the dead. That Saturday night, the two men met with Brad Orsini, a former FBI agent and local community security officer, and spoke with Rabbi Jeffrey Myers, the rabbi of Tree of Life, who gave them his blessing to enter the synagogue and begin their work.

At about 10:00 p.m., the FBI agreed to allow Orsini, Rabbi Wasserman, Rabbi Admon, and another security officer to walk through the building, without touching anything. They were there only to get a sense of the scope of the work that would be ahead. A large contingent of the local *chevra kadisha*—men, women, young and old—stood outside in the rain until almost 1:00 a.m., ready to volunteer their services if needed. No one else was allowed to enter that night.

The eight men worked until 4:35 p.m. on Tuesday, completing their work on the areas that had been made available to them. At this point the Secret Service, coordinating the visit of President Donald Trump to the site, had them remain in the basement of the building until about 6:00 p.m. The FBI agents on the scene were also on lockdown, and the two groups sat together in the basement. "This was the first time they have ever let civilians inside the building," said one member of the *chevra kadisha*, "and they had never seen anything like it before, so they were pretty curious about our work." In turn, the *chevra kadisha* asked them about FBI work, and, of course, which FBI television shows were the most accurate. "They said only *The Wire* was even remotely accurate," this member added. He doesn't know when the FBI will open up access to the next two areas of the building and ask him to return to complete the work. The men are also busy this week preparing the bodies for funerals and attending to details of the burials, and they remain on call.

The bodies themselves were removed on Sunday, starting around 3:00 a.m. Rabbis Wasserman and Admon had returned about two hours earlier, to sit with the bodies, which had all been moved to a staging area within the building, and then to help assist with the transfer of the bodies to the vehicle that would take them to the medical examiner's office, a task done with the help of two other members of the *chevra kadisha*. By this point, the community had organized a rotation of *shomrim*, those who guard the body before burial and ensure the dead is never alone, to sit in the medical examiner's office. Naomi Balaban, who coordinates the *chevra kadisha*, sent out a Google doc with one-hour time slots to community email lists, and over forty volunteers answered the call to sit and guard the bodies. The dead were never alone.

At that point, one task remained: what remained of each victim was to be collected from the building.

Along with the FBI presence, which accompanied them throughout their work but did not participate in it, the *chevra kadisha* scrubbed under sinks, behind counters, over countertops, using blacklights and hydrogen peroxide to search for every speck of blood. They brought scrubs and wipes and brushes and sprays and biohazard bags. They wore bodysuits and gloves and headlamps.

The building has been described as a scene of otherworldly carnage. According to officials and others who've been inside, there is blood in multiple areas, on multiple surfaces, and bullet holes riddling multiple areas, including some of the holiest artifacts of Jewish life. Because it is important in Jewish law to keep the blood of each person distinct—so that it can be matched and buried with the particular body that housed it for so many years—these men had to identify each area in the synagogue with the specific person killed there, in order to collect the material meticulously and, in consultation with the family, reunite the remains with the body.

This is what is left for the Jewish community to gather.

The blood and human elements were then bagged, along with all of the materials used to collect them—the gloves and the brushes and the wipes. Throughout the course of this week, each bag will be buried in or alongside the coffin. Material that cannot be identified with a specific individual will to be put into a communal grave, laid to rest with all the dignity that accompanies the burial of an individual with a name and identity.

"When asked about my reaction, what I say is I haven't had it yet. I just haven't had time," said Rabbi Wasserman on Monday morning. "I can tell you: I don't know if the word *carnage* is good enough. It's terrible." And here he paused, his voice cracking. "Just terrible."

> "The hardest part of what we do is that we can't tell people what we've seen and experienced here. I wish people could know and see what had happened here."

Another member of the *chevra kadisha* told me he is "emotionally dead" right now, steeling himself for this work. "I'll deal with this later, not now," he explained of his own reactions to the events. Another member spoke to me after his afternoon prayers. "It hit me when I walked over the threshold of the building this morning. This is it, this is where these people were." A longtime paramedic and volunteer firefighter, he struggled to find the words for the loss and the tragedy.

Unlike in Israel, where the 2014 stabbing at a synagogue in Har Nof and the 2008 attack at the Mercaz HaRav yeshiva were each reported in news outlets alongside pictures of bloodstained prayer books and blood-soaked steps and bloodied prayer shawls, there has been no visual horror to add to our emotional horror. We cannot see their blood, as everyone involved is under strict orders by the FBI to say and show nothing of the scene inside. "The hardest part of what we do is that we can't tell people what we've seen and experienced here," one *chevra kadisha* member said to me. "I wish people could know and see what had happened here."

We now live in an America that has eleven new Jewish martyrs, men and women murdered for being Jews. Most of us are strangers to this experience, a reality so foreign to the history of Jews in this country. But we also live inside a Jewish history that for thousands of years accepted the Jewish martyr as fact, and which accordingly developed an entire subset of laws to address the burial of those murdered because of who they were.

For millennia, Jews have been collecting and burying the blood of our martyrs. This week, the Jews of Pittsburgh have joined that history.

Contributors

Patrick Blanchfield is an associate faculty member at the Brooklyn Institute for Social Research.

Tara Isabella Burton is the author of *Strange Rites: New Religions for a Godless World* (PublicAffairs, 2020) and the novel *Social Creature* (Doubleday, 2018). She is a contributing editor at the *American Interest* and a columnist for Religion News Service.

Daniel José Camacho is an associate web editor at *Sojourners*. His work has previously appeared in publications such as *Christian Century*, *Religion Dispatches*, *America Magazine*, *ABC Religion & Ethics*, *TIME*, the *Guardian*, and the *Washington Post*.

Nat Case is a cartographer and writer and remains a member of Laughing Waters Friends Preparative Meeting. He blogs irregularly at maphead.blogspot.com. He lives in Minneapolis with his family.

Simon Critchley is Hans Jonas Professor of Philosophy at the New School for Social Research in New York. He is series moderator of the Stone, a philosophy column in the *New York Times*, to which he is a frequent contributor.

Erik Davis is an author, award-winning journalist, and independent scholar based in San Francisco. His work focuses on the intersection of alternative religion, media, and the popular imagination. He is the author, most recently, of *High Weirdness: Drugs, Esoterica, and Visionary Experience in the Seventies* (the MIT Press, 2019).

Faisal Devji is professor of Indian history and fellow of Saint Antony's College at the University of Oxford. He is the author of four books, on militant Islam, global politics, Gandhi, and Pakistan as a political idea. Devji is an intellectual historian focusing on political thought in South Asia and the Muslim world.

Burke Gerstenschlager is a writer and former academic book editor, contributing to such publications as the *Los Angeles Review of Books*, *Image Journal*, and *Killing the Buddha*. He has an MDiv from Yale Divinity School and writes at his blog, *Bleak Theology*. He lives in Brooklyn, New York.

Emma Green is a staff writer at the *Atlantic*, where she covers politics, policy, and religion.

Sands Hall's work includes the memoir *Reclaiming My Decade Lost in Scientology* (Counterpoint Press, 2018), the novel *Catching Heaven* (Ballantine Books, 2000), and the craft book *Tools of the Writer's Craft* (Moving Finger Press, 2005); her stories and essays have been published widely. She is also a singer/songwriter and teaches for a number of conferences. Please visit sandshall.com.

Peter Harrison is a professorial research fellow and director of the Institute for Advanced Studies in the Humanities at the University of Queensland. Former professor of science and religion at the University of Oxford, he is the author of seven books, including *The Territories of Science and Religion* (University of Chicago Press, 2015), based on his Gifford Lectures.

David Bentley Hart is an Eastern Orthodox scholar of religion and a philosopher, writer, and cultural commentator. He is the author and translator of fifteen books, including *That All Shall Be Saved: Heaven, Hell, and Universal Salvation* (Yale University Press, 2019).

Jim Hinch is a senior editor at *Guideposts* magazine and an occasional contributor to the *Los Angeles Review of Books* and other publications.

Briallen Hopper is an assistant professor of creative nonfiction at Queens College, CUNY, and coeditor in chief of *Killing the Buddha*. She is the author of *Hard to Love: Essays and Confessions* (Bloomsbury, 2019), a Kirkus Best Book of the Year.

Joel Looper holds a PhD in divinity from the University of Aberdeen. His work has appeared in the *Los Angeles Review of Books*, the Australian Broadcasting Company's *Religion and Ethics Report*, Notre Dame's *Church Life Journal*, the *Other Journal*, *Sojourners*, and other outlets. He lives in Waco, Texas.

Ann Neumann is the author of *The Good Death: An Exploration of Dying in America* (Beacon Press, 2016), a visiting scholar at the Center for Religion and Media at New York University, and a former editor in chief of the center's publication, the *Revealer.*

Kaya Oakes is the author of four books, including *Slanted and Enchanted: The Evolution of Indie Culture* (Henry Holt, 2009); *Radical Reinvention: An Unlikely Return to the Catholic Church* (Counterpoint Press, 2012); and *The Nones Are Alright: A New Generation of Seekers, Believers, and Those In Between* (Orbis Books, 2015).

Meghan O'Gieblyn's work has appeared in *Harper's Magazine*, the *New Yorker, Bookforum, n+1*, the *Believer*, the *Guardian*, *Ploughshares, Tin House*, the *Point,* the *Los Angeles Review of Books*, the *New York Times Book Review*, and elsewhere. She is the author of the essay collection *Interior States* (Anchor Books, 2018), which won the 2018 Believer Book Award for nonfiction.

Jennifer Ratner-Rosenhagen is the Merle Curti and Vilas-Borghesi Distinguished Achievement Professor of History at the University of Wisconsin–Madison. She is the author of *American Nietzsche: A History of an Icon and His Ideas* (University of Chicago Press, 2012) and *The Ideas That Made America: A Brief History* (Oxford University Press, 2019).

Marcus Rediker is Distinguished Professor of Atlantic History at the University of Pittsburgh. His ten books have won numerous awards and been translated into sixteen languages. His most recent work is *The Fearless Benjamin Lay: The Quaker Dwarf Who Became the First Revolutionary Abolitionist* (Beacon Press, 2017).

Leigh Eric Schmidt is the Edward C. Mallinckrodt Distinguished University Professor in the Humanities at Washington University in Saint Louis, where he is part of the John C. Danforth Center on Religion and Politics. He is the author of *Village Atheists: How America's Unbelievers Made Their Way in a Godly Nation* (Princeton University Press, 2016).

Nathan Schneider is a journalist and author who covers social movements in the United States. Since 2015, he has been a professor of media studies at the University of Colorado Boulder.

Shira Telushkin covers religion, fashion, and culture for such places as the *New York Times*, the *Atlantic*, the *Washington Post*, and *Teen Vogue*. She is also a regular contributor to *Tablet Magazine*.

Daisy Vargas is an assistant professor in the Department of Religious Studies and Classics at the University of Arizona. She is currently writing a book manuscript tentatively titled *Mexican Religion on Trial: Race, Religion, and the Law in the US-Mexico Borderlands*.

Sam Washington is a lover of all things Star Wars and a student of faith, life, and politics. He currently resides in San Antonio, Texas, with his family. A military veteran, Sam entered seminary in 2011 and holds a master's in ministry and a master's in theology.

Brook Wilensky-Lanford received her MFA in nonfiction writing from Columbia University and is currently a PhD candidate at the University of North Carolina at Chapel Hill. Her book reviews and essays have appeared in the *Boston Globe*, the *San Francisco Chronicle*, and *Lapham's Quarterly*. She is the author of *Paradise Lust: Searching for the Garden of Eden* (Grove Press, 2011).

Permissions

Part I—Personal Agon: Experience & Identity

Briallen Hopper, "Learning to Write about Religion," originally published in the *Revealer*, December 10, 2019. Reprinted here with the author's permission.

Nat Case, "I Contradict Myself," originally published in *Aeon*, August 26, 2013. Reprinted here with the author's permission.

Tara Isabella Burton, "What Is a Cult?," originally published in *Aeon*, June 7, 2017. Reprinted here with the author's permission.

Sands Hall, "Light a Candle," originally published in *BLARB*, October 13, 2019. Reprinted here with the author's permission.

Brook Wilensky-Lanford, "How to Talk to 'Nones' and Influence People," originally published in *Religion Dispatches*, June 16, 2016. Reprinted here with the author's permission.

Burke Gerstenschlager, "The Lonely Boy," originally published in *Image*, February 4, 2019. Reprinted here with the author's permission.

Patrick Blanchfield, "Soul Murder," originally published in the *Revealer*, August 15, 2018. Reprinted here with the author's permission.

Part II—Political Agon: Politics & Society

Simon Critchley, "Why I Love Mormonism," originally published in the *New York Times*, September 16, 2012. Reprinted here with the author's permission.

Emma Green, "Will Anyone Remember Eleven Dead Jews?," originally published in the *Atlantic*, October 15, 2019. From *The Atlantic* © 2019 The Atlantic Monthly Group, LLC. All rights reserved. Used under license.

Nathan Schneider, "No Revolution without Religion," originally published in *Occupy! An OWS-Inspired Gazette*, April 25, 2012. Reprinted here with the author's permission.

Kaya Oakes, "Forgiveness in the Epoch of Me Too," originally published in *Killing the Buddha*, May 10, 2020. Reprinted here with the author's permission.

Sam Washington, "A Welcoming Church No More," originally published in the *Los Angeles Review of Books*, April 29, 2018. Reprinted here with the author's permission.

Joel Looper, "How Would Bonhoeffer Vote?," originally published in the *Los Angeles Review of Books*, July 31, 2019. Reprinted here with the author's permission.

Jennifer Ratner-Rosenhagen, "Zen and the Art of a Higher Education," originally published in the *Los Angeles Review of Books*, July 15, 2018. Reprinted here with the author's permission.

Part III—Natural Agon: Science & Technology

Peter Harrison, "Why Religion Is Not Going Away and Science Will Not Destroy It," originally published in *Aeon*, September 7, 2017. Reprinted here with the author's permission.

Leigh Eric Schmidt, "Monuments to Unbelief," abridged version of an essay originally published in *Aeon*, October 25, 2017. Reprinted here with the author's permission.

Erik Davis, "Amma's Cosmic Squeeze," originally published in *Salon*, July 19, 2007. Reprinted here with the author's permission.

Daniel José Camacho, "Who Am I?" (Alternate title "On the Threshing Floor") originally published in *Sojourners*, July 2019. Reprinted here with the author's permission.

Meghan O'Gieblyn, "Fake Meat," originally published in the *Paris Review*, January 28, 2019. Reprinted here with the author's permission.

Ann Neumann, "Opioids: A Crisis of Misplaced Morality," originally published in the *Revealer*, November 16, 2017. Reprinted here with the author's permission.

Part IV—Divine Agon: Theology & Philosophy

David Bentley Hart, "Christ's Rabble," originally published in *Commonweal Magazine*, September 27, 2016. Reprinted here with the author's permission.

Marcus Rediker, "The Forgotten Prophet," originally published in *Aeon,* May 3, 2018. Reprinted here with the author's permission.

Jim Hinch, "Evangelicals Are Losing the Battle for the Bible. And They're Just Fine with That," originally published in *Los Angeles Review of Books*, September 7, 2017. Reprinted here with the author's permission.

Daisy Vargas, "La Llorona Visits the American Academy of Religion: A Tribute to Luís de León," originally published in the *Revealer,* November 7, 2019. Reprinted here with the author's permission.

Faisal Devji, "Against Muslim Unity," originally published in *Aeon*, July 12, 2016. Reprinted here with the author's permission.

Shira Telushkin, "Their Bloods Cry Out from the Ground," originally published in *Tablet*, November 1, 2018. Reprinted here with the author's permission.